DECISIVE BATTLES
of the
KOREAN WAR

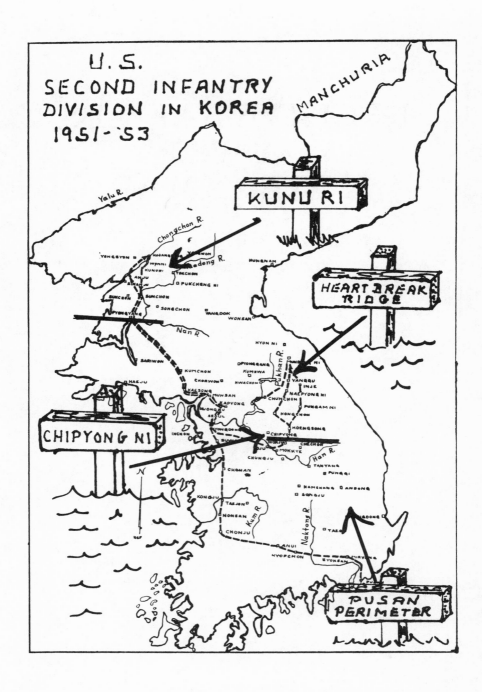

DECISIVE BATTLES
of the
KOREAN WAR

An Infantry Company
Commander's View
of the
War's Most Critical
Engagements

**Lt. Col. Sherman W. Pratt,
U.S. Army, Ret.**

VANTAGE PRESS
New York

FIRST EDITION

Published by Vantage Press, Inc.
516 West 34th Street, New York, New York 10001

Manufactured in the United States of America
ISBN: 0-533-09584-0

Library of Congress Catalog Card No.: 91-90897

0 9 8 7 6 5 4 3 2 1

Contents

Foreword

This work about critical phases of the Korean War is written by a participating observer, which makes it unusually realistic and authentic as a chronicle of that historical struggle. It is "must" reading for war and history buffs who seek a firmer foundation for their understanding of the importance of the Korean War in our country's history.

The author, retired Lt. Col. Sherman W. Pratt, highlights three points in the war that he feels were particularly critical in determining the outcome of the American and United Nations efforts. In two of these the author was personally involved as a company commander in a rifle-infantry company of the 2d "Indianhead" Infantry Division, and writes from his own experiences.

Colonel Pratt is aware of and concedes that there were countless other actions throughout the war by his and other divisions and units that were bloody, cruel, and painfully costly. He argues, however, that most of them, regrettably, did not contribute decisively to the survival or outcome of the UN effort, and certainly to the extent of the turning points he here describes.

It is usual, and understandable, that vets from nearly any military unit in war will feel that their outfits bore the brunt of the battle and played the most indispensable role. They especially should find Colonel Pratt's argument fascinating, challenging, and thought-provoking. Others should find his narrative informative, historically helpful, and captivating.

DICK ADAMS, President
Korean War Veterans Association

Motivation and Credits

This narrative was generated by, and is an outgrowth of and an expansion on an interview in March 1988, in Arlington, Virginia, between Thomas M. Ryan, official historian of the U.S. Eighth Army in Korea, and retired army Lt. Col. Sherman W. Pratt, former captain of infantry with the U.S. 2d "Indianhead" Infantry Division in 1950–51.

Photographs and artwork, in whole or in part in some instances, are by the author unless otherwise indicated. Some artwork is enhanced from graphics by the arts office of the Army's Office of Public Affairs in the Pentagon.

Other sources or individuals who contributed to this work are identified in the text.

The author's profits from this work are to be donated to the funds for the establishment of a memorial to the Korean War veterans on the Mall in the nation's capital, or elsewhere.

The narrative is dedicated to all veterans of the Korean War and their families, and especially those of the author's U.S. 2d "Indianhead" Infantry Division.

A Word of Caution

This work contains wartime conversations from many years ago. In so writing I am reminded of the caveat of no less a distinguished and honored historical person than our late general and president, Dwight D. Eisenhower.

In Ike's book *At Ease—Stories I Tell to Friends* (Tab Books, Inc., Blue Ridge Summit, Pennsylvania), he warns his readers:

> I am usually opposed to the author who puts within quotation marks conversations he never heard or who pretends to recollect with absolute fidelity conversations he heard a long time ago . . . On the latter, the key phrases are indelibly imprinted in my memory. But I have engaged in some reconstruction. I urge the reader to take all the quoted materials, particularly that recollected across the decades, with the necessary grain of salt.

My wartime involvement as a lower-echelon infantry-company commander was obviously far less complicated than that of Supreme Allied Commander Eisenhower. I have much less detail to remember, and therefore can do so with perhaps better accuracy. Nevertheless, I would urge readers not to completely discard their salt-shakers when ingesting conversations herein.

Preface

Korea is a country, or an area, that few Americans, in our short history, have been able to either locate on a map or to identify, except for the period around the early 1950s when the United States and the UN were engaged in hostilities there.

The country called by Koreans "the Land of the Morning Calm" is essentially a peninsula about one hundred miles wide and almost a thousand miles long at its extremities. Offshore to the west is the Yellow Sea and to the east is the Sea of Japan. The country has a common frontier of several hundred miles with Manchuria to its north, and with the Soviet Union for about a dozen miles just south of the port of Vladivostok.

The Korean peninsula, on the Asian Pacific coast, has been said to "point like a dagger" at the heart of Japan. Most of the country consists of rugged mountains terraced with rice paddies and interlaced with countless valleys that are dotted with towns and villages. It is a land of striking beauty when not laid waste by the ravages of war.

Throughout most of history, Korea has played a relatively quiet and obscure role on the world stage. There have been several instances, however, when certain developments in Korea overlapped those of America, or the rest of the world, and in a way that should command the attention of all who pride themselves on knowing something of Korea's place in the family of nations.

Korea has long been overshadowed by its more powerful neighbor, China, and has been more or less dominated or controlled by that country. From 1905 until the end of World War II, Korea was occupied and controlled by Japan. Since that time Korea has been divided into a republic in the south and a Communist-controlled country in the north.

In the early post-biblical era, Korea was ruled internally by an arrangement known as the Three Kingdoms, which was followed by various dynasties to include the Koryo, Hideyoshi, and Yi Chosum.

A notable event in Korean history relating to world developments elsewhere occurred in the late 1200s, during the height of the Mongol expansion. The "Golden Hordes" of Genghis Khan had swept out of the Siberian steppes and had overrun most of the civilized world except Western Europe. By the 1260s the Mongols had reached China and Korea, and in 1267 attempted to cross the Sea of Japan and invade Japan. That attempt failed because of a sudden and ferocious storm at sea known to Orientals as the *kamikaze*, a name applied centuries later in World War II to Japanese suicide pilots who operated in a like manner. Since the Mongols advanced as far as Korea, but no farther, Korean territory has the distinction of constituting the high-water mark of the Mongol invasions in the east.

Another event in Korea that would certainly have made the nightly news at American supper tables, had there been radio and satellite TV-transmissions, occurred in 1866 at a time of heightened American activity in the Far East. In the 1850s Com. Matthew C. Perry had sailed units of the American fleet into Japanese waters and took the first steps toward "opening up" Japan to trade.

At the end of the American Civil War, from 1861 to 1865, those trade efforts resumed and, together with those of other nations, were extended to Korea. The American merchant ship *General Sherman* sailed up the Taedong Gang [river] to P'yongyang in the summer of 1866, dropped anchor, and released many of its crew for shore leave.

On shore the *General Sherman* crew got drunk and committed riotous acts of looting and insulted Korean women. The indignant and offended local population, thereupon, killed and imprisoned many of the crew and attacked and burned the ship. Five years later, when an American flotilla arrived to retaliate for the *General Sherman* incident, it too was beaten back, although eventually, in the 1880s, a treaty was signed that resulted in the opening also of Korea for trade.

Korea entered the American news columns again shortly after the turn of the century, when Russian and Japanese interests conflicted in that part of the world. By the 1890s Western powers entered the area in force and Chinese influence in Korea waned. Japan invaded Korea, later annexing the country, and the Russians pushed their boundaries to the Pacific, intent on becoming the dominant power there.

When war broke out between the two countries in 1904, Russia invaded Manchuria and the tsar sent his fleet around the African Cape of Good Hope. The Russians suffered disastrous defeat both at sea and in heavy land battles on and around Korean soil. By the middle of 1905, the war had reached a stalemate.

The American administration of President Teddy Roosevelt became concerned about the regional instability resulting from the Russo-Japanese War because of its threat to our position in the Philippines and for other related reasons. Secretary of War William Howard Taft offered to mediate the dispute, and in August of 1905 the American government hosted the conference that resulted in the Treaty of Portsmouth, which ended the war. The treaty recognized the undisputed supremacy of Japan in Korea and began a period of oppressive Japanese control that lasted through World War II.

Neither the events surrounding or following the visit of the merchantman *General Sherman,* nor those consequential to the provisions of the Treaty of Portsmouth, did much to create respect, admiration, or appreciation of America by Koreans.

Upon the ending of World War I and the announcement by Woodrow Wilson of his Fourteen Points declaration that included the "self-determination of peoples," another milestone in Korean-American relations occurred. Korean independence leaders, including one Syngman Rhee, later to become the post–World War II president, considered that the concept applied to Koreans as well as Czechs and others, and they rose in revolt against the Japanese. An estimated 2 million Koreans joined in demonstrations against the Japanese rulers as waves of students and citizens took to the streets. On March 1, 1919, a declaration of independence was read at a rally in Seoul. Many assumed the Americans would come to their support. But the Americans did not. Japan had been an ally during the war and American policy did not countenance a confrontation with a former ally. There were other complex issues involved as well.

When the Japanese caught their breath they responded with brutal repression, arresting almost fifty thousand people, killing and jailing thousands more, and stopped the demonstrations. Their ruthless and exploitive colonial policy continued through World War II as Korean independence leaders fled the country and formed an exile provisional government in Shanghai.

Again, the great American nation, the birthplace of modern-day democracy, the advocate of freedom and human rights, had let the Korean people down. It was hardly a path designed to generate appreciation among the cruelly oppressed Korean people.

Korea next came to the blunt attention of American leaders after the fighting had ended in Europe at the end of World War II. Korea had hardly been mentioned at the summit conferences during the war in Cairo, Teheran, or Yalta. At the Potsdam Conference in July 1945, only days before the dropping of the atom bombs on Japan, it was determined that the Russians would enter the war against Japan.

With the ending of the war in Europe, the advance of Allied armies in the Pacific to the shores of the Japanese homeland, and the entrance of the Russians into the war against Japan, there was the necessity of establishing a line of demarcation so that Russian and Allied armies would not clash upon meeting.

An Allied goal in the Pacific was to disarm the Japanese forces on the mainland and in Japan. With the Russians advancing from the north through Manchuria and the Allies advancing through Japan and Okinawa, Korea was decided to be the area of contact. American planners noted that the 38th parallel ran about halfway up the Korean peninsula and suggested that the line would make a feasible point of demarcation. The Russians, surprisingly, agreed.

Although it appears clear that both Russian and Allied intentions at the time did not contemplate that the 38th parallel would be other than a tactical boundary for the benefit of field military-commanders to avoid confusion on the battlefield, the line has, nevertheless, become a permanent, to date, boundary between two separate and hostile politically controlled sections of the country, one Communist in the north and the other non-communist in the south.*

Nor did the American administration of the southern half of Korea after the assumption of control in September of 1945 do much to reverse or correct the dismal prior history of American mistreatment of and insensitivity to Korea and its people.

Many prominent and scholarly historians have documented in detail the pathetic and almost amateurish efforts of the Americans in Korea during that period. A picture emerges of a country in the throes of demobilization, thrust into a remote part of the world about which it knew little and in which it had no long-range strategic interests, and

---

* Readers interested in learning more of why and how the 38th parallel line of demarcation came about could refer to an extraordinarily in-depth treatment of the subject by Michael C. Sandusky in his *America's Parallel* (Alexandria, Virginia: Old Dominion Press, 1983). The book may be out of print but should be available in many libraries or by contacting the author c/o Vantage Press.

at a time when it was greatly preoccupied with conditions and problems elsewhere, especially in the homelands of the countries it had just defeated and that lay in shambles.

When Gen. John Hodge's troops of the U.S. XXIV Corps landed at Inchon in late August of 1945, there were all the ingredients for disaster. Some troops were fresh from stateside training camps, others were weary from the Pacific campaigns and not happy upon arriving in an unknown land rather than being sent home.

General Hodge himself arrived with conflicting or no instructions. At first he was told to treat the Koreans as "liberated people," or as "semifriendly." He then proceeded to brief his officers to treat the Koreans as "enemies of the United States." Guidance from MacArthur's headquarters was scant. When Hodge requested instructions, he was told to "use your own judgment."

Under these circumstances, mistakes and misjudgments piled upon each other. Perhaps among the greatest, to the intense irritation of the Korean people, was the American reliance on, and continued use of, the Japanese officials in senior positions who remained in the country during the early days of the American occupation.

With the ending of the war and the defeat of Japan, the Koreans did not find that they were relieved of the presence of and control by their hated Japanese oppressors. On the contrary, the same Japanese secret police, or their Korean lackeys, stayed on, with America's blessings, to torment, mistreat, and oppress the Korean population.

Politically the American actions were filled with miscalculations that further alienated the Korean people from their occupiers. With the advent of the cold war in the late 1940s and American preoccupation with the threat of Communist activism in Europe and elsewhere, American support for Korean political movements tended to be more and more conservative. As the months passed, this trend isolated and shut out large numbers of Koreans who were not necessarily Communist, for they knew little of Communism, but who were not disposed toward conservatism which they related to past Japanese control.

An additional cause of friction developed because of the American support for and help in returning the self-proclaimed independence leader Syngman Rhee, who had lived abroad in America for many years but was not well known or liked by many Koreans. Rhee managed to win the United Nations–sponsored election of 1948, which was boycotted by the left, including the Communists. His regime has been characterized widely as dictatorial, ruthless, and repressive. It was friendly to the Americans, however, and, to a point, received U.S. military and economic assistance.

By June 1949, Russian and American troops had left Korea, except for small military advisory groups, as had been earlier agreed. The Americans left behind a partially trained South Korean military force without tanks or heavy artillery or aircraft, capable only of interior control or limited defensive efforts. The Russians, on the other hand, left behind a considerably stronger North Korean military establishment with definite offensive capabilities. The North Korean government was vocal in a torrent of threats to unify the country by military action if necessary. The American objective of limited military equipment and training was to prevent Rhee from "marching northward," as he was known to want to do.

By early 1950 yet another blow at the Korean people was to be struck by America, as if the long and devastating record of harmful actions over the past hundred years or so were not enough.

In 1949 the Communist forces had consolidated their position in China and had gained control of the entire mainland area. The National Forces of Generalissimo Chiang Kai-shek evacuated to Formosa and set up government there, thus creating two Chinas.

In January of 1950, President Harry Truman and his secretary of state, Dean Acheson, plus Senator Tom Connally, chairman of the Foreign Relations Committee and a known friend of the administration, made public statements outlining America's defense perimeter in the Far East. They indicated that the mainland, including Korea, was not within that perimeter. Many observers interpreted the remarks to be a warning to Peking that America would not stand by idly if an attack were made on Formosa.

The Washington statements were received in Seoul like a bombshell. Rhee complained bitterly that the comments were an open invitation for the Communist north to attack across the 38th parallel, where there had been constant clashes and disorders for weeks, and a near-battlefield situation existed.

Rhee was proven correct. Only a few weeks into spring "campaigning" weather on June 24, the North Korean Communist forces crossed the parallel in an all-out invasion. The Korean War was launched and was to continue in all its fury until a cease-fire was agreed to at P'anmunjom three years later in 1953. President Truman ordered full-scale American military support for the South Koreans and the United Nations called upon its members to assist.

Too much has been written in detail about the Korean War by such capable and prolific authorities as Clay Blair, Max Hastings, S. L. A. Marshall, official historians, and many others for us to dwell on it excessively here. Suffice it to say that the fighting consisted of several major phases that can be identified briefly. First, the Communist aggressor pushed through all South Korea until stopped by South Koreans and hastily thrown in American forces from Japan and elsewhere at a perimeter around the southeastern port city of Pusan.

The next phase involved the American–UN counteroffensive with the North Koreans driven back to or near the Manchurian border at the extreme northern end of the peninsula. The Chinese Communists intervened near the end of 1950, and the UN forces withdrew to positions roughly again along the 38th parallel.

In the first half of 1951, UN and Communist forces attacked and defended in a series of "seesaw" actions, mostly in the middle or eastern portions of the Korean peninsula. By the end of 1951, the front had stabilized along a line running slightly below the 38th parallel in the west and a few dozen miles above the parallel in the east. The front remained essentially unchanged thereafter until the cease-fire in 1953 and to date.

Much bloody, severe, costly, torturous, courageous, and sometimes pointless fighting took place during the three years of the Korean conflict—by the troops of both sides—at various times and places.

It is my belief, however, that the truly decisive engagements of the fighting can be limited to only three phases, or battle periods, and in all my research and study of the campaigns I have not found any writer who has put the matter in quite that context. I think there is a need to do so for the record and in fairness to the memories of those brave and hapless troops who participated.

Decisive, in military terminology, as any neophyte in strategy or tactics will well know, applies to an action or major engagement that by its very nature determines, or significantly affects, the outcome of the struggle, or an important part of the struggle.

Not every confrontation on the battlefield is, of course, decisive, no matter how costly or violent, or even if enormous numbers of troops are involved. World War I ground on for over three years, with millions of casualties, without any really decisive battles. Nor would anyone be likely to contend that Leonidas with his 300 Spartans fought a decisive battle to his last man at Thermopylae in 480 B.C. against the Persian invaders. The stand has earned a spot in history as a model of courageousness, but it was not decisive in any meaningful way. The Persians were delayed, but only briefly, and went on to overrun Greece.

The battle of Marathon, however, ten years earlier, was clearly decisive. When the Greeks threw back the Persians they decided the outcome of the whole invasion—at least for the time being.

Meade's defense at Gettysburg in the American Civil War in early July of 1863 was also clearly decisive. The attacks by Lee to include Pickett's charge of the Virginians through the cornfield was the high-water mark of the Southern cause, and the South never again enjoyed the initiative and the outcome of the war was foretold.

Just as decisive was the D-day invasion of Europe across the English Channel on June 6, 1944. The outcome of the war thereafter was never doubted—only the timing of the end.

In the Korean conflict, as stated, there were three actions, two relatively short, the other longer, that I consider to have been quite decisive and would have drastically altered the outcome of the action to the detriment of the UN–American cause with the Communists in sole control today of all Korea.

The first of these actions, and the most drawn out, in which I had no part, was the initial commitment of American troops immediately after the Communist North Koreans crossed the parallel. Those troops, mostly Japanese garrison and peacetime occupation-forces, for the most part were ill-trained, inexperienced, pathetically few in numbers, scared, disorganized and disoriented, and not highly motivated to fight in combat for a cause they little understood or agreed with.

Upon arriving hastily on Korean soil, the American troops were thrown into combat in unfamiliar areas with little idea of the tactical and enemy situations. Seldom in modern history, if ever, have men been called upon to lay down their lives in battle in a more unprepared condition.

These earliest participants in the Korean War were expected to slow down the advance of the North Koreans and then establish a defensive perimeter around the port of Pusan until sufficient reinforcements could be sent to deal effectively with the invasion. They succeeded in doing so, but at terrific cost and with nerve-wracking uncertainty. Had they not stood their ground for those critical weeks in the summer of 1950, the Communist forces would for certain have conquered all of Korea. A later UN return, involving an enormous amphibious landing on hostile shores occupied by the Communist forces, would have been clearly beyond military and political feasibility. The performance of those forces was clearly decisive in determining the future course of the fighting and the fate of South Korea pending further developments.

The other two decisive actions of paramount importance in determining the outcome of the Korean War occurred upon the entry of the Chinese Communist forces and a few weeks thereafter in the winter of 1950–51.

Both of these decisive actions involved the U.S. 2d "Indianhead" Infantry Division. The rifle company that I commanded played a key and also decisive role in a way that has never been documented or even fully known to other than my troops, the men of Company B, of the 23rd Infantry Regiment. It is to these two combat situations that I will direct primary attention herein.

The first of these decisive situations occurred only hours after the Chinese Communist Forces, or the CCF, launched their all out offensive in the last days of November 1950. In the west the UN forces, including my division, were only a few miles from the Yalu River and the Manchurian border. In the east, the forces of Gen. Ned Almond's X Corps were mostly on the Manchurian border.

In the face of overwhelming numbers of Chinese, the Eighth Army was in danger of being surrounded and cut off. To prevent that, a general withdrawal to a more defendable position in a narrower part of Korea was undertaken. One division, my 2d, was left behind sacrificially to hold off the Chinese until the rest of the army could retire in an orderly manner and in shape to fight another day.

If the 2d Division had not held off the enemy for a few precious hours at that time, it seems clear that the whole Eighth Army might have been cut off and surrounded, or damaged so severely that withdrawal from Korea would have been necessary.

Two of the regiments of the division, the 9th and 38th, were almost wiped out themselves as they withdrew and were ambushed, as described graphically by Marshall in his *The River and the Gauntlet.* Even in their despair, they contributed to the salvage of the Eighth Army to the extent that the massacre by the CCF took some hours and delayed the enemy's advance, allowing time for the escape of nearly all of the rest of the army.

With the preoccupation of the other two regiments in the Gauntlet holocaust, the main task of delaying the waves of Chinese blanketing the landscape fell upon my regiment, the 23rd. To implement its mission the regiment went into defensive positions on high ground south of the town of Kunu-ri. Its presence there, straddling the main bridge and road to the south, held up the Chinese for critical hours and permitted the safe withdrawal of other forces as planned.

The action of the 23rd Regiment at Kunu-ri was clearly decisive in the most dramatic meaning of the term. Had the division and regiment failed in their delaying actions, there can be but little doubt that the combat operations of UN forces would have been fatally impacted. Again, a withdrawal from Korea would most likely have been ordered. Most historians seem to be in full agreement with that conclusion.

The division and regiment, however, almost did not succeed because of a predawn attack on my rifle company by waves of Chinese that, if successful, would have provided the CCF with commanding terrain over looking the whole regiment so as to make its positions untenable. Had the regiment at that point been routed and overrun, its ability to delay the Chinese forces would have been terminated and the whole Eighth Army might not have escaped encirclement.

Ironically, the desperate engagement by my company, remotely and on the forward slopes of a high hill, was not even known to the regimental commander, Col. Paul Freeman, or his staff, far away in the valley below and behind. The circumstances of the critical, decisive, and desperate engagement are revealed in more detail herein.

The second major decisive engagement that took place in the

Korean War, and the decisive role played in it by my Company B, occurred in February 1951, about fifty miles southeast of Seoul in what has become known as the battle of Chipyong-ni.*

In the weeks after the Chinese intervened at the end of November, the UN forces withdrew to positions along the 38th parallel, and the X Corps evacuated the northeast section of the country around Hungnam on the east coast. During December and January there was much talk of evacuation of Korea and we witnessed the burning and destruction of large quantities of supplies and materials. In that period, contacts with the Chinese consisted mainly of a series of actions labeled "rolling with the punch," by lower echelon commanders and others.

The capabilities of the Chinese to launch an attack and maintain the momentum of their advance was not well understood and it was not known whether, or for how long, the UN forces could prevail against the Chinese, especially after the winter ended and there was time for the enemy to build and advance their logistical stockpiles from the far north. A period of testing took place. We took defensive positions to inflict the most damage possible on the enemy before being overrun and then withdrew through another unit to our rear that would repeat the cycle.

We learned from these operations that once the Chinese massed for an attack and followed through with their assault, they were not able to keep going. What would happen, it was asked, if instead of defending briefly, and then withdrawing, we stayed in position. Could the Chinese dislodge us by sheer force and firepower? The high command decided to find out.

My 23rd Regiment was in positions on high ground around the communication center of Chipyong-ni, where several roads and a railroad met. Gen. Matthew Ridgway, the new army commander, had recently arrived and was infusing a new spirit of encouragement in the command. Talk of defeat and evacuation had subsided. But it was still

---

* The names of Korean towns are often, and quite inconsistently, shown with suffixes such as "dong," "ri," or "ni," sometimes hyphenated, and I so refer to them thusly herein, depending on the sources. My Korean contacts advise me that while there is no exact English equivalent for the terms, they can be roughly translated as "city" for *dong*, "small village" for *ri*, and "smaller village" for *ni*.

not known just what were the relative strengths and weaknesses of the UN and CCF forces.

When the situation maps began to show an enormous enemy buildup in the areas around Chipyong-ni, a decision was made not to prepare withdrawal plans, but to stand and fight. A test of enemy and UN capabilities was to be made.

The 23rd's regimental commander, Col. Paul Freeman, was ordered to reposition his forces into an all-around, or perimeter, defense, to dig in deeply, and to stockpile ammunition and supplies in anticipation of the forthcoming Chinese attack.

Freeman did so and in mid-February the Chinese struck continuously for several days in all their fury, with everything they had. In the end, the regiment prevailed and after inflicting sickening casualties on the Chinese, the enemy withdrew. The engagement marked a turning point in the war by establishing that the Chinese were not, after all, invincible, and that a well-organized and prepared American or UN team could hold their ground and turn back the best and most the enemy could offer and at great loss to them.

The battle of Chipyong-ni and, to an almost equal extent, the battle of Wonju to the east by the other regiments of the division, and a subsequent engagement to the northeast by the British Brigade at Kap'yong were decisive engagements of major consequence in the Korean War. The battles, especially Chipyong-ni, marked a turning point from a UN attitude of uncertainty and trepidation and talk of defeat and fear into one of confidence and reassurance that UN forces were as good or better than those of the enemy.

The victory at Chipyong-ni, however, hung precariously by a thread for several crucial hours on the last day. The defense line on the south had been breached by the CCF and the high ground gave the enemy direct observation of, and fire upon, the center of the regimental perimeter, including command posts and armored and artillery-fire support centers. That breach had to be closed and the ground retaken by the regimental reserve company. If that reserve company failed, the outcome of the defense at Chipyong-ni almost certainly would have been reversed, and we would not have established that UN forces could prevail against the CCF and that they should abandon plans to evacuate the peninsula.

The reserve company, my Company B, did not fail in its

counterattack on that occasion. The security of the perimeter was preserved intact, although at staggering cost to Baker Company, with over half the unit wiped out. As at Kunu-ri, the action took place over the crest of a hill and mostly out of sight or hearing of higher commanders, and has thus escaped the attention of unit historians and others. I hope that the more detailed treatment herein will set the record straight and place historical records in better perspective, and thus correct that oversight.

There will, of course, be those who will disagree with me as to the significance of the events that I cover in this work. I will welcome their opinions, and I hope for the benefit of posterity that they will set forth their views if they conflict with anything herein so that the objective observer can draw his or her own conclusions or give such weight to contrasting views as they deserve. It is said that we all draw from our own experiences, so impressions can be expected to vary.

For example, some may feel the spectacular landings at Inchon rate a "decisive" label. The brilliance of the Inchon landings in September of 1950 as other forces were breaking out of the Pusan perimeter and racing toward the 38th parallel has been emphasized often. My own feeling has been that, admirable as that exercise was, under most trying tidal, weather, and other conditions, it did not qualify as a particularly decisive part of the war.

The landings at Inchon certainly facilitated and assisted the advance of the main body of troops from the south by relieving pressure, and thereby probably saved many lives. But I think it is clear that the southern forces had the North Koreans on the run and would have reached the parallel in short order whether or not there had been Inchon landings. I have not found any works by other writers who contend otherwise. Nor would the overall outcome of the war have been different, in my judgment, had the landings not taken place. Participants, of course, will be reluctant to agree, but this is not meant to detract in any way from the sacrifices they made in that operation.

Additionally, there was no shortage of bitter, painful, agonizing, and costly fighting at times and places other than the three I contend were the decisive highlights of the Korean fighting. Even bloody Heartbreak Ridge and Porkchop Hill and the Punchbowl fighting later in the war do not qualify in my judgment as decisive, sad as it may be to so state in deference to the many who were there, including myself.

The eventual outcome of the war, or even the location of the front lines, was not affected to any particular degree by those engagements, although it can be argued that the fighting there did persuade the enemy to resume meaningful negotiations at P'anmunjom, looking toward a cease-fire.

It is my hope that this work by someone who was personally involved in the war will contribute to a better understanding of the conditions that then prevailed and that it will fill in some important ingredients not heretofore revealed and not contained in available records.

Acknowledgments

In addition to the comrades and others named herein, I am especially indebted to the following for support or assistance in preparing and completing this work:

The staff and personnel at the U.S. Records Center at Suitland, Maryland.

Col. M. J. Lundberg and Mr. Earl Young in the graphic-arts office in the army's Office of Public Affairs in the Pentagon.

My son, Paul, for relinquishing his claims on my time for cruises on our sailboat.

My daughter, Christine, for her sharp and highly critical editing abilities.

Most of all to my wife, Anastasia, for her patience, encouragement, and indulgence on numerous occasions when I was expected to be otherwise occupied for her convenience.

DECISIVE BATTLES
of the
KOREAN WAR

CHAPTER ONE

A Combat Replacement for Korea

"So you think you won the Korean War all by yourself, eh, Mr. Pratt?"

I took a slow sip on my glass of rhine wine and studied my questioner for a drawn-out few moments before attempting to respond. I knew he was playing the role of the provocateur—to evoke a full and candid answer for him to note.

The scene was my rec room in my home in Arlington, Virginia, on a March evening in 1988. My intimidator was Mr. Thomas M. Ryan, the official historian of the U.S. Eighth Army in Seoul, Korea.

Ryan was in the States as an army historian to gather additional information from such veterans of the long-ago Korean War who might still be around. Among others, he had visited and quizzed retired army Gen. Richard Kotite* nearby in Fairfax County, who had

_____
* Kotite died in 1991.

been a first lieutenant in my rifle company of the 23rd Infantry Regiment in Korea, beginning with the winter of 1950–51.

During his exchange with Ryan a few days earlier, General Kotite had related that his former company commander, myself, was in the area and that Ryan might want also to brain-pick me for whatever info I might still recall. Ryan had replied that he did indeed want to do so, and he contacted me and set up a get-together.

"No, Tom," I said, "I never intended to convey any impression that I had any exaggerated concepts of my contribution to that effort. There were a lot of guys over there. My part was relatively insignificant, and I am sure I was lost among the many."

"But you said that your company played an unrecorded role in two battles that could have changed the entire course of the war—and even if you were defeated, it could have resulted in the withdrawal of UN forces from Korea altogether."

"Yes, I did say that. And I think it's true. But I don't claim any particular credit for it happening. It's just that my company was in a particular spot, at a critical time—on two occasions. I think our efforts saved the day and it has never yet been realized by historians—or even my own superiors—at the time or since."

"Well, I would like to hear about it and include your story in our official records. We can let others make their judgments on the extent to which your version has merit. Fair enough?"

"Of course," said I.

"You were, as I understand it, in Korea from mid-1950 at the Pusan perimeter breakout until Heartbreak Ridge in the fall of 1951. Isn't that correct?"

"Yes."

"And you were CO of Baker Company of the 23rd Infantry Regiment of the 2d Division?"

"Yes, at first. Later in the summer of 1951, when my promotion to major arrived, I was assigned to regimental headquarters as the exec."

"For the record, how about giving me a rundown on the highlights of your prior military service?" Ryan too sipped his wine and leaned into his memo pad, ready for data. "And spare me any false modesties," he added. "I want my notes to be as complete and factual as possible."

"Well," I began, "when I enlisted back in '39 fresh from high school in North Little Rock, Arkansas, I was assigned to the 7th Infantry Regiment of the 3rd Infantry Division at Vancouver Barracks, Washington, on the Columbia River." I continued and told Ryan that I had begun and ended my Third Division duty with Company L, with an intervening assignment with the regiment's Anti-Tank Company, to include wartime service in campaigns in Morocco, Tunisia, Sicily, Italy, southern France, and Germany. "I received a battlefield commission in France and soon commanded Company L, one of the two rifle companies of the regiment that captured Berchtesgaden, Hitler's Alpine retreat, in the closing days of World War II. I rose from first sergeant to captain in only three months, a record in the 3rd Division, if not in the army, I've been told. After the war, I had an interesting, but sad, assignment with the war-dead return-program out of Chicago."

"What were you doing when the Korean fighting broke out in June of 1950?"

"I was assigned to the military district in my old hometown of Little Rock."

"What was a military district?"

"In those days," I explained to Ryan, the youngster, "each state had an army headquarters called a district. It was responsible for coordinating reserve, National Guard, ROTC, and certain recruiting activities. My job was as the PIO, or Public Information Officer."

"Do you recall the reaction there when the news flashed that the Communist North Koreans had crossed the 38th parallel?"

"Yes, rather vividly. Like the rest of the country, and world I guess, we were startled and shocked. We immediately received instructions to recall to active duty all possible reservists as individuals, but not units or members of specific units. The desperate need was for individual replacements to increase the badly understrength combat divisions that were hastily being sent from Japan and that were rapidly falling back to the Naktong River and adjacent areas in what was to become known as the 'Pusan perimeter.'"

"Didn't those reservists object to being recalled to duty?"

"You better believe it! Most of the individuals who found themselves suddenly on orders were quite flabbergasted. They had been inactive, in administrative-holding detachments for up to five years, since the end of World War II. Most thought they no longer even had any military connections at all. There was much anger, bitterness, resentment, especially from those with new and firm community ties or family obligations. There was an appeal process established for extreme hardships, but overall the desperate need for replacements in Korea far outweighed most compassionate reasons for deferring most of the reservists from new active duty."

"You were not a reservist. You were on active duty. How did it happen that you also soon wound up in Korea?" Ryan wondered aloud.

"Yes. I asked myself the same thing at the time. To understand the matter, one must realize how utterly desperate was the need for bodies, of any kind and of no matter what backgrounds, or where located, or what doing. Divisions on routine peacetime occupation duty in Japan were being suddenly airlifted to Korea and dumped in strange and unfamiliar surroundings. Regiments had only two battalions instead of three, battalions had only two companies instead of four or five, and even they were in most instances only at half strength. Further compounding the matter was the fact that most divisional personnel, other than senior leaders, had no combat experience or even training."

"Yes," said Ryan, "the records show that in those desperate days the military combed its active rolls also for any personnel who could be spared for reassignment to the Korean theater. So they sifted through the roster at your headquarters and tagged you?"

"Exactly. The staff knew that anyone could be on orders at any moment, but most of our people were from the administrative or service, and not the combat, branches of the army. They felt they were not very vulnerable for frontline needs in Korea. There were only a few of us combat-branch officers in the office, and the talk was that Pratt would not likely be selected for reassignment in view of his many campaigns in the last war. It developed they were wrong, and I was on orders well before the summer was out."

"Upon arrival in Korea what did you first experience?"

"After processing through Japan, at the Pusan replacement center I was assigned to the 2d 'Indianhead' Infantry Division then on the line. The division was moving out of the Pusan perimeter as part of the all-out offensive to drive the communist forces out of South Korea.

At the division I was assigned and moved to the 23rd Infantry Regiment and met the regimental commander, Col. Paul Freeman. He personally interviewed me and the several other officer replacements with me."

I was profoundly impressed with Colonel Freeman on that first contact in a burned-out Korean village somewhere near the Naktong River. He was a pleasant, sincere, and warm individual. He looked people straight in the eye, and radiated interest in them. He listened closely to the answers they gave to his questions. He exuded confidence and control. I had a feeling of gratitude that I had been assigned to Freeman's regiment. He asked if any of the incoming officers, except for one fellow with a medical administrative background, had any objection to being assigned to the battalions. None did, although I wondered what would have been his action if they had objected. He told me I was to go to the 1st Battalion.

Upon arriving in the 1st Battalion, a day or so later when I caught up to them in the supply trains, I was interviewed by the commander, Lt. Col. Claire Hutchin. I was to form a liking and admiration for Hutchin that would equal, if not exceed, that which I would have for Freeman. I was, of course, to see much of Hutchin in the coming months. I was never to see him when he was not in full control of the situation for which he was responsible. He would always be collected, courageous, decisive, and infectiously inspiring to his staff and commanders. Even in the darkest moments he would glow.

As time passed, my battalion commander and I were to develop somewhat the classical "mutual admiration society," as he was to write on my efficiency report, among other things, ". . . a real ball of fire, with imagination and ingenuity."

Freeman and Hutchin were truly two of the most remarkable and outstanding commanders under whom I ever served in combat—which is saying a lot considering the high caliber of many of my World War II commanders in the 3rd Infantry Division.

I paused for Ryan to catch up on his notes and after a bit, he asked me where Hutchin had assigned me in the 1st Battalion.

Hutchin said, "I guess you want a staff job, Captain Pratt, since you have had so much combat in the past war? Most of my line officers are lieutenants, and you are a captain."

"Not necessarily, Colonel," I told him. "Don't do me any favors.

Assign me to a line company if that is where you need officers the
most." Hutchin was obviously pleased with that answer, and he assigned me to Baker Company. He probably was impatient with people
whose main obsession was to gain a rear area, and relatively safe,
assignment. Understandable as that desire may be, no war would ever
be won if everyone succeeded in reaching that goal.

"So what happened then to you, and your Baker Company?"
asked Ryan, stretching his fingers to ease his writer's cramp.

"Well, just as I arrived and assumed command of Baker Company, everyone was on the up and go from long weeks of stagnation
on and around the Naktong River positions. Things were happening
fast and furiously." Ryan smiled and nodded his head in agreement.
No doubt he was recalling his own readings on that phase of the
fighting.

POW Interrogation

As our advance northward picked up speed, we initially met some
rather stiff resistance. Day by day, however, the enemy's will collapsed
and soon a general rout developed. The remarkable landings at Inchon
took place and as our forces from the south rushed forward, there was
a linkup with those pushing eastward from Inchon.

My recollections of events of that hectic period are somewhat
blurred by the rapidly changing combat situation. We engaged the
enemy with actual contact from time to time, but usually only briefly,
and they scampered to elude our grasp. Sometimes we advanced by
foot, other times by motor convoy over crowded and primitive roads.
Our problem was not to guard against counterattacks but, rather, to
try to keep up with the fleeing North Koreans.

I had to learn in those early days of Korean duty to cope with a
command that was largely composed of people with whom I could not
communicate. About 80 percent of the rifle companies were comprised of Republic of Korea, or ROK, soldiers because of the dearth
of American personnel to round out unit strengths.* The ROK troops

* Korean troops were also known as KATUSAs or Korean Augmentation Troops
  with the United States Army.

were far better than none, and in many ways they were more hardy and reliable than our own Americans. They did, though, present problems in other and strange ways.

One day when we had left the Seoul area behind and were nearing the 38th parallel, I heard some commotion and screaming in my company area. It seemed to be emanating from some partially burned-out and damaged native houses.

I hastened to the source of the noise, and upon entering I found a group of my ROK soldiers with a half-dozen or so North Korean army prisoners. One prisoner was on the floor with his arms outstretched and a ROK trooper was grinding his hands and fingers into the floor with the heel of his heavy, cleated GI boots. There was blood all around and on several other prisoners over in a corner.

"What in the hell is going on?" I shouted to a ROK who knew some English and whom I recognized as one of our makeshift platoon interpreters. "Stop this instantly!" I ordered.

The ROK to whom I spoke and the others looked at me, and each other, in not a little surprise. The interpreter peered at me meekly.

"What is wrong, Captain, Sir?" he said in apparent innocence.

I then asked the young fellow what they were doing to those prisoners and why were they treating them so cruelly. He floored me, figuratively and almost literally, with his answer.

"We are interrogating them, Captain-san. We always question prisoners in this way. Otherwise they will not talk. How else can we do it?"

Needless to say, I explained to him, as best I could, that there were other ways of conducting an interrogation, that his way was not acceptable, and that it must never again be used in an American outfit. At the next opportunity when I met with my platoon leaders I informed them of the incident and laid down the law in no uncertain terms that such practices would not be condoned in my company henceforth. I never heard of it happening again.

In later years, and a war later, when I read of the frustrations and stresses in Vietnam and the somewhat frequent occurrence of cruelties by our troops there, I have wondered if I would be quite as sanctimonious if we had been confronted with similar conditions in Korea. I don't know. But I would like to think that I could never be guilty of abusing any person without just cause. But what is just cause? Perhaps only the philosophers can say.

Ryan asked me what happened to the prisoners.

"They were routinely evacuated. I was told they got medical attention at the battalion aid-station and were questioned by the S-2, intelligence staff." At that point they were no longer my problem. I had other challenging matters to attend to.

Across the Parallel

At that point the war and the advance were racing madly on. We were at the 38th parallel, where the fighting had started months before. Of course that famous cartographical line that runs around the globe almost through Washington, Madrid, and Athens does not race along the landscape like a white-painted strip to be easily seen and recognized. We were not exactly aware of the precise moment we crossed over and could not say, "Behold! We are now in North Korea!" but the time came when word spread through the ranks that we had crossed the parallel.

There had been that brief period of uncertainty just before we crossed the parallel. For us it seemed only a breath-catching moment or two. We did not know whether we were to stop at that point and if the war was over, or whether we were to continue on. In later years I would learn of the momentous deliberations between General Mac-Arthur and others over and under him, and all the way back to the Pentagon and Truman's White House as to whether the advance should continue. As we know now, more than then, it was a highly controversial matter on which there was bitter emotional disagreement, which has not to this day, half a century later, been resolved to the full satisfaction of many writers and others.

The pros and cons of the UN crossing the parallel are well documented by numerous historians in great depth. I do not flatter myself that I could add to or detract from their conclusions. I only know that for us doggies on the ground, at the time, we knew of some hesitation and uncertainty as to whether we were to move on.

"But the uncertainty did not last for long, did it?" asked Ryan.

"Not at all. It's a matter of history that MacArthur wanted to move on. Some say he had only implied cautious and hesitant permission to do so. Be that as it may, he ordered the Eighth Army commander Walton 'Bulldog' Walker to resume the advance and pursue the disorganized and disintegrating Communist North Korean army. Whereupon we did so."

We pushed on into and through P'yongyang, the capital of North Korea. The city was quiet as we rolled through, and mostly deserted. The 23rd Regiment did not remain in the city, although many of us wished we could do so. The housing and urbanization, such as they were, looked inviting. Damage was not heavy as compared to most of the villages through which we had been passing, which were nearly always totally destroyed.

When our forces cleared P'yongyang moving on northward from some high ground, we looked back upon a spectacular panoramic view of the whole valley in which the capital was located.

A few miles farther on, and an unrecalled number of hours later, we witnessed an even more galvanizing scene. Slowly the air off on the southern horizon filled with aircraft that we recognized as troop carriers. Moments later the sky was dotted with parachutes, and at a briefing Colonel Hutchin explained that the 187th Airborne Regiment had dropped. He said it was intended to be a tactical assault to capture key road-junctions and other areas near the capital but that, ironically for the paratroopers, their targets were mostly in friendly hands by the time they dropped, although some units were opposed. To us it was a bit humorous, with the laugh on the 187th. We doubted that they found it to be funny. In fact, I find now that the drop was much analyzed and debated with the strongest feelings by both airborne critics and supporters.

The airdrop by the 187th near P'yongyang, no matter how gallantly executed by the troopers themselves, can hardly be described as a smashing success and an argument for the continued use of large-sized airborne units. The question of the proper size of units had long been debated as a highly controversial matter. Fiascos in Sicily in World War II when much of the 82d Airborne Division was shot out of the sky by friendly ack-acks and widespread disorganization among airborne divisions dropped in and around Holland had not done much to settle disputes boiling around the issue over the years. Nor would the questionable and belated drop by the 187th in North Korea help much to resolve the dispute.

Few people in the military whom I have ever known have contended that there was not a need for airborne troops. Students of warfare continue to admire the success of the German drop on Crete and the drop of the 503rd American Regiment on New Guinea in 1943 in World War II and a few other instances of effective use of airborne operations. Clay Blair treats the disagreements surrounding the matter in some detail in his *Ridgway's Paratroopers*. He describes the sharp differences of opinions at the highest levels of military command during the war.

Although airborne enthusiasts such as Generals George Marshall, Matt Ridgway, Joe Swing, and James Gavin had consistently and successfully pushed for division-sized forces, other prominent and influential top generals to include Eisenhower, John Lucas, and Lesley McNair felt that divisions were too large and unwieldy and that units no larger than battalions were the best approach. It seems to me that our experiences in combat bear out the smaller-unit arguments, although to date we still cling to the division with the 82d Airborne at Fort Bragg at this writing.

I think it pertinent too to note that the airborne troops dropped in late 1989 during the Panama "intervention," which I gather is considered a successful operation, were of battalion size at each drop, although they were from a division, the 82d Airborne, at Fort Bragg. Just where that leaves us seems to remain to be seen or to be worked out by future tacticians. For sure, however, the Panama experience was not proof of the justification for division-sized airborne units, since the full division was not all at once employed.

It Was Rape, She Wrote

Ryan had almost snoozed off when I paused for breath. I rose to enrich his wineglass and to hand him a potato chip. Suddenly he came to life. "So what happened after the parallel, P'yongyang, and the 187th drop were behind you? No doubt you took your troops and headed for Japan for R and R?"

"We wished. But not quite. Ever on we pushed, Tom. Day by day, kilometer by kilometer, and ridge by ridge. The going was not really very tough so far as the enemy was concerned. For the most part they were hard to find, and if found, they had little stomach for standing against, by now, such an overpowering opponent. Our movement was largely by vehicle—either in trucks or piled on armored vehicles like swarms of hornets after the division reconnaissance-people had determined the roads to be clear."

The weather had been getting tougher and colder by the day. In October and November the first harsh winter winds blow into Korea from the Manchurian inland plateaus and valleys, and living outdoors begins to be an ordeal. Now and then scattered snow squalls would occur, especially in the higher hills and mountainous areas.

At about that point I had one quite unpleasant experience involving shameful and criminal misbehavior by one of my American soldiers. While halted overnight in and around a small village, one of the platoon sergeants came into the company CP and reported that one of his men had just raped a local woman.

I rushed down the street to the house where the incident had taken place, and upon entering, observed a Korean family huddled in a corner, shaking with fear. The husband, apparently a peasant rice-farmer, was comforting his wife, whom it seemed was the target of the assault. He looked at me pleadingly and in terror. Several small children were also in the room, cowering against the wall and sobbing. Presumably they had been present and witnessed the rape of their mother.

Needless to say, I was furious. I told an interpreter to apologize to the family and to assure them that someone in the American army would try to make amends to the extent that it could be done, and that the soldier would be duly punished. I tried to convince the family that the American and UN forces did not sanction such outrageous acts by their troops, who were there to help, and not harm, the Korean people.

I then ordered the soldier to be brought before me. I told him he was under arrest, for whatever that meant, if anything, in a combat situation, and that he was to be evacuated to the rear for confinement pending court-martial as soon as I had a chance to draw up and file charges.

One of the tragedies of justice and ironies of war, as often happens, is that the fellow involved was never court-martialed and made to pay for his crime. The only American soldier nearby who could have testified was later captured by the Chinese farther up north when they intervened, and he was reported to have died in a POW camp. We felt great compassion for the victim and her family and would like to have helped in some way. But we had no opportunity to do so. Moments after the incident we were ordered forward and quickly left the town far behind. The town and its rape victim were later inaccessible when the front returned to South Korea. The whole matter became moot anyway. Less than a month after the incident, the offending soldier was killed in fighting near the Yalu River. Sometimes fate and justice work in strange ways.

CHAPTER TWO

Race to the Manchurian Border—UN-High-water Mark

Tom Ryan sat for a while on my rec room couch, feet comfortably up on the coffee table, as I had invited him to do. It was obvious he knew his business as a historian. His brow was wrinkled. He was pondering what I had told him so far. One could almost see his brain wheels turning as he put the pieces together and scribbled copious notes on his pad. Finally, he looked up at me and, after a bit, fired his next question.

"So your division, the 2d, finally reached almost to the Yalu River and the Manchurian border on Korea's west coast?"

"That's correct," I confirmed, "and a matter of record. Perhaps a sad record, in view of the ultimate developments that were to follow within days. We crossed the Namdae River northwest of Sinanju and

13

Anju and by mid-November were within about fifty miles, and less in some places, of the border."

The area I was describing on Korea's west coast, far up north, is the section where the mostly narrow peninsula suddenly broadens from a hundred or so miles in width to almost a thousand miles, meandering along the Manchurian border.

"And there you halted. Were you stopped by enemy forces?"

"Not really. Or that is, not by North Korean forces. They continued to be hard to find. In fact, as a tactical threat, they had all but ceased to exist. But various divisional units, including our own, had started to encounter enemy forces of a different kind—not North Korean, but Chinese."

The intentions of those Chinese, or CCF for Chinese Communist Forces, were by no means clear to us in contact with them on the ground in the local area. Nor, as I have since learned much later in life, were their intentions much understood on strategic levels in the theater by Generals Walker and MacArthur, or even back in Washington.

"How did your division fit into all this?"

"About the time we had our Thanksgiving dinner with the traditional turkey and trimmings, served in the field by dedicated and striving mess personnel, our regiment went into bivouac in a broad valley, with rice fields, near the Ch'ongch'on River a few miles north of the town of Kunu-ri."

"You mean you had Thanksgiving dinner while on the lines in position?"

"Well, sort of. But not exactly. Our battalion was in regimental reserve and behind the 9th Infantry Regiment, which was in position ahead a couple of miles. I'm not sure how they handled their Thanksgiving dinner. It must have been a bit antsy. But for us, our mess teams brought up the dinner in the standard hot-food containers and served a few men at a time—cautiously."

The high commands were quite pleased with the ability to serve Thanksgiving dinner to as many combat troops as possible in forward areas, and lost no opportunities to brag about it, perhaps justly so. It was actually no small logistical and tactical accomplishment, considering the terrain, weather, and many other adverse conditions at the time.

"About that time, as the reserve regiment, we were being used for motorized patrol missions out in front of the other units on line. The name of the game was to find the enemy's location and strengths—and capabilities—and, for the intelligence people, their intentions.

"But some puzzling things were happening with the CCF that added greatly to the general uncertainties about their intentions."

"Puzzling things? What kind of puzzling things?" Ryan was showing renewed interest.

"Well, the Chinese were doing things that could lead one to assume they were not interested in fighting—at least for then, or so long as we did not advance any further toward their territory across the Yalu in Manchuria."

In those days, and on our patrols, the Chinese had actually shown what seemed to be signs of friendliness. For example, one day I was ordered to take a company-size patrol out and up the road northward leading toward the Yalu and in the direction of the town of Kanggye. The day was clear and cold in early winter. We passed through mostly barren, hilly country. Patches of scattered snow were on the rice paddies and adjacent slopes. Our convoy, with several armored vehicles, some jeeps and 3/4-ton personnel carriers with pedestal-mounted 50-caliber machine guns, and a couple of antiaircraft artillery "flak wagons," pushed cautiously along the twisted and winding gravel road up a long and slowly rising valley floor.

Our patrol had advanced about five miles when the troopers began noticing increasing numbers of figures on the skylines of the hills on each side of the valley. We were quite nervous and halted immediately. The platoon leaders quickly confirmed that the figures were not refugees, but military personnel, and in uniforms they identified as Chinese. I knew we were in a most dangerous and vulnerable situation in the bottom of a valley with enemy on the high ground on both sides of us. I had visions of the American cavalry in the far West during frontier days, being ambushed in a gorge by the clever Indian chiefs and warriors.

As a precaution, I ordered the convoy to turn around and reverse direction so that we could haul ass in a hurry if fired on by surprise. We then spent some time just sitting and watching the Chinese on the skyline. They seemed relaxed, wandering around as though oblivious to a potential bloodbath.

As we sat watching the Chinese, and they peered at us, I could not recall in all my wartime combat-duty in World War II, or in the Korean War thus far, ever being in quite a similar situation—so close to a formidable number of the enemy and yet not engaged in a fire fight. As the minutes ticked by, I had the platoon leaders take counts and try to assess the Chinese armaments. There were no vehicles in sight, but one squad leader reported what he thought were some machine-gun positions, but no other heavy weapons. I knew, of course, that mortars or artillery would hardly be on the skyline, but could be readily available for support just over the hill beyond.

Some of the men wanted to open fire on the Chinese and asked if they could do so.

"Did your patrol then start firing?" Ryan interjected.

"Absolutely not! I hastened to put out the word that under no circumstances were we to fire the first shot, especially from our very vulnerable positions." We were a reconnaissance, and not a combat, patrol and could hardly have been in a more "trapable" and dangerous position with all the ingredients of the classic oater "last stand." As stated, we seemed to be almost completely surrounded, by a numerically superior enemy, with unknown reserves, occupying all the high ground, with us in easily destroyed column formation at the bottom of a long valley.

To open fire ourselves would have been little less than suicidal. My fear was that if we provoked the Chinese into opening fire on us, we could not withdraw without heavy losses, if at all. The situation was most delicate and potentially explosive and yet, when my troops waved at the Chinese, some so close you could even determine the expressions on their faces, the Chinese would smile and wave back. It was all most mystifying. Here they were, all exposed in full view, as though hostile action was the furthest thought from their minds.

After a few more minutes of the standoff, I gave the order to commence withdrawing and returning to our own lines. The lead vehicles started moving, slowly and cautiously, with everyone fully alerted and ready to return fire if the Chinese opened up. As we gradually left the area, the Chinese continued to watch us, but they never fired a shot and we returned to our lines safely, but thoroughly puzzled by the whole experience.

"When you reported all this upon returning from the patrol, what was the reaction of Hutchin, your battalion CO, or others?" Ryan wondered aloud.

"At first, disbelief. Or at least stunned skepticism. Colonel Freeman was at battalion headquarters and grilled me and some of my leaders over and over. We also talked with the regimental intelligence officer for extensive debriefing. I learned that they had, in turn, consulted at length with the division intelligence people."

"Was that the end of the matter?"

"It was as far as Baker Company, or myself, was concerned, but a day or so later, when I was at the battalion CP, Colonel Freeman arrived again in his jeep. He spotted me and came up. We saluted and greeted each other and I could see he had something apparently hot on his mind."

"Pratt, you wanna hear something real weird?" Freeman asked me.

"I guess so, Colonel," I answered with some hesitation. I was not sure I wanted to hear his little tidbit, especially if it meant another hairy patrol by my company or me.

"You remember that patrol you took out?" I admitted apprehensively that I did. "Well, we sent a follow-up the next day, reinforced with more firepower, with instructions to push farther to see what the Chinese would do."

"And what happened?" I asked, not really sure I wanted to know, but at the same time keenly interested in learning whether a later patrol would have gotten off as easy as we did earlier.

"They got as far as you did, without any problems, but when they began to advance beyond that point, the Chinese opened fire, and the patrol had to withdraw, which the Chinese permitted them to do. It did not seem they were interested in wiping them out, or inflicting heavy damage on them. But they did have to leave behind some men wounded in the confusion."

"So we now have some missing POW casualties from that patrol?" I asked.

"No, and that's the really bizarre aspect of the whole matter. When a third patrol returned the next day to the same area, they found the wounded men all bandaged up and warmly covered with blankets on litters by the sides of the road where they had fallen. Our patrol picked them up and brought them back to our positions."

"By George," I said, or perhaps similar but more expletive words, "that's truly eerie! What does our side make of all this, Colonel Freeman?"

"We wish we knew. It's all so very puzzling to our intelligence people, and the whole matter has gained the attention all the way up the line, even to 'ole Mac' 's headquarters. It's as though the Chinese are attempting to communicate to us that they do not want to fight, or intend to fight. But, on the other hand, could it be only that they do not want to fight at this particular time? There's a huge difference, I think.

"No one can say for sure," Freeman continued, "whether this telegraphs an enemy intention, or is mere deception. It's been no secret, as we all know, that they are here. We've spotted them for days. Earlier this month, the Chinese were spotted by aerial reconnaissance crossing into North Korea from Manchuria by the bushels. But then, a few days later, as we approached this area close to the border, they were seen in long columns recrossing the Yalu bridges into Manchuria.

"I don't like it at all," Freeman added, as he shivered in the cold and munched on a C-ration candy bar. "Last thing I think should happen to us, having been so successful thus far, is to lock horns with any masses of Chinese in this remote area, far forward of our supply sources, and the enemy so close to theirs, in some of the world's most treacherous terrain, and with winter descending upon us. Even our air support is operating at the absolute maximum of their range and can spend only minutes over the combat zone. They certainly could not provide us with close support for any extended period."

Little did Freeman then know how prophetic and on point were to be his comments in that windy, open, and bleak cornfield in far North Korea in late November of 1950. Almost within hours, he was to have answers to his questions as to the intentions of the Chinese and whether they would defend in force, put up only a token rearguard action, or would attack in full force and fury. General MacArthur, fully convinced that the Chinese would not intervene in strength, in spite of regular Peking announcements to the contrary, and my commanders were soon to have dramatic answers to these questions, to their dismay and to our grief.

I hung on at that exchange to Freeman's every word. The words burned into my memory like engravings. I have long remembered such comments from Freeman and Hutchin when they favored me with them. I had great respect for their judgments and felt flattered when they shared them with me, a mere company commander. But that was the nature and modus operandi of those two superb officers. They took great pains to insure that their men were fully informed and knew as much as possible about what was going on in their areas and in the general combat zone. I once heard Hutchin express his conviction that a soldier well informed as to what he was doing, and why, could be expected to fight better.

Strangely, if our good Freeman, 2d Division commander Keiser, army commander Walker, and even the Pentagon were having trouble figuring out the Chinese's intentions, MacArthur, as stated, was not. As is written by many historians, MacArthur was convinced the Chinese had no intentions whatever of becoming involved in the Korean War. He attributed Peking warnings, to the contrary, as so much paper-tiger propaganda. Clay Blair, in his *Forgotten War,* wrote: "MacArthur was on record from the President on down as unequivocally assuring that the CCF would not intervene in Korea in force." Coming events would show just how wrong was MacArthur.

"What was your next role?" asked Ryan, rousing himself somewhat from deep meditation.

"After our Thanksgiving dinner on Thursday, November 23, we prepared to move forward into an assembly area when the word came, as is now long since recorded, that the Eighth Army would launch a general attack all along the front with the X Corps in the northeast sector over the central mountains."

We learned that the Division's 9th and 38th infantry regiments, with supporting artillery and other units, had already moved up on line in the area around Kujondong on the right, and east, bank of the Ch'ongch'on River, some twenty miles or so from Kunu-ri. Colonel Hutchin summoned his company commanders for a briefing on the morning of November 25.

"As soon as transportation arrives," he began, "we are going to move by motor to our assembly areas in the division sector. The Eighth Army has launched its final assault to reach the Yalu and the Manchurian border so close by. The X Corps has been on the border for some days, as you know, over in the east.

"The 2d Division will spearhead the army's attack in the west.

The 23rd will initially be in reserve. The 9th and 38th are already on line. Theater intelligence believes the CCF in the area will fall back into Manchuria. It is hoped this will be the final stages of the war. With luck we should be home by Christmas."

I did not have the feeling that Hutchin much believed the last part of what he was saying. But it sounded nice. The reports, though, of fighting already underway by other regiments of the division hardly sounded like an enemy who was not going to fight but, rather, who was pulling back into his own country.

Transportation arrived as planned in late morning. We loaded and spent much of the sunny but cold day, with piercing and biting winds, bouncing torturously along, over a narrow and twisting road, stopping and going, with almost constant gridlocks from heavy military traffic of all kinds.

"Did you have any contacts with the CCF along the way?" interrupted Ryan.

"Not much, or at least directly, although we could hear artillery and small-arms fire from time to time off to our right front, which would have been the ROK II Corps or perhaps the Turkish Brigade sectors."

We completed our move by mid-afternoon without any serious incidents and closed into our assembly area in another open valley. There were a few isolated Korean houses scattered around and a mixture of cornfields and rice paddies. There were some low and rolling hills a few hundred yards to our left, and some rather higher and challenging ones to our right.

Settling into an Assembly Area

As Baker Company pulled into the assembly area farther north of Kunu-ri and not very far from the Yalu River, I assigned positions to the platoon leaders and others. I had the first sergeant select a spot for the company CP, or command post. He picked the reverse slope of a small embankment that ran athwartship of the valley and across a cornfield. A couple of my ROKs began digging in. I told the platoon leaders to carefully check their men, ammunition, and equipment and make ready for any eventuality, since we did not know at all what we might be up against in the next few hours or through the night. We could hear small arms, and explosions in the distance and mostly up the valley toward what we thought was the direction of the enemy front.

On the side of precaution, even though we were in reserve, I told the platoon leaders to displace their platoons in a defensive tactical alignment looking upward toward the direction of the firing, and to dig in to the extent they could in the partially frozen soil. To our front there extended a harvested cornfield with broken stalks scattered here and there. Beyond that, about four or five hundred yards away, we could see friendly troops moving about and some trucks and other vehicles, and what we thought were field-artillery pieces in position.

The battalion CO had sent Able Company off to our left to occupy ground between us and the Ch'ongch'on River. While my company was getting settled down and carrying out my instructions, I walked through the cornfield and over to the Able Company CP. The CO, Capt. Melvin Stai, and I chatted for a bit and I could see that he was as uneasy about the situation as I was. We agreed that we were like sitting ducks in this open valley and at the mercy of the enemy if they chose to put mortar or artillery observers on the high ground on our flanks, especially on our right front. We were not as much concerned about enemy small-arms fire from the high ground, since it was at least a mile or more from us and beyond the effective range of most small weapons.

Stai advised me that he too had deployed his company in a tactical defensive arrangement. We both felt better with each other's precautions. As I returned to my company area, I looked out and saw the regimental and battalion COs bearing down on my CP. I hastened to meet them.

"Is everything OK, Pratt?" asked Hutchin, speaking first. I said yes and explained what the Able Company commander and I had done about deploying our troops in defensive positions. Hutchin was clearly pleased. He turned to Freeman and said, "You see? I told you Pratt and Stai would not need to be told to do the obvious." Hutchin enjoyed praising his officers and men when in the presence of higher commanders. He had a sharp grasp of the requirements for good leadership and morale building.

"How about an update on the big picture now that we are here?"

I asked, looking at both and waiting for an answer from either. This time Freeman spoke first.

"Well, Pratt," he started, "I wish I could give you a complete picture overall, but unfortunately I can't. There are more things about this action that I do not understand than I do understand. Intelligence from above seems to me to be unduly optimistic. They believe the CCF is capable of delaying us as they withdraw, or attacking with weak forces against our positions around here—but they think they will do the former—that is withdraw if hit. Based on this estimate, the general advance has been ordered."

Freeman's frustration and deep concern came through loud and clear. Hutchin was nodding his head in agreement.

"I'm not sure I follow your concern, Colonel Freeman," I said. "If the Chinese do withdraw with only token resistance, isn't that cause for rejoicing? Can't we roll out the barrels and do some singing and dancing in the streets?" A brief smile crossed Freeman's face as he noted my feeble attempt at metaphorical humor.

"Perhaps so," he said slowly. "God knows I hope so, but we have Chinese all the way down in the Sunch'on area, almost fifty miles to our south. We know too that there are swarms of CCF all around us near here. We are one hell of a distance from our supply dumps but the enemy is almost on top of theirs. All the while, the Chinese government is continually saying they are going to intervene. In the face of this I simply do not see the wisdom of going on the offensive. I can only hope that 'ole hot Doug' knows something that we don't."

We were all silent for a good long period as we tried to digest and contemplate Freeman's pearls of wisdom. No one knew quite how to feel and least of all what lay ahead for us.

"Chinaman's Hat"—Hill 329 Gets a Name

The regimental commander was obviously quite worried about the situation and the fate of his command. He turned to Hutchin and asked about the disposition of the rest of the First Battalion. He shot me another glance and then as he was about to depart, he said, "Then you think you are all set for the night and can repel all attacks, Pratt?"

"I didn't quite say that, Colonel," I responded. "I would like, however, to know more about our nearby compatriots. Who, for instance, are these folks out to our front?"

Freeman looked out at the direction I was pointing, and returned for a moment to his map board.

"Oh, that's the 61st Field Artillery from the First Cavalry. They are on loan and supporting the 2d Division."

"Also," I followed up, "aren't you two, with your CPs here in the valley with us, concerned about the high ground on both sides? Suppose it becomes occupied by the enemy. They would sure be looking down our throats, wouldn't they?"

Both colonels looked around and studied the terrain.

"Which high ground in particular?" one asked me.

"Well, any of them for that matter, but I guess the most threatening is there," I said, pointing to our right front at a peak that was particularly close and high. "The pointed peak that looks like a coolie's hat. We've started calling it 'Chinaman's Hat.' "

Freeman studied the hill I pointed to for a moment and then returned to his map board and chuckled.

"Well, that hill is shown as Hill 329 on the map, but I think I like your designation better. It's certainly descriptive." After that, he and Hutchin mounted their jeeps and sped away, leaving me and some of my men standing forlorn in the cornfield.

In later references and communications, and in most or all historical accounts in later years, Hill 329 would routinely be identified as "Chinaman's Hat." Whether I can claim credit, or the blame, for that, based on my exchange with Freeman that evening in our valley, I shall never know for sure. Perhaps there are others who also referred to the hill in that way, and before I did so. Either way, the little hill has occupied a slot in fame and history, not so much because I or others may have given it a recognizable title but, rather, because of the critical role it was to play in the scheme of things over the next few days.

The sun was now low on the western horizon. The bitter wind had picked up and was sweeping down the valley. The thoughts of darkness settling in and what the enemy might do under its cover were not very comforting. I watched my men digging in. Some were attacking cans of cold C rations and pulling their jacket collars tight up around their necks and heads. At such times, combat men's minds must surely drift longingly to families or others far away and more pleasant places and wonder just how they offended fate to wind up in a place like North Korea in an open cornfield at such a time. No matter what thoughts raced through or lingered in their minds, they had little conception or forewarning of the grisly events that lay just ahead.

CHAPTER THREE

The Chinese Strike

"So you and Baker Company of the 23rd were snug in the valley, gazing up at 'Chinaman's Hat' to your right front and laying plans for your forthcoming ski resort, eh?" Historian Ryan smiled at his casual try at injecting some humor into an otherwise thoroughly unhumorous predicament.

"That would perhaps have been a desirable course of action I suppose, but hardly within the scope of our capabilities at the moment—if ever. That night as the UN offensive was supposed to be in full swing all over the front, the Chinese instead struck in full fury just at dark, like swarms of ants. It would seem that they were literally everywhere one turned."

In later years I have learned more of the extent of that attack in sectors other than my own immediate area. The 9th and 38th regiments of our division, in the early hours of the Chinese attack, were engaged in particularly heavy and bloody fighting from CCF units that came at them from all directions and in great and overpowering numbers.

The ROK Corps on our right and the Turkish Brigade collapsed and were routed to the peril of our division by exposing our right flank. The sad and devastating experiences of those units are graphically recorded by historians and also veterans far more personally involved and knowledgeable than I. An especially gripping account is available from the incredibly prolific writer S. L. A. Marshall. In his *River and the Gauntlet* he described the tribulations of those units, including our 9th and 38th, in ghastly details.

Marshall, however, devoted scant attention to the 23rd Regiment, for reasons that have never been clear to me. In his chapter "An Affair at Chinaman's Hat," he alluded in a paragraph or two to the fighting by Able Company on the first night of the attack, and then concedes on page 50 that "Baker Company also was drawing its share of the fire." The more expansive facts are that we did indeed have our share of troubles, although probably not to the hair-raising extent of our sister regiments. Still, I have long felt that Marshall's characterization of our participation is perhaps one of the major understatements of the war.

Be that as it may, our troubles began around midevening. Artillery and mortar fire began falling rather haphazardly to our front and our rear near the regimental CP. Off to my left, at about 2200 hours, there was intense small-arms fire, very close and undoubtedly in the Able Company area. I remember being completely bewildered.

We were several hundred yards behind the 61st Field Artillery, which in turn was at least a mile behind the 9th Infantry, through which we were supposed to attack the next morning. What then, I asked myself, could Able Company be firing at? By then, I had fully alerted all my platoons and, as the firing continued, I decided to take my radio operator and a few men to see if I could work my way over to Able's CP to find out what was causing all the firing.

"Hey, Rodriguez!" I shouted, "Grab a couple runners and a couple ROKs and come along. We're going over to Able's position to see if we can find out what's going on."

Domingo Rodriguez was my indomitable radio operator. My "right arm" as it were. He was constantly by my side night and day with the walkie-talkie SCR-300 without which I would be out of communication with higher headquarters and almost the rest of the world. But Rodriguez, a Mexican-American from my birth state of Arizona, was no ordinary radio operator—or run-of-the-mill soldier. He was exceptional. Whether needed or not, he was there. Not always awake, perhaps, in the wee hours or even with the sun high overhead, but he was there at my side responding when called upon.

Rodriguez was for me a source of humor and support when the going would be roughest. He was my constant companion, running up and down hills at my side as I routinely checked the platoons and their positions and fields of fire and possible avenues of enemy approach in the countless defensive positions we had taken, or were to take, over the months.

Rodriguez and I were to grow very close to each other, occupying usually the same foxhole, eating and sleeping together, and learning each other's every idiosyncrasy, strength, and weakness. If either of us had any homosexual tendencies, which we did not, I suppose we would eventually have seriously considered matrimony if we survived the war. Before he himself was to be killed, he was to save my life on more than one occasion, as we shall see.

"Si, Si, Capitano. Presto," Rodriguez said, leaping to his feet and shouldering his beloved signal corps radio. In short order he had our group together, and we headed out through the cornstalks.

"Were you then under fire?" Ryan inquired. "Did you make it to Able Company OK or are you still lying out there in a Korean valley?"

"Not funny, Tom, but good try," I retaliated. "I don't recall that there was any incoming small-arms fire just in those moments, but for sure it existed in the surrounding hills, and over in the direction of Able Company or beyond, where we were headed."

We started through the cornstalks, about waist-high in most places. I retraced in the moonlight, as best I could, my route earlier before sunset. We had left our own positions and had gone only a few dozen yards when one of the runners tripped and fell flat on his duffer. I remember scolding him somewhat, cautioning him to be more careful and quiet when stepping over the furrows.

The fellow said, with a bit of indignation, "Christ, Captain, it ain't no furrow. It's a body!"

I paused and returned to the trooper who had fallen. Sure enough, in the glowing moonlight, I could see that the "furrow" was indeed a body. By his quilted uniform, tennis shoes, and long "sock" of rice around his neck, he was recognizable as a Chinese soldier. We glanced around and spotted two other Chinese, and then also the body of an American GI.

I then warned the men to be extra careful. To me this was especially alarming. I feared there must be more Chinese nearby and that we could be ambushed at any moment—not exactly the kind of stuff to restore calm and serenity. Of course I was right with my worries, but we pressed on and shortly came to some GIs whom we identified as Able Company troops. It was Able's Third Platoon, and the nearest unit to our Baker Company. I asked for, and found, the platoon leader. Some of the men were laying down a blanket of fire on something out ahead. Just what, if anything, I was not able to ascertain. I knew it not to be uncommon for nervous troops around the front lines to fire simply out of uncertainty or fear.

"Lieutenant, I'm Baker Company CO," I said in a low voice, almost a whisper. "Can you tell me what is going on? Are you actually being hit, or are your men just trigger-happy."

"Trigger-happy, my butt," he shot back, not sure whether I was annoying or baiting him. "We've got gooks out the anus. They are everywhere. They've been pouring into our area since dark and we've had an almost constant fire fight. We've been mowing them down and still they come. Not sure whether they are driven by fear, force, or confusion. Perhaps a little of all."

"How about your losses? How hard are you hurt?"

"We've got losses all right, but nothing compared to the Chinese who are piled out in front of us. Must be dozens and dozens, but won't know before daylight. Sure as hell not going to send my men out now to find out."

"Of course not," I agreed. "But how in God's name can all those Chinese be here? There's a whole artillery battalion just ahead of us, and the entire 9th Regiment ahead of them. Could that mean they are all wiped out and this is now the front?" I chattered. I was shaking like the proverbial dog passing peach seeds and not sure whether it was from the bitter cold, with the temperatures in the teens, or from fright—or from both.

"They seem to be pouring across the shallow Ch'ongch'on River to our left flank."

"But there are companies over there from the 9th Regiment."

"Are?" the lieutenant said. "Better say 'were'! Gangs of GI stragglers have been pouring into our positions all evening and almost getting shot themselves by our men, who are confusing them with the gooks. The stragglers are panicky and thoroughly shook up—a real mess—most are wet from wading the river and almost frozen. They say their whole outfit has been overrun. Don't know whether they are exaggerating or not. No time to check. We have our hands more than full and all we can do to hang on. Hasn't Baker been hit yet?"

"Well, I'm not sure yet, Lieutenant," I answered. "Certainly nothing like you're going through. We did stumble over some bodies back in our left platoon sector—both Chinese and our own. So apparently the enemy is around in our company too—could be anywhere, I guess. For sure we are in for a rough night. I'm going to get back. Let your CO know I was over if you get a chance." He didn't, as I later found out. He was killed shortly after I left him there in the moonlight.

Rodriguez and I and the others started our return and had almost reached our nearest platoon positions when I dimly saw several men moving about just ahead of us in the night air. A welcomed and reassuring development, I recall thinking. As we got closer, straining to see, I gradually realized they were not our men. I could make out the quilted clothing and the absence of helmets. One of the runners also had seen the figures, recognized that they were not our GIs or ROKs, and urgently whispered to me, "Captain, they're gooks!" I did not need convincing. They had also seen us and were swinging around to open fire.

Almost instantaneously the dreaded "bur-r-r-r-p" of a sub-machine gun ripped through the cornfield. Dirt kicked up at our feet and the air around our heads made the familiar snapping "crack" that occurs when a slug passes close by—sort of a miniature sonic boom. The runner at my side fell to the ground with, as I later confirmed, a bullet through his eye and out the back of his head. I felt a tug at my right sleeve as though someone were trying to get my attention. I recognized the feel of a bullet smashing into or through clothing. I hoped it had missed me. By then, it seemed, everyone on both sides was firing madly.

I aimed my carbine at the closest Chinaman who had fired the first volley, but the hammer went forward slowly and softly and barely made a sound as it struck the firing pin in the bolt. I knew instantly what the problem was. The freezing cold had solidified the lubricant and prevented enough force on the firing pin to detonate the cartridge. It would not be the last time during the winter when such a phenomenon would occur. Desperately, with dry throat and pounding pulse, I worked the bolt by hand to recock the carbine and pointed it as accurately as I could at the shadow of the enemy trooper. This time it fired, but I missed, or at least the Chinaman showed no indication of being hit. Again I fired. This time the man let out a yell and I saw him fall to the ground. Several more Chinese emerged from the background and joined in the exchange. The fire fight continued for at least several more minutes and then gradually began to subside. Firing became sporadic and then finally completely stopped. We saw no more of the enemy and we eased away. In the daylight the following morning we returned and counted seven dead enemy troops. One of my ROKs was shot in the leg. Rodriguez had a bullet dent in his helmet and his radio antenna was shot away.

I paused to let Ryan catch up on his notes. Finally he asked, "What was your company doing during all this firing?"

"I wasn't sure, of course," I said. "We were vaguely aware that small-arms fire was continuing in the Able Company zone from whence we had come, but we still were not aware of any firing in our own Baker area. But if there were any, and the rest of my company were also being hit, I knew it was quite possible that I would not have heard it over and above the firing we were doing."

As we left the vacant, we had thought, area between our companies and approached my First Platoon's positions, we were challenged by nervous riflemen who had for sure heard our firing. We hastened to identify ourselves with our limping, wounded ROK trooper. I ran into Sgts. Louie Burch and Paul Buswell, both squad leaders, and we exchanged what info we had as to the situation.

I was about to leave the company area and check on the other platoons—I am not sure which at this late date—when suddenly the air was again filled with the crack and spurt of small-arms fire. Bullets cut the cornstalks all around us and several of my men yelled, "Here they come! We're being attacked! There's gooks everywhere!" And indeed, there were. They were running straight at our positions, seeming not to care as they were mowed down by our well-directed and controlled fire.

My men too were being hit. Some at almost point-blank range. I joined in the firing, unavoidedly, as the Chinese bore down directly at me and Rodriguez and some others immediately nearby. Several of the Chinese fell at our feet and almost on top of us. Some rushed on by as though to run around or through our positions. Events were unrolling at a frantic, noisy, and clamorous rate.

I also knew this was no place for a company commander who must be concerned about the operations and welfare of all his company and not just about one of the platoons engaged in a fire fight. I knew I must get back to the company CP so that I could monitor and assist all the platoons with support and direction. I had not forgotten the fate of Gen. William Dean, CG (commanding general) of the 24th Division, who had gotten himself captured the previous summer. He had not been at his division CP, where division commanders usually stay, but had been with a rifle platoon firing a bazooka. His action was reported at the time as an example of courage, but years later, when he was released as a POW, he acknowledged that he had not been especially prudent. I did not think I would serve my troops best by being another Dean. I knew I must inform the battalion commander of my predicament and promptly.

"Come, Rodriguez," I said. "We must get the hell out of here. There's lots to be done before bedtime."

"Right behind you, Capitano," as he loved to call me, and we ran, crouching among the cornstalks, toward the company CP.

Upon arriving I immediately let the other platoons know of the Chinese strength fighting our left platoon and then tried to contact battalion. It was difficult because of the shot-away antenna. The signal was weak, but fortunately we were only a few hundred yards away from the battalion CP. After a bit Hutchin came on the radio and he let me know that the Chinese had launched a major attack of their own, were overrunning units across the front, and had overrun our own regimental CP. Freeman had been forced to relocate. "Hang in there," Hutchin told me. "Be ready for the worst, and keep me informed," he admonished. I "rogered," or acknowledged, his message but was by no means certain as to how I was going to comply.

"As you were reporting to Hutchin, what was happening to your first platoon which was so heavily engaged?" Ryan wondered.

"They still had their hands full with wave after wave of the enemy assaulting their positions, but after about an hour, the fighting eased. The platoon leader had let me know that after the Chinese ran into his wall of fire, they lost interest in maintaining their attack. Bit by bit they disengaged and withdrew. But we could not, through the night, be sure just how far they had withdrawn and whether they had abandoned the assault or were simply regrouping."

"What about artillery or mortar support? Did you use your 60s, or did you call on battalion for 81-mm, or artillery, or other fire?"

"No, hardly at all. And that was frustrating. Ordinarily that heavy-fire support is the infantryman's salvation. The problem was that we had, as far as we knew, friendly artillery and other troops to our fronts in various stages of disorganization wandering around exactly where, we knew not. I could not ask for heavy-weapons fire-support without the risk of clobbering all those friendly folks. Nor could we shell the closest Chinese, who were almost on top of us and mingled among us in our own positions. I certainly did not want to shell my own troops. They would frown for sure on such a development. Had we been in the usual frontline positions, with no friendly troops ahead, such a limitation on the much-desired use of our own heavy-fire support would not have existed. We could have made excellent use of various support fire regularly available to assist the foot-slogging infantry."

Chinese Food or Pizza?

"So then what happened in the absence of ordinary artillery support? No doubt everyone saddled up and adjourned to the local pizza parlor? Or was it the Chinese-food carry-out?" Ryan looked a bit proud of his lighthearted injection.

"That of course would have been most welcomed, but it was hardly in the cards. Around midnight, or a bit before, our sector and the nearby environs became strangely silent, rather nervously so.

There was lots of rumbling of explosives and chattering of small arms away in the distance in almost every direction, but not exactly near to us.

"Then, about a half-hour after midnight, all hell broke loose smack in the center of my company as the platoons opened fire on new waves of Chinese. This time they were ringing bells, and tooting horns and making all sorts of noise and racket. We thought they even had pots and pans on which they were banging with clubs or sticks. They even whistled and yelled. Several of my men were hit, but the heavy toll taken on the Chinese was little short of ghastly and pathetic. They simply piled up all around."

Chinese Willingness to Die

We were never able to determine with certainty just what drove the Chinese on. Did they think we were not there? Or were they pushed from fear of dire consequences from their leaders if they did not charge forth as they did? I could never believe that an ideological brainwashing in Communist philosophy could so fanatically motivate peasant people to the point of such apparent disregard for their lives.

It has been suggested by some analysts that routine life for the Chinese poor was so burdensome that they did not try as we would to hang onto it. For sure, strong religious convictions and a belief in rewards in the hereafter can drive men to willing sacrifice of their lives on a battlefield for a cause.

We've seen fanatical fighting in history in the Crusades, the Islamic Jihad, or Holy War, in the Sudan deserts at the time of Gordon of Khartoum, and even in the 1980s in the Iran–Iraq war. But surely the intensity of those religious convictions cannot be equated with the religious or political beliefs of the Chinese soldiers that we were facing.

The matter of Chinese disregard for life has been given much study in years after the Korean War, but I do not know that any of the think tanks have ever emerged with a dispositive answer. There are many theories, but none that I know of that attribute the Chinese blind charge into certain disaster in the Korean War to merits of the Communist cause. One can only speculate and wonder.

Under the circumstances then I had no time, however, for such

philosophizing. There was work to be done for the combat infantrymen. I worked my way up at one point in the fight and located
Sgt. Jessie Hilton, who I found was with Cpl. Edgar Halloway, one of
the squad leaders. Both of them were almost surrounded with dead
and dying Chinese.

"What's the scoop, Sarg?" I asked. "Do you think you can hold?"

"We don't know, Captain. So far we are hanging in here, but pretty
soon we've got to have some ammo. Lots of our damned weapons are
jamming and won't fire. I think they have iced up from moisture, or
may be gumming up from the cold grease. We're freezing our balls off
too. Did some one blow the pilot light out in the heating system? How
many gooks do you think are around us, anyway?"

"I sure wish I could tell you. No one seems to know. This is part
of a front-wide general assault. No one seemed to have expected an
attack of this size, if at all. Seems to me we have no choice but to
withdraw unless there are a hell of a lot of reserves somewhere that I
haven't heard about. If we do withdraw, I sure wish I could tell you
when."

As we talked there in the middle of the cornfield, we thought we
detected an easing of the firing. It seemed to be tapering off, and in
fact it did. Soon the battlefield became quiet again around us.

Ryan asked if we had prevailed over the Chinese.

"Not at all," I hastened to assure him. "I suspected and feared the
little rascals were still out there and in great and dreadful numbers.
But it was likely, if the truth were known, that they did not cotton to
being shot up any more than any other soldiers. They had borne the
cross to a point, but might have finally concluded that there had to be
a better way to make a living—so they fell back to regroup or go into
a pondering session somewhere out there in the darkness."

Chinese Strategy

In retrospect, I have long felt the Chinese were feeling us out and
trying to find out where we were not, and then advance in that area.
They had tried to pass through Able Company's area, probably not
knowing for sure that Able was there. When they learned, at their
bloody cost, that Able was there, the Chinese then withdrew,

regrouped, and tried to move through our area, either not knowing, again, that we were there, or not thinking we were there in force.

I figured the Chinese would not likely hit us again, but would try to swing around us to the right. But, of course, I couldn't be sure. Nevertheless, since they had concentrated on the center of my positions earlier, I sent a message to my right platoon to be extra careful and alert and to expect an attack.

Near-Slaughter of Fleeing GIs

"Surely Baker Company earned a letup in the fighting for the rest of the night?" Ryan volunteered, but not really with much conviction in his voice. "Did more attackers arrive?"

"Not exactly as expected, but the night's excitement was far from over."

About an hour after the last fire fight, with an uneasy calm prevailing, we suddenly heard all kinds of commotions along the Baker Company front—but no firing. I hurried forward again to investigate. I found the platoons trying to cope with quite a different kind of situation.

Out in front of the platoons there were large numbers of men who were trying to come through our lines, but hesitating for fear of being fired upon. They were shouting, "We're GIs! Don't shoot!" But they were not convinced that my men believed them. There had been instances in wars, and elsewhere in Korea that same night, where English-speaking enemy troops had shouted and pretended to be Americans.

My men exercised commendable restraint, however, and did not fire, even though many felt very uneasy and not sure the men shouting were in fact friendly troops.

Gradually, the straggling GIs came out of the cornfields and approached our positions. They were a pitiful sight to behold. Most were wet and near freezing to death. Some had no shoes and their feet were injured and bleeding from stumbling across the frozen ground. Nearly all were disoriented and nearly hysterical with fear.

As we questioned these men, we learned that most were from the 61st Field Artillery battalion that we had seen ahead of us the previous evening before sundown. Some were also from the 9th Regiment, which had been in positions in front of the 61st.

Over and over, the fleeing troops told us of being "overrun" by "swarms" of Chinese. They claimed the CCF had hit so quickly and with such little warning and in such overwhelming numbers, that the GIs had no chance at all to grab their weapons and put up any resistance. Many had been caught in their sleeping bags, trying to rest or stay warm. The artillerymen confessed that they had simply run off and left their guns intact. I could only hope that the Chinese in our area were not 105-mm howitzermen who knew how to turn the guns on us.

As we talked with these pathetic, scared men, more fleeing troopers continued to pour through, some at a dead run and literally out of control. I soon noted that the panic of these men began to spread contagiously among my own men. Some actually bolted, or were clearly about to do so. I knew some fast command action was necessary.

Quickly, I ordered the platoon leaders to circulate among their men so they could see that the situation was under control and that their leaders were on hand, that there was no cause for panic, and that the men were not about to be deserted by the rest of the command and left alone to face the enemy assaults. Strong reassurances at such times I knew to be absolutely essential to avoid a collapse of resistance by frontline troops. I knew that panic could spread like wildfire on a moment's impulse.

As I urged the platoon leaders into action to prevent panic and what was later to become known as "bug-out fever," I was not too sure just how much of what I said I believed myself. But I knew far better that the effort had to be made, and urgently, if control was to be maintained.

Off and on for most of the rest of the night, stragglers from the overrun units to our front continued to filter through the lines. We were lucky that the Chinese did not hit us again. If they had, I don't know how we could have differentiated between them and our own men to avoid shooting up the fleeing GIs.

As the firing again died down and some sporadic quietness returned to the battlefield, I spent about two hours moving up and down the Baker Company front. I felt my troops needed all the encouragement they could get in such a hairy situation. Above all, I wanted them to know that their officers knew they were out there. Also I wanted to assure myself that they remained alert and as well prepared as possible if the enemy struck again. Those were simply some of the most elementary requirements of sound, and safe, command.

"So the remainder of the night passed without incident, eh Pratt?" Ryan chimed in again.

"Not so. There was more to come, unfortunately for us, as is now well recorded, but not, to my knowledge, in much detail."

At about 0200 hours, as I was circulating cautiously and, admittedly, nervously about in my Third Platoon area, I came upon a machine-gun position with several troopers staring intently out to their front. I eased up quietly to see what so captivated their attention. Two of the men, as I recall after all these years, were Sgt. Guy Gillett and Cpl. Richard Holmes.

"What's up fellers?" I asked in my lowest voice.

"There's gooks out there, Captain," Gillett whispered back.

"You're sure right about that," I agreed, after peering out myself for a bit. I could see shadowy figures poking around not more than fifty yards or so away. "Why aren't your gunners firing at them?"

"We were about to," Holmes added, "but they haven't fired at us, and we think they are only carrying away their dead and wounded. If so, they may be like medics with red crosses, and we aren't sure they should be shot."

"No, they shouldn't if they are medics. It's against the Geneva rules of warfare and much more. Would not be a very polite thing to do," I said. We watched a bit longer and felt sure we could see the Chinese dragging bodies away in the night. I was about to instruct the troopers to continue to hold their fire unless fired upon, and to move on myself, when suddenly we began to hear the most God-awful racket off to our right front.

From the slopes of Chinaman's Hat we began hearing the by-now familiar horns, bells, rattles, screaming, and countless other unidentifiable noises the Chinese had been making when on the attack. We thought we saw, additionally, flashlights or lanterns of some sort. It was clear there was to be no return to normalcy that night. Moreover, with the Chinese on the Hat, overlooking our positions, a far graver

"Ordnance? Ah'm havin' trouble with mah shootin' arn."

As in all modern warfare, artillery in Korea played a major role, but its effectiveness was often limited because of rough terrain, great distances behind remote troops on hilltops, and foggy and inclement weather. Many an artilleryman in the Korean War would consider Mauldin's message in the above World War II drawing a masterpiece of understatement.

element was being injected into the fighting. Now I was not so sure I wanted an end to the darkness that concealed us from the enemy's gaze.

Came the Dawn at Chinaman's Hat

The long night eventually passed and the first rosy fingers of dawn crept over the hills to our east. As daylight broadened, we peered anxiously at the slopes of the Hat to our right front, but could see no Chinese, even though we knew they must be there in force. As we waited and licked our wounds and assessed our losses and situation, we continued to be confronted with other matters.

Even after daylight, stragglers from the 9th Infantry units on both sides of the Ch'ongch'on River, and from the 61st, continued to filter through our lines and kept us constantly on edge. It was another night we thought would never end.

Hill 329, known as "Chinaman's Hat," on Korea's west coast near the Manchurian border. Author's foxhole can be seen in foreground.

Cornfield battleground in front of Baker Co./23rd Reg. positions in valley below Chinaman's Hat on Korean west coast, November 1950.

CHAPTER FOUR

Chaos at Chinaman's Hat

The occupation of Chinaman's Hat by the Chinese was to put an entirely new and critical complexion on our whole presence in our Ch'ongch'on valley location and situation. We had thought the previous afternoon that we might have seen movement on the slopes of the Hat. Freeman had commented that it was not any American units, according to know friendly troop dispositions. We had withheld fire because of some uncertainty on that point. Actually, the Hat was just beyond practical small-arms fire-range, although certainly within easy range of mortars, tanks, or artillery.

We knew that if the Hat was occupied by the enemy, the Chinese would be in an extraordinarily favorable position. They would be looking straight down our throats and be able to observe with ease our every position and activity. Although we would mostly also be beyond the range of their small arms, they could certainly bring devastating artillery or mortar fire on us through forward observers almost anywhere on the crest or slopes of the Hat. Also, on the Hat, the Chinese would be outflanking the whole 23rd Regiment, if not much of the 2d Division.

I felt the situation required immediate action of some sort and I hustled back to the CP area to contact Hutchin. "Good ole Hutch," however, was at least one jump ahead of me. He did not need convincing on this point. Freeman, from his relocated command post, had already ordered Hutchin to occupy the Hat, and I heard orders going out to Charlie Company to do just that. That order, it was to turn out, proved to be easier said than done. It was to be a tougher nut to crack than either the battalion or regimental commander realized. Still, there could be no question that the attempt had to be made. The whole command was in serious jeopardy.

The day and night passed as all awaited H hour on the following dawn. In the last predawn moments of that crisp, cold November 26 morning, Charlie Company began moving out in battle formation for the attack. Its platoons were, wisely, well dispersed. We were shivering and watching as we saw the platoons reach the far side of the valley and begin ascending the Hat's lower slopes. We lost sight of the troops off and on as they disappeared briefly from view amongst the low brush on the hillside. We looked in vain for any sign of the enemy. Surely they were there, lying concealed and waiting, but no one knew for sure just exactly where. Nor could we guess at their strength or their intentions. Would they resist or withdraw, or just what?

Before Charlie had advanced more than about a hundred yards up the slopes we had our answer. So did the poor Charlie troopers. They came suddenly under small-arms fire and artillery or mortar fire exploded in their ranks. It steadily increased in intensity. The company was clearly locked in a deadly fire fight and could hardly have been in a more disadvantageous situation. Its troops were exposed, on lower ground, and against a well-concealed enemy vastly superior, it turned out, in numbers. Charlie's attack was being aborted almost before it began.

As the morning wore on, the sun climbed ever upward, bright and shining. Its warm rays were a thankful blessing after the misery and cold of the past night. We learned that the temperatures had dropped below the teens. Only our intense activity and preoccupation with the enemy all through the dark hours prevented the cold from having a greater impact on us.

By midmorning the Hat was under almost constant artillery barrages. We saw little or no activity by Charlie troops who seemed well "pinned down" all over. We watched the familiar puffs of white phosphorous shells as forward observers adjusted their fire, and then a whole area would literally explode in ear-shattering blasts as the high explosive shells from a battery or battalion salvo landed over a wide area.

We felt, surely, that the Chinese must be paying dearly in casualties from both Charlie Company's small arms and the highly explosive shells landing all about.

"Was there any other fire delivered on the Hat?" Ryan asked from his comfortable sofa seclusion.

"Yes, in fact, there was. The tankers, that had joined us during the night from the regimental tank company and also from, I think, the 72d Medium Tank Battalion had started raking the Hat with their 50-caliber machine guns and also their tank cannons. There were also numerous air strikes. The fighters would come in dramatically and low, strafing and dropping napalm."

Under different circumstances, the firepower delivered on the Hat on that unforgettable morning, from almost every kind of air and ground weapon, would have been spectacular entertainment on the most grandiose scale, justifying top prices for admission tickets. We did not view it quite that way, however, with our fate hanging in the balance.

Our thoughts were both hopeful that the firepower would be successful and very apprehensive. I knew, perhaps even more than most of my men, who did not have World War II combat experience, that even the heaviest concentrations of firepower are often not enough to overcome enemy forces if they are well protected and dispersed.

The minutes ticked by as noon approached. We moved about with relative ease as the battle near the base of the Hat and up its slopes dragged on. Our supply people came up with ammo and rations and other items of equipment. I felt some guilt that we were carrying on with such ease with our Charlie Company locked so tightly in a continuing engagement.

At one point, the artillerymen from the 6lst Battalion were marched through our area on their way to their guns ahead. They had been rounded up and were being returned. Marshall was to write in his *River and the Gauntlet* about the events of the night: "Baker Company of the 23rd was given a hard time and the 61st Battalion did not fight but was stampeded" (page 51). I understand that vets of the 61st Battalion disagree with the criticisms of their conduct in the "Hat" engagement, but be that as it may, that morning we watched them return to their guns. They, surprisingly, found the guns undamaged by the Chinese and ready for use. Apparently the Chinese attacking in the valley were uninstructed or ignorant on the subject of destroying captured artillery pieces. I don't know that it is fair to greatly fault artillerymen not experienced in infantry fighting for not standing their ground when suddenly surrounded with swarms of the enemy in the middle of the night. Some vets may feel otherwise.

Shortly after noon, Rodriguez advised me that a message had been received for me to report to the battalion CP a short distance to the rear, whereupon I scurried back to comply.

At the battalion CP I also found the Able Company CO. The S-3 (operations officer), with Hutchin in attendance, proceeded to inform us that Colonel Freeman had received permission from the division commander to use the 23rd's 2d Battalion, which had been in division reserve, in an effort to "take" the Hat and that forthwith, the 2d Battalion, together with my company and Able Company, would undertake to do just that. He quickly briefed us on our routes of advance and our objectives and stressed speed in moving to and crossing the line of departure some several hundred yards away, and in closing on our objectives.

"Division is convinced that our only hope of remaining in this valley is to eject the CCF forces from Hill 329, where they have complete observation of all of us here below," Hutchin explained. "With the enemy on that high ground, our position here is completely untenable. The division is in certain danger of being surrounded and cut off."

Hutchin then went on to bring us up-to-date on the overall situation along the front. He said the Chinese had launched a general assault and had committed masses of troops. We did not disagree with that. He said that General Walker was profoundly puzzled and could not understand how such huge forces could have invaded North Korea and not have been more accurately detected. He said that the army commander had reported to MacArthur that it was still too early to know whether the attacks in strength were local counterattacks or a major offensive. As we now know, that position was dreadfully in error and understated.

Hutchin also told us, I recall strongly, even at this late date because I was very worried about our own fate, that the 24th Division on our left, nearer to the coast, had not yet been attacked and that the ROK II Corps on our right might be in deep trouble, but not to worry because the lst Cavalry Division and the Turkish Brigade were in reserve just behind, and were available to shore up the army's right flank in case matters got out of hand. Hutchin said that General Ed Almond's X Corps on the east Korean coast had also been hit, but that details were as yet quite sketchy.

I had the feeling that Hutchin was not completely squaring with us and that the situation might be much graver than he was letting on. But that was his optimistic nature. He was always the encouraging and inspiring leader. Subsequent events, as we now also know, were to show that my skepticism was more than fully justified. But for the moment there was much to be done. I had my orders and knew I must move fast in my own interest and in that of my men.

Within the hour after returning to my company, the platoon leaders had received their briefings and instructions, and we were on the way to the line of departure, that point at which the tactical assault is considered to be technically underway.

"Do you recall your company formation in the assault?" Ryan again chimed in.

"I feel sure I had two platoons forward abreast, followed by the weapons platoon, then company headquarters and with the reserve platoon bringing up the rear. It's been a long time, and my memory is not infallible, but that's the usual approach when attacking and I doubt that I would have deviated from it on that occasion."

"Did Baker Company pass through Charlie Company already engaged?"

"No, I have a clear recollection that we went in on their left, with the 2d Battalion companies on Charlie's right."

I do recall also, most vividly, that we had not quite gotten abreast

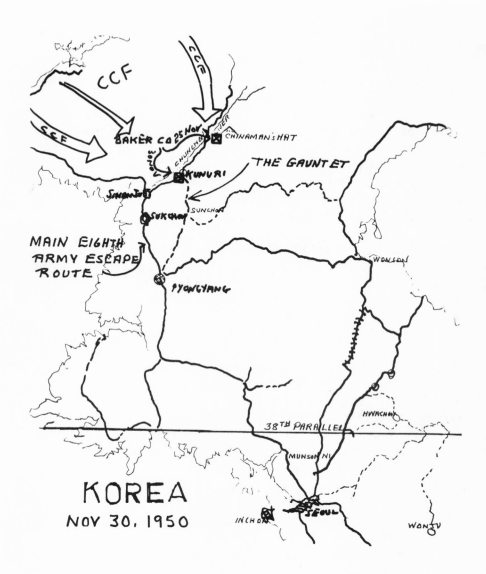

CCF

CCF

CCF

BAKER CO 25 Nov CHUNGHON CHINAMAN'S HAT

KUNURI

THE GAUNTET

SINANJU

SUKCHON SUNCHON

MAIN EIGHTH
ARMY ESCAPE
ROUTE

PYONGYANG

WONSON

38TH PARALLEL HWACHON

MUNSON NI

KOREA
NOV 30, 1950

INCHON SEOUL

WONJU

of Charlie's positions when we came under fire. Shades of Pickett's charge at Gettysburg on July 3, 1863, must have flashed through my mind. Even with a tremendous preparatory barrage by supporting artillery and mortars, the Chinese brought fire to bear on us that constantly increased, and steadily ground us to a halt.

In spite of the withering enemy fire, platoon leaders were courageously and stubbornly urging the men forward. No commander could ask more of his officers, but still the men were dropping like flies and were going down all across my front. I could hear heavy firing also over on the right, where Charlie Company and the 2d Battalion positions were. Our attack was not more than an hour old when we found ourselves all pinned down like Charlie Company. Every time a squad tried to move forward, devastating enemy fire forced it down again. In addition to the small-arms fire, mortar rounds were constantly dropping amongst us. Bit by bit we were being decimated, or worse.

At one point I thought perhaps if I took a more direct part, we could resume the advance. I decided, not with a great deal of wisdom, to see if I could get closer to my platoon on the left, which I believe was my second platoon with no officer, but under the command of an acting platoon leader, Sgt. John Crawford.

I waited until what I thought was a break in the firing, and then jumped up with a runner and began dashing forward and toward the area where I could see the platoon spread out. I crouched and zigzagged in the best Hollywood fashion, and as I did so a Chinese machine gunner opened up. He hit my runner in the leg and the runner went down. I had no choice but to keep going, since I was in a wide-open spot. The dirt kicked up around me and I felt a bullet tear into my left combat boot, but I didn't feel any pain.

"Then you were not hit?" Ryan said with what I thought was justifiable renewed interest.

"I wasn't sure at the time. Very often men can be hit or wounded and not feel pain or, sometimes, even not know they are wounded. But I had lucked out as I had on numerous occasions before and after—the bullet played hell with my boot, to my discomfort for some time afterwards, until I could get another pair. Almost the whole side had been sliced open."

I ran on a bit and literally dove behind a small mound of "bushy" rock, where I had a measure of protection. The machine gunner eased up and I had to see whether he would resume. He didn't, so I presumed I was out of his line of sight. A stone's throw away I spotted one of the squad leaders, Cpl. Ray Nolte.

"What the hell you trying to do, Captain? Get yourself killed?" he blurted out at me.

"Not deliberately, Nolte. But we are in deep trouble. No one can move forward, and I sure don't like all the company out here in the open providing the Chinks with unlimited targets. I gather you have also tried to advance without success?"

"You got that one right, Sir," he shot back, and pointed to the body of one of his men and motioned to two others only three or four yards away who were bloody with wounds.

"Why can't we get some fire support on that hill?"

I knew his remark was his way of trying for a bit of humor. He knew, as did I, that the hill had been all but blasted off the earth by hours of the heaviest imaginable barrages. If there was anything that we did not have, it was lack of fire support. Our dilemma could not be attributed to that.

The facts were that we simply were in a too disadvantageous and horrendous situation. We were in the military nightmare-predicament, like Charlie, of attacking from below an enemy who had superior observation and concealment and perhaps, insofar as we knew, outnumbered us pitifully. I knew the hill could be taken, at least later by night, providing enough strength were thrown at it and the command was willing to pay the price in casualties. After all, the marines had taken Iwo Jima, but at what a ghastly cost in dead and wounded. I admitted to myself that if it came to that, that I had no great, uncontrollable urge to be a part of the exercise.

After a few moments, while contemplating my next move and sure that I was at a loss as to what it would be, I heard a commotion behind me. I glanced to the rear just in time to see Rodriguez come tearing up and slide in along the side of me, with his trusty radio strapped firmly between his shoulder blades.

"What the devil are you doing up here, Rodriguez?" I scolded. "I thought I told you to stay back in the CP. Already you got your antenna shot off. You want your arse shot off as well? You might feel you are expendable, but I can't risk losing my only means of communicating." I thought he might think it a little funny if I placed the safety of the radio above his own scalp. But I don't recall that he exploded in sidesplitting laughter.

"It's battalion, Capitano," he blurted. "Battalion Six (code for commander) insisted that I locate you. He wants to talk to you—says it's most urgent."

I immediately got on the "box," as we referred to the portable radios, and called battalion. Hutchin came on. We started talking, as we routinely did, in our self-devised impromptu code, using sports or other jargon in an effort to conceal our meaning in event that the enemy was listening. We knew that some Chinese must have spoken excellent English. Someone had to teach the enemy the English phrases they had been shouting at us when they were pretending to be GIs. At least on some occasions they had been successful, to the sorrow of some of our troops.

Bit by bit Hutchin made me understand that I was to hold fast and not risk any further casualties. He indicated that the enemy resistance was far more determined than Keiser and Freeman had thought, and that we would probably get instructions to disengage as soon as it became feasible to attempt to do so. He also let it be known that there were "big troubles" over on the division's right flank in the ROK zone. Except for the latter, those were welcome words and I breathed a qualified sigh of relief—probably loud enough to be heard along the entire length of the line.

The minutes had been dragging on, I felt, somewhat monotonously. I thought I detected Ryan snoozing. I decided to give him a break. Being a historian and constantly listening to others tell of their experiences must not be the most exciting way to earn one's pay, I thought. Interesting overall, perhaps, but certainly with its boring moments.

I decided to pause and give Ryan a breather and replenish our refreshments. Just then a jet zoomed overhead on its approach to Washington National airport, and an eighteen-wheeler whined by on nearby Interstate 395, which we call "Shirley Highway" in our neighborhood. The noise startled Ryan and he sat up with a jolt.

"Catching forty winks, Tom?" I needled him.

"No, no," he protested. "Wide awake. Keep going."

I smiled, but waited a long moment before resuming, to insure that this wide-awake fellow was again with me, duly armed with pad, pencil, and portable tape recorder.

When I was satisfied that I again had his attention, I resumed. I could not leave him to believe that I and my company had perished in North Korea on those miserable days of November 1950. I felt I had to let him know whether we had gotten out of the mess, or to what extent.

Prepare to Disengage

As darkness steadily closed in that bleak winter night far up in North Korea in a valley never heard of by the faraway American public before or since, we were in a numbing state of uncertainty and apprehension, to put it in the mildest of terms. The painfully bitter cold returned.

For the moment we remained in position. Under the cover of darkness, we tried to distribute food and supplies and to locate and evacuate our wounded and dead with priority to the living. Hutchin ordered some units to relocate.

For the next twenty-four hours or so, there was to be renewed fighting, at times bitter and deadly, not just in our immediate area on the slopes of the Hat, but also in adjacent areas, including what was left of the 9th Regiment, mostly to our left along the Ch'ongch'on. Freeman was repositioning his forces into something of a perimeter defense. Writer Clay Blair, in *The Forgotten War,* was to put it this way:

> That night, as Freeman was shifting his forces around to tighten the perimeter, the CCF again attacked in massive numbers. The attack carried through to Freeman's CP, forcing him and his staff to abandon it. . . .
>
> Chin Sloane (9th Reg CO) ordered his 2d battalion (on the west bank of the Chongchon) to cross the river and reinforce Freeman's 23rd sector. As the 2d battalion prepared to respond it was suddenly and overwhelmingly attacked by other CCF troops. In a matter of minutes Companies F and G were decimated by swarms of enemy; in G Company alone, seventy three men fell dead or wounded. . . . Collecting what was left, battalion CO Barberis led them east across the river to tie in with Hutchin's 1st battalion of the 23rd for a Custer's Last Stand.

"... I'll never splash mud on a dogface again (999).... I'll never splash mud on a dogface again (1000).... Now will ya help us push?"

Many of the combat conditions depicted by famed cartoonist Bill Mauldin in World War II were equally applicable to the Korean fighting. Korean mountain roads, used mainly for oxcarts, were narrow and unpaved and were rapidly transformed into quagmires by heavy military traffic, especially during the spring and summer rainy seasons.

By that time . . . the CCF had mysteriously withdrawn from the battlefield and Freeman had reoccupied his CP. . . .*

"How can you be sure your recollections are correct?" The
historian's bent for accuracy was coming through from Ryan.

"Well, I'm not infallible," I conceded. "But I feel I am acceptably
correct, at least in substance of any consequence. There may for sure
be some veterans of the fighting whose recollections may vary from
mine. The version of some other and more famous writers of the hectic
Chinaman's Hat fighting, including that of S. L. A. Marshall, Max
Hastings, Blair or others may stray here and there from mine. That is
understandable and has to be expected, as any student of history will
know."

Events in hectic combat are complex and change rapidly. Most
historians do not personally witness each occurrence in a battle but
must rely on the often sketchy and fuzzy recollection of those who
survive or on official records that often may be incomplete.

Available witnesses, or participants, including myself, may be so
preoccupied with developments in their immediate area as to be
relatively uninformed on what may have happened elsewhere, even
nearby. Their perspectives may certainly be limited, and their
memories are seldom completely reliable.

I am reasonably confident of the substantive accuracy of this
version of my experiences in the Korean War, but confess to the
possibility of some error concerning details, or names, or exact times.
If others spot such slips, I told Ryan, I must ask their forbearance and
I am more than willing to be corrected.

"Fair enough," Ryan agreed. "But about that time your regiment
must have gotten the OK to pull out? We know there was to be a
general withdrawal from those far north lines."

"Yes, but not right away, or soon enough to suit us. As I now recall,
we stayed at the Hat for about another day. The Chinese did not again
try for a frontal assault on our positions, nor did our regiment on theirs.
They did keep up pressure at various and changing points. As we were
to later learn in the following days and weeks, their tactics were not
to try frontal assaults and smash their heads against an enemy like us

* Clay Blair, *The Forgotten War* (New York: Time Books, 1987), p. 446.

with heavier firepower and armor. With their lightly equipped and highly mobile foot soldiers in tennis shoes and with socks of rice around their necks, they could exist for days away from supply lines, so they used unique tactics. With superior numbers they would fan out and try to outflank, surround, and isolate our units and then close the roads or routes of withdrawal to our rear. They could then ambush and slaughter us as we were on the road trying to withdraw.

"But aren't you contradicting yourself? You've said the CCF hit you frontally in the valley of the Ch'ongch'on."

"That's true, but from what we later learned of their tactics and intentions, it seems that those assaults were probably miscalculations. They either did not know for sure our dispositions, or perhaps they thought we were ROKs whom they had no hesitation to hit."

The Chinese experience some days earlier in October when first entering Korea was that the ROKs would fold and disintegrate when faced by Chinese. That theory seemed to hold in the following days. If they stumbled upon us, they would most often fall back and fan out to our flanks.

Will the Koreans Fight?

I had learned in my contacts with Ryan, the modern historian, that he had a lot of respect for the professional capabilities of the Koreans in the 1980s, since he had been with the Eighth Army. He looked as though he was about to do battle with me in my own rec room.

"Are you saying the ROK units were less reliable in combat than the American units or units from other countries?" Ryan asked challengingly. Ryan was no dummy. He knew full well of the staying problems of the ROKs during the fighting, but I knew he was trying to intimidate me for a better response. I had the feeling that Ryan would have made a good cross-examiner in court.

"No. Not exactly," I said carefully, picking my words slowly. "I cannot say so based on my personal experience and at my level of command in an infantry company. I am sure that others are in a better position to rate the ROKs overall, and many have done so." It is, of course, a well-established matter of record that the ROKs did indeed

have their share of problems and repeatedly demonstrated their unreliability. And the Chinese seemed to know it well. They hit the
ROKs, instead of us, whenever and wherever they would find them.

"But it's a matter of record that they did scatter when hit, no
matter how reluctant we may be to admit it. Do you have an opinion
as to the cause? Why didn't they perform better?"

" 'Better' is certainly a relative term. Accepting that, I would only
point out that the Korean country and its army was only about five
years old when the 38th was crossed and fighting broke out. Therefore,
its army and its officers, even including the most senior, could not have
had more than about that much experience in the military and, unlike
Americans, no experience at all in combat or warfare. Our senior
officers were mostly well along in their careers, with as much as
twenty-five or more years of service. Nearly all were graduates of the
world's finest and most sophisticated military schools, including the
National War College at Fort McNair and the Command and General
Staff College at Fort Leavenworth."

"So you think it surprising that the ROKs fought as well as they
did with so little experience and military background?" Ryan asked
after a long and pondering silence.

"Yes, I think so. But as I say, I am not much qualified to pass
judgment based on personal contact, of which I had little. The ROK
II Corps was some miles off to our right. With respect to the ROK
soldiers in our units, I think I am in a much better position to rate them
and I would give them all above-passing grades." The ROKs were
almost childishly loyal, eager to please, dedicated to us and our mutual
cause of defending their country and resisting a Communist invasion.
Most helpful in that cold and brutal climate and mountainous country
was the ROKs' ability to withstand hardship. Our ROKs seldom
complained, no matter how hard the going, and never fled so long as
their American companions did not.

American units went into the Korean War desperately understrength and we were assigned large numbers of ROKs to fill up our
squads and gun crews. My company consisted of about 75 percent
ROKs, as did most other infantry companies in that first winter of the
war. We liked them and they literally worshiped us. Our main problem
with the ROKs was the language barrier. In those days, few Koreans
spoke English, at least very fluently, so it was often difficult to give

them instructions so they could effectively take part in the fighting. Also, most were not very highly educated and could not comprehend many technical matters such as map reading, compass work, weapons adjustments, fire direction, or vehicle maintenance. Nevertheless, they contributed much by just being there. We had no problem finding useful things for the ROKs to do, and in time many were gradually given more and more complicated tasks.

"But the Korean army was almost five years old. Surely they had learned something of warfare in that time?"

"True, the Korean military had a few years of existence after the end of World War II, but I think the history books record that in those days the big fear of the American government was that President Syngman Rhee would carry out his threat to 'march northward' and start a war to unify the country by invading North Korea." American policy was to work for unification, but not by war. So we permitted South Korea to have an army that was essentially only a police force. It had no heavy artillery or armor, very little transportation, and never conducted any tactical combat operations or training of any consequence. So the South Koreans were almost totally unprepared for the large-scale military operations that were then in full swing. Nor were they especially equipped psychologically to combat the Chinese. For hundreds of years the Koreans had been dominated by their Chinese neighbor. The Koreans feared and were awed by the Chinese. With all these handicaps, one could hardly expect the Koreans to excel on the battlefield against the CCF. It seems remarkable to me that they fought as well as they did. And in the fighting along the Ch'ongch'on River and in upper North Korea in general, it was not just the ROKs who were in trouble. We too, as is now well known, were having more than our share of problems.

"So in your 'Hat' fighting you had no contacts with the ROK units?"

"No, I don't think so, unless perhaps there might have been some vehicles or convoys on the roads behind us as units were moved around in those confusing and hectic days."

A day or so after the aborted attempt by our battalion and the regiment's 2d Battalion to take the Hat, and with scattered skirmishes continuing throughout the area, we grew more nervous by the hour. Rumors abounded of drastic developments in areas all around us. Late in the afternoon of, I believe, Nov. 26, I made my way back to the battalion CP and found Hutchin arriving in his jeep from a meeting with the regimental commander. Hutchin's expression told a thousand tales. His operations and intelligence officers and I, and some others, gathered around him, eager for any information that he might possess in these critical moments.

"Fellows," he began, "I have some bad news and some good." He paused to catch his breath and to lay out his map board on the hood of his jeep, and then continued. "Freeman and General Keiser [the division commander] are furious and frustrated. They say they can't get higher headquarters to understand the magnitude of this Chinese attack. Both are convinced this is a major offensive, that there are far more Chinese involved than anyone imagined. The ROK II Corps is all but wiped out on the division's eastern flank and the Chinese are pouring through and threatening to run around behind us. The 24th Division on the coast to the west is still in pretty good shape, but the 25th Division on our immediate left is being pounded hard and has incurred heavy casualties. Over the mountains to the east, the X Corps is under attack all along its front."

"For God's sake, Colonel," someone gasped, "what the hell's the good news?"

"Well, the good news is that General Walker has finally permitted the 2d Division to begin a withdrawal, but my question is whether or not it is too late to get out. At first I was told to set up a roadblock outside Kujang just to our rear, but before I could leave Freeman told me the pressure was too great for us to hold there, so now we are to move back to the best defensible position just south of Won."

"How far back is Won from Kujang, Sir?" one of the staff officers asked.

"About eight to ten miles," was his answer.

I remember all too well the tension and stress on everyone's faces. This was truly a time of crisis and everyone knew it.

Ryan's brow was wrinkled. His expression was one of skepticism. "How can you be sure now what was said so long ago?"

"Fair question," I answered. "Of course I can't recall verbatim what was said on all occasions. But many things said in times of crisis and peril burn themselves into a person's mind." I once had a commander who characterized it as "indelible impressions," ones that do not go away. But, for many conversations, even if not recalled exactly word for word, I can remember the thrust of the exchange, and the timing and circumstances in sufficient detail so that I can narrate the substance of what was said with a reasonable degree of accuracy.

"Did your battalion commander have instructions for you?"

"He did indeed. He said that Able Company and my Baker Company were to promptly move out with whatever transportation, including the tanks, that we could round up and start moving to the rear down the MSR (main supply route) to the town of Kunu-ri, halting just south of the town where he or someone on his staff would meet us and let us know where to go into position. He said if there was not enough transportation we would have to leapfrog, alternately marching and riding. He also cautioned us that we were likely to encounter Chinese, perhaps in strength, at any, or many, points along the road to our blocking position, and that we should be on alert accordingly."

Hutchin also explained that our battalion was to be the rear guard once the 9th and 38th Regiments passed through our roadblock. He said some of the 9th's 2d Battalion were still on the west side of the Ch'ongch'on, but had been ordered to start out.

As Hutchin had been talking to us, he instructed his radio operator to contact Charlie Company, which was still engaged heavily and in tight contact with the CCF, and instruct the CO to start withdrawing. As Hutchin completed his briefing and instructions to us and we started to leave, he received word that Charlie Company was pinned down and was unable to withdraw.

Hutchin became quite alarmed. He quickly rounded up some nearby troops and took off on foot to Charlie's position across the field and up a slight incline. In the distance, upon reaching Charlie Company, we could see him in the fading twilight rounding up troopers and directing them with their gear to the rear even as the Chinese continued to fire at them and inflict casualties. It was an impressive thing to see. Not many battalion commanders take such personal charge of their troops in close combat, but had "good ole Hutch" not done so, it might well be that we would have left behind what remained of poor Charlie Company. If Hutchin was not decorated for this achievement, he should have been.

CHAPTER FIVE

Operation "Bugout" from Chinaman's Hat

"Along about this time, with a sickening casualty rate, CCF on almost all sides, with the ROK II Corps collapsing on your division's right, and word that the 24th and 25th divisions on your left were pulling back, and into your third or fourth day of steady fighting, you must have thought it might be about time for your outfit to think also of relocation to the rear?" Ryan could hardly have put it more succinctly and on target.

"You better believe it," I was quick to respond.

"So you started moving out?"

"Well, we started. And with not a little eagerness. I tried not to communicate my anxiety and growing alarm to my officers and men. But with each ticking minute I could well see us cut off from the rear and surrounded and then only God would know the next steps. We knew very little about the Chinese other than that they were Orientals with a long history of caring little about human life or rights, and we thought of them as not having much compassion. Spending time in a Chinese POW camp, even if one survived, was not high on my list of desirable fates."

"I can see you personally did not wind up as a POW, so I suppose you succeeded in withdrawing?"

"Yes. I hurried back to my company, briefed my officers and senior NCOs, and within the hour we were on our way back down the MSR. We spent most of the night on the road and alternated between marching and climbing on the scarce vehicles. Just as Colonel 'Hutch' had predicted we were hassled by Chinese almost all the way. It seemed they had just about blanketed the countryside."

At every landmark we passed on our start from the Hat we encountered more Chinese. But they also seemed to be more than a little disorganized themselves. On the move I lost some half-dozen or more men to CCF fire but I could have lost far more if the Chinese had a better grasp of what they were doing or why. I had the feeling that they were as confused as we were.

Sometimes during our withdrawal the Chinese fired or threw grenades at our column or our vehicles, but others would just mill around on the road shoulders or the adjacent fields and not fire at us, almost as though they did not realize we were the enemy and constituted a danger to them. In retrospect I have concluded that they must have expected mainly to occupy the area of North Korea but not necessarily to meet any UN forces in the process and they did not have precise instructions on what to do if they did meet us. Or perhaps, as individuals, they actually meant us no harm. But I'm not sure I really believe that, either.

It must have been shortly before dawn when we passed through the ruins of the village of Won and just beyond we were met by the battalion S-3 known as the "operations" officer. He instructed me to go into position on the left side of the road, and that Able Company would be opposite on the right side.

"We are to hold here," he said, "for the 9th and 38th and the rest of the division to pass through us. Most are badly clobbered. The last of the 9th 2d Battalion is crossing the Ch'ongch'on from the west. They have had to wade the icy waters. Who knows how many got out, or exactly what shape they are in. We'll be the last out of here."

"With the Chinese nipping at our heels?" I asked.

"Well, somewhat," he answered. "But our mission is to hold until one of the other battalions can set up a block behind us, through which we then will pass. We're to cover each other so no battalion will be completely exposed to the enemy."

I was somewhat encouraged in the cold, bleak dawn. At least it seemed that our withdrawal was to be undertaken with some degree of organization and control, and not turn into a rout, or a "bugout," to use a term that was then beginning to be bandied about. Little did I then know what was shortly to be in store for the division.

"How long did you stay in that position?"

"I think it must have been all that day, and into the night. Things were happening at a fast clip all around, as I later learned, but I did not know much about it at the time. Its always intriguing how such monumental happenings can be taking place in combat all over the landscape without an individual in a particular location knowing very much about the big picture."

"How did you or your men bear up under the cold during this period?"

"In a word, horrendously!" We suffered constantly and greatly. This has been covered graphically and in gruesome detail by many writers, including the marine and other historians covering the long, cold withdrawal from the northeastern section of the country and the heroic naval embarkation at Hungnam.

Most Americans have endured winter weather somewhere, at some time, except perhaps in the deep South or across the Sunbelts. There are heavy winters or frosty mornings with thorough chillings, and perhaps numb feet, hands or ears. But for most people such experiences are usually relatively brief and are followed by a return to the heated indoors and a cup of hot coffee or other drink to help them thaw out. Soon all is back to temperate normal and the chilling event is soon forgotten.

In combat in North Korea near the Yalu, and to a lesser extent later around the 38th parallel, such a scenario did not exist. The bitterness of the cold seemed to know no limits. The temperatures hovered around zero much of the time, or well below, and the chill factor in the merciless Manchurian winds drove the apparent cold to points far below zero. The combat soldiers' exposure was not for brief periods, but continued on endlessly through the days and nights.

For the combat soldier outdoors, the bitter cold penetrates and permeates to the deepest interiors of the human body. A trooper was not merely cold, he was in debilitating pain that greatly restricted his ability to move, or to think, or to react. All this is greatly compounded if heavy winter clothing is inadequate, or nonexistent, or if the clothing next to the skin has become wet from perspiration and is followed by a prolonged period of inactivity.

Nights on hilltops or at lonely outposts, even if there was little or no enemy activity, became eternities and the daylight with its possible sunshine seemed never to arrive.

Apart from the disastrous effects of cold on our persons, the extreme low temperatures also disabled or seriously limited the usefulness of our equipment. Vehicles would not start. Batteries died. The grease on our guns turned to glue and the guns wouldn't fire. Our rations remained frozen like stone and were nearly impossible to eat, or to digest if they could be chewed on. Some men carried cans inside their clothing next to their bodies in an effort to keep them from freezing solidly.

But far worse than all this, men died, sometimes from rather minor wounds, simply because of the shock induced by the extreme cold. Others emerged from the war with amputated feet or legs, due to frozen members, or from trench foot.

"Then you think you had to leave men behind who were wounded and might have survived under less cold conditions?"

"No doubt about it. Repeatedly, I witnessed men with light wounds, from my company, or others, expiring on litters either while lying around a CP or a collection point or being carried down a hill to a road for evacuation. As any medic knows well, a wounded or injured person must be kept quite warm. In the cold outdoors in the bitter North Korean winter, with inadequate blankets or bedding, our people could seldom keep the wounded warm enough. So they died not so much from their wounds as from the elements."

Roadblock at Won

"How long did your company remain at the Won roadblock?" Ryan wanted to know, with pencil and pad ever at the ready.

"As I recall, it must have been for the rest of that day and through the night. While we were there, all kinds of hairy and scary things were happening. Most of the 2d Division passed through us down the road to Kunu-ri, about ten miles or so to our rear."

The only bridge across the Namdae River was just south of Kunu-ri. If that bridge were blown or collapsed, for sure our withdrawal would have been greatly complicated, or perhaps impossible. I paused to study my maps of the Korean northlands to reorient myself all these years later and in the comfort and ease of my rec room. It all seemed so far back and remote, like a dream, and yet startlingly vivid and threatening still.

I forced my thoughts to journey again back to that cold and distant Korean setting. Again I was in Korea, on a noisy and nameless road, manning a block to allow others to pass through to the rear.

All through the day and into the night, the troops and vehicles streamed. At times, traffic was so heavy the motor column would come to a complete halt—harbingers of the frustrating, if less deadly, gridlocks that would plague countless American commuters later in the century in nearly every major American city.

Troops and equipment in our intermittent gridlocks were mostly in a very pathetic state of disarray. Equipment was often just thrown haphazardly on vehicles. Tanks had clusters of infantrymen riding on them who in appearance were every inch the forlorn-looking Korean War "Willies" and "Joes" of Bill Mauldin's artistic creations in World War II.

Many troops walking along the road had no weapons or helmets or packs. Some were wounded. Their appearance attested to the severity of the fighting in which they had been engaged now for almost three days. They were all dirty, unshaven, weary looking beyond description and with blank expressions on hollow and gaunt faces. They would not have passed a Saturday-morning white-glove inspection.

"What were the Chinese doing during this withdrawal?"

"They stayed busy. I don't recall that there was ever a moment when some firing was not going on in various directions from us. During the day the troops on the road, either motorized or walking, would be sniped at from CCF forces in the hills a few hundred yards off the road, or much closer in places."

Sometimes the burp of a submachine gun would be heard and we knew there were casualties during the daylight hours. Here and there, withdrawing troops or my own would return the fire, aiming generally at unseen targets somewhere in the direction from whence the enemy fire had come. Several times the tank gunners joined in during halts, or even while slowly moving.

Nor were there any times, that I witnessed, when our withdrawing column of troops stopped and took up battle formations to make a stand against the harassing Chinese. The prevailing thought was to simply get the hell out while the getting was possible, and pass through our rearguard roadblock, which the 1st Battalion of the 23rd Regiment was manning.

We were interested in seeing the operation continue without a hitch because we realized that when all had cleared our blocking position, it would then be our turn to withdraw through another block behind us manned by another battalion of the division or the regiment.

"Are you suggesting a condition of widespread cowardice?"

"Not necessarily. Considerable alarm and fear, but not cowardice. On the contrary, the incidents of courage and heroism over the past several days were enough to boggle the mind. I remember few times, if any, when I had cause to complain about the performance of my troops, either American or ROKs."

The preceding thought brings me to another long-standing gripe of mine. I have always bemoaned the fact that combat commanders have so little opportunity to write up their men for much-deserved decorations. The public commonly sees the much-decorated military man strutting around with a chest full of ribbons. Usually, however, they are senior officers or generals or admirals. Not that they necessarily do not deserve their awards, but so, or more so, do the lower-ranking people if they are frontline combat personnel engaged in exchanging fire with the enemy. The difference is in the opportunity and the availability of clerical or other personnel or commanders to witness the deeds or to record the circumstances. Those conveniences usually exist in the rear areas far more than up front, so the combat soldier is more often than not simply overlooked, unrecognized and unrewarded. But more on this later.

Around noon at our roadblock, we witnessed the remains of the 2d Battalion of the 9th coming through. It was one of the very few all-black infantry battalions still in existence. The 24th Division, I think, had a couple of black battalions.

The 9th's men on this occasion were certainly a motley-looking group of guys. Not because of their race, but because they had been heavily engaged for days, crossing and recrossing the Ch'ongch'on from the west side.

We counted only a little over a hundred men of the 9th's 2d Battalion coming through our positions from what we assumed must have been a battalion strength of at least a thousand only a few hours earlier. We had leapfrogged through them on the way to our Won position. There was a report that the battalion CO, Lt. Col. Cesibes Barberis, had been wounded. One of their few remaining officers told me they were falling back to our rear to set up another roadblock. So lst Battalion 23rd and 2d Battalion 9th were getting to be quite chummy. Misery loves company, as the saying goes.

Late in the afternoon, I wandered down near the lst Platoon area and slumped down by a trooper whom I remember as Ernie. His last name slips me. I wanted to compliment him on his performance the day before, when we were trying to help Charlie Company on the Hat. He had helped hold off a passel of Chinese who were almost on top of us, and we were about to be done in.

I always think of Ernie when I see in recent years a guy by the same name who makes TV commercials in the Washington-Baltimore area. Like the TV "Ernie," my Ernie was also a rural-looking fellow, and also not really very handsome. He had grown up in the South. I had taken a warm liking to him because of his noncomplaining attitude and his willingness to carry out about any task assigned him when others around might well look for excuses not to do so.

Ernie and I had talked before, and he enjoyed telling me about his lean childhood days as one of several children in a sharecropper family in Mississippi. Now Ernie did not appear to be particularly elated.

"Cheer up, Ernie," I told him. "We'll get out of this OK."

He looked at me quietly for a bit, then said, "Wish I could believe that, Captain, but I doubt if you very much believe it yourself."

"You're right, fellah," I admitted. "It's a dark hour just now, but I'm supposed to encourage you lads. It's part of the requirements."

"OK, Sir. I'm encouraged and cheered up. Now why don't you get yourself somewhere else less exposed? No point in both of us getting shot up. I want you in one piece to get us out of this mess. Anyway, you might be drawing fire on me," he added with a faint smile.

I didn't have a chance to respond to all he said. Just then a mortar barrage started sweeping through the area. Some rounds landed smack in the midst of one of my platoons. Someone called for the medics. I concluded, as Ernie had admonished, that perhaps my time could indeed be better utilized elsewhere. I notice that the barrage was walking on around the area and that rounds were falling near what I thought was the battalion CP.

"OK, Ernie. Perhaps you're right. I've things to do. Carry on." It was to be my last contact with Ernie. He was killed that night by a Chinese grenade. In our desperation and helplessness, we could not even remove his body or many others who had fallen in that remote and bleak North Korean valley.

A perceptive and inquisitive historian, Ryan sat silently for a bit and studied me as the minutes ticked on without me saying anything. Finally he asked, "Are you dozing off? You want to stop?"

"No," I answered. "Just trying to put my thoughts in some sort of order. But it's also hard not to drop into reminiscing from time to time. We can carry on."

"Then did the Chinese seriously attack your company in its roadblocking position at Won?"

"I'm not sure it could be characterized as 'serious,' but attack us they did, in a disorganized sort of way. The withdrawing elements of the 2d Division, and various attached units, continued through that day and well into the night. I think it must have been November 28, but I could be off a day. I think, especially in hindsight, that the Chinese at that early point were still trying to avoid frontal assault and heavy commitment."

The aim of the CCF was, it seemed, as I've said, to bypass, and block and then annihilate, or inflict heavy damage from ambush as we tried to withdraw—on the road, in column, and exposed.

As evening fell, the enemy closed in and under cover of early darkness began to attack the withdrawing troops at close range, sometimes firing their burp, or b-r-r-r-p, guns and throwing grenades from the ditches right next to the moving column. They would even climb on vehicles, or try to pull marching troops from the road.

The Chinese were continuously meeting with success. In the darkness our troops had great difficulty in identifying the enemy and differentiating them from the friendly troops. Many men were reluctant to open fire for fear of hitting American troops.

Repeatedly, my men would stare into the darkness at withdrawing troops and see that there were Chinese soldiers intermingling with the Americans. Some men would call to other Americans to inform them that there were Chinese mixed up in their ranks.

The confusion that resulted from all this is impossible to adequately describe. The challenge to the GIs, in the dark, was to capture or kill the Chinese without shooting up our own people. Combat operations are extremely confusing at best, under conditions that might be called normal, if combat ever is. But that night at the Won roadblock defies comprehension and reconstruction.

As the night wore on and evening stretched into midnight, the withdrawing columns began to thin out. There were dead and wounded Chinese, and some Americans, almost everywhere. We also had by then collected about fifty Chinese prisoners in a paddy near the company CP. I had been alerted that soon after the signal that all the withdrawing troops had cleared our roadblock, we too would be given the order to withdraw. I did not want to withdraw with the Chinese prisoners, so I made an effort for one of the units in the columns to take the POWs along with them to the rear.

At first my effort to dispose of the POWs was resisted. One infantry officer in the column refused. "We can't handle them," he said. "We've got more than we can handle trying to save our own asses. Just shoot the bastards," he threw back over his shoulder as he disappeared down the road in the dark.

Of course I am thankful today I did not follow his advice, although I guess I must have been tempted. I would not want it on my conscience that we had lowered ourselves to the level of the animals that we were claiming the enemy to be. I contacted another passing unit and insisted that they take the Chinese POWs to the rear for evacuation, and they did.

I never learned what finally happened to those Chinese POWs. In the days to follow, when we could not even take out our own dead, and many of our wounded, it may be that they had to be turned loose and left behind. If so, then I suppose they were fighting us again later on. Perish the thought.

Although it may not have been shared by many others, I think I never lost completely my feeling of compassion for the enemy troops, as individuals, whom we were fighting. Deep within, I recognized that the poor coolies, like many on our side, may have had nothing to do with their selection for frontline duty in a war, and might have meant us no harm but were only carrying out their orders so as not to be shot themselves for disobedience.

I had no doubt that few of the Chinese we faced had any conception at all of the Communist philosophy for which they were made to fight by their leaders and that, given their druthers, they probably would have much preferred to be back in their home villages or planting rice in their paddies. How could one stomach killing such people other than strictly in self-defense? Most of the Chinese we encountered that night at Won were not especially aggressive. I think, mostly, they were separated from the massive number of other Chinese in the area. Many must have been as startled as we were.

On the other hand, their harassing attacks on the withdrawing columns may have been a deliberate and calculated tactic to slow our withdrawal. In so doing, other outlying Chinese columns would have more time to swing around our flanks and set up blocks further south to cut off the entire Eighth Army, which is exactly what they almost succeeded in doing.

Colonel Freeman shed some light on the Chinese intentions at his debriefings. He spoke Chinese and I saw him on several occasions quietly interrogating POWs at one of the CPs. This was another of the characteristics that made Paul Freeman a truly remarkable field commander.

Things were relatively quiet for several hours after midnight. Still we encountered some stray Chinese, and I was ordered to maintain sporadic fire for the express purpose of satisfying the Chinese that we were still there. Otherwise, they might come charging down the road and right up the posteriors of the troops in the withdrawing column.

As dawn approached, I became increasingly apprehensive. I felt sure we could not withdraw in broad daylight, and if we were not gone by then, we would be cut off for sure. I tried to go over the head of the S-3 and asked to speak to the battalion commander. My radioman Rodriguez was told the CO was not available. I later learned why. Hutchin had been badly wounded by shell fragments in the face. I later learned that he refused evacuation, however, and continued leading his battalion. He did leave later, but I'm not sure just when.

Withdrawal from the Won Roadblock

"But you did get out before dawn?"

"Yes. Sometime about an hour or two before the rosy fingers of dawn were expected to stab through the eastern sky, the much-awaited order to withdraw came crackling over Rodriguez's backpack SCR 300. It's hard to imagine our relief. My troops needed no persuasion to 'saddle up' and get on the road. It's also hard to realize the condition of my weary and decimated troops by that time."

Baker Company, as well as the other units, had been in almost continuous contact and engagement with the enemy for several days. Few men had ever slept at any time during the nights, but had only grabbed short, restless naps occasionally during the days. Food had been only cold, and usually frozen, C rations.

The awesome experience of constantly losing buddies and seeing death and destruction all around and ever-present fear for their own safety had exacted its price on my men. They were weak and thoroughly drained—physically and emotionally. Many had serious physical problems with colds, flu, hemorrhoids, torn ligaments or muscles, intestinal problems, macerated and swollen feet, and almost any other ailment to which field troops are vulnerable. Their bodies ached and their whole beings cried out for rest and relief, while they realized that none was available and that there was no recourse but to push on until they simply dropped in their tracks.

Many writers have graphically and ably depicted the state of mind and body of exhausted combat troops in such situations, and I need not try to compete with their literary efforts. Suffice it to say that under those conditions, my company and the 23rd's lst Battalion assembled in the predawn of that day and headed back down the road toward the town of Kunu-ri, staggering, numb, and not very hopeful for their prospects for survival.

Sunrise arrived as we hiked. We kept constant vigilance over our shoulders toward assumed Chinese positions to our rear, but nothing particularly perilous occurred, and after a couple of hours and about four or five miles, we passed through the blocking position of the 9th Regiment. At this point my recollection becomes a bit fuzzy.

I knew the 23rd was to withdraw to the south side of the Namdae River at Kunu-ri and set up rearguard blocks so that the rest of the Eighth Army could withdraw to the south, and that my lst Battalion was to do the main blocking from the high ground just south of the river. I am uncertain whether we moved straight to our blocking positions that night or whether we paused overnight en route.

In either event, we spent the early hours of the night of November 29 moving through the town of Kunu-ri. In some places there was eerie silence as we trod along the streets and past dark and foreboding Korean houses or shops in various stages of destruction. It was all like a dream in our dazed state of mind.

Other sections of Kunu-ri were scenes of frenzied activity as Eighth Army service units, which had been supporting us up front, were busy loading and obviously getting ready to move out themselves. On we marched, and sometime near midnight we were on the bridge over the partially frozen river. Ahead in the moonlight we could see the skyline of the high hills just beyond the river and some rice paddies in the floodplain.

Crossing the river at Kunu-ri, we could also make out the cut in the hills through which the road we were on passed. That road, which forked a mile beyond with the main road swinging west toward Sukch'on near the coast, and the other southerly toward Sunch'on, was to be the main route of withdrawal for the bulk of the Eighth Army. Much of the army had already cleared and was on its way to P'yongyang, about a hundred miles away. The 2d Division would be the last one out, and the 23rd would cover the withdrawal of the rest of the 2d.

CHAPTER SIX

A Night on Bald Mountain—Baker's Stand at Kunu-ri

Eighth Army historian Tom Ryan and I had covered many items, days, fire fights, kilometers, anxieties, and a constantly lengthening list of other critical events in our discussion of the bitter winter days of the first year of the Korean War in 1950. There was a long period of silence in my Arlington home as he and I tried to get a grip on the complexities of what we had thus far covered.

For several more minutes we sat in deep thought and simply gazed into the fire, and at times, at each other. I poured a bit more wine, but not enough to dull my recollections.

At long last, Ryan spoke.

"So in those closing days of November, with the Chinese overwhelming you at the Hat, and your stand there, the roadblock at Won, and now your pullback from the town of Kunu-ri, as you crossed the bridge over the Namdae chon, you must have thought the worst was over for you?"

"We might have thought so, but it was not to be. My company's problems, and most of those of the 2d Division, were just beginning." The town of Kunu-ri, and the withdrawal south therefrom was to be burned into our memories and combat histories like the tablets on Mount Sinai. It was to be, in my humble judgment, one of the most crucial engagements of the Korean War, and while I note that most historians give the events there some play, most do not seem to recognize just how important they were to the safety and continued fightability of the entire Eighth Army.

"How so? Aren't you overstating it?"

"Not at all. The rearguard stand there by the 2d Division permitted the rest of the Eighth Army to safely withdraw from the far north, substantially intact, and stand again later around the 38th parallel, instead of being routed and possibly ejected entirely from the Korean peninsula."

The stand on the high ground over the river south of Kunu-ri by my battalion of the 23rd, in turn, allowed the rest of the 2d Division and the 23rd, to also withdraw, although the other two regiments did so at ghastly costs further south on the Kunu-ri-to-Sunch'on road in what historian Marshall calls the "gauntlet" and "pass" areas. But let's set the scene a bit better for the benefit of anyone who might later read this account who is not familiar with the surrounding circumstances that then prevailed. It's an intriguing and exciting development in this historical period, and well worth careful concentration.

"As you and other historians know well," I told Ryan, "and as we've here briefly seen, when the Eighth Army in the west and the X Corps over the middle mountains in the east approached or reached the Manchurian border in October 1950, many Chinese divisions and corps appeared in North Korea." The intentions of the Chinese were not known with certainty, I reminded Ryan, and were a matter of great speculation from the lowest units to the Pentagon and the White House.

After a pause by UN forces at and near the Yalu River and the frontier of Korea, General MacArthur, convinced the Chinese did not intend to make a major commitment, ordered a final drive in the west to the Yalu River for November 24, 1950, the day after Thanksgiving.

History and the following events, however, proved General Mac-Arthur wrong. Far from returning to Manchuria as the UN resumed its advance, the Chinese themselves launched their own offensive—suddenly and in overwhelming numbers. It then became almost immediately apparent that if the UN forces were to avoid encirclement and annihilation, they must quickly withdraw to the south and to a more narrow and defendable front.

For the UN forces to withdraw successfully, some part of the Eighth Army would have to hold back the advancing waves of Chinese, even if the rearguard units were sacrificially lost in trying to do so. As has often been the case in battle, a few might have to be lost to save the many.

The 2d Division was assigned that mission, which it accomplished effectively at Kunu-ri, although at crippling costs, and the rest of the army carried out a congested but reasonably orderly withdrawal and preserved its combat effectiveness. Had it not been permitted to do so, it seems inescapable that the UN forces, in all likelihood, would have been compelled to evacuate Korea. Even so, serious consideration was later given to doing just that. Had the 2d Division not prevailed at Kunu-ri, the withdrawal surely would have turned into a disorganized rout at enormous cost to the whole UN command.

Kunu-ri was, and is, located about fifty miles inland from the west coast of northern Korea and the Yellow Sea. To its east are high mountains running up and down the Korean peninsula with few, if any, serviceable roads for heavy military equipment.

That rugged terrain of central Korea separated the Eighth Army on the west from the X Corps on the east, commanded by Lt. Gen. Edward Almond. While it constituted a barrier for the highly motorized and mechanized UN forces, it did not stop the less sophisticated Chinese foot soldiers. They swept into the mountains and down the right flank of the Eighth Army in an effort to encircle and cut off the UN forces. They very likely would have done so had our 2d Division not held them back, or at least slowed them down, at Kunu-ri and along the roads south.

The two main roads that provided escape routes southward from Kunu-ri were the road westward through Anju, Sinanju, and Sukch'on to P'yongyang, and the secondary road due south to P'yongyang through Sunch'on. It was down these roads, and principally the western route, that UN forces would withdraw while the 2d held off the Chinese in the Kunu-ri area. Elements of the U.S. I and IX Corps and the ROK II Corps, including the 2d, 24th, and 25th infantry divisions, the lst Cavalry Division, and the Turkish Brigade, were among those units to be withdrawn.

The role of my own battalion, the lst of the 23rd, was to hold the pass on the south bank of the river at Kunu-ri until the rest of the 2d Division could get safely out. We succeeded in holding the pass, thanks largely to the determined and unrecognized stand by Baker Company, but by a hair's breadth, as we shall see. The rest of the division, to a sad and disastrous degree, did not get safely out. It was on the road south to Sunch'on that the 9th and 38th were to be ambushed in the "gauntlet," as graphically and shockingly described by Marshall.

The Role of Baker Company in Kuni-ri Defense

"So on the night of November 29 your company and battalion were about to play a most critical role in the overall action?" Ryan asked.

"Yes, and as I look back on that night and the following days, I have ever marvelled at how we managed to press on and survive. We simply must have had some divine or outside help, as I suppose many others must have felt in those brutal days."

As we cleared the town of Kunu-ri and the bridge to its south, we hiked past about a half-a-mile of flatlands and rice paddies. Back in Arkansas, where I entered the army, we would call them "river bottoms," I think. For sure the area was the river floodplain. There were several buildings of some sort off to our left. Beyond the flat area, we could see rising hills. Ahead the road rose slightly and then entered a cut in the hills.

There was intense motor and other activity on the road ahead of us, and also behind us. It was about 2200 hours and bitterly cold, with a stiff wind. We had hiked several hours, however, and were quite hot and sweaty, which makes for an exceedingly dangerous situation. To be wet with perspiration and then remain outdoors in severely cold weather can greatly frustrate a soldier's efforts to avoid freezing and remain alive. Moreover, we had been in constant combat for almost a week without any letup or rest, and most of the men were on the verge of complete collapse. Many were little more than walking zombies. In this condition, my weary company approached and entered the pass between two high hill-masses on either side.

As I was about to clear the pass, a couple of figures materialized out of the darkness and approached me. It was Maj. George Russell, the battalion executive officer, and Maj. Harold Shoemaker, the regimental S-2.

"Pratt," said Russell, "you are to take your company up the hill behind me," pointing to the high ground on the east side of the road, "and go into position. Be prepared to defend from the river and Kunu-ri to the north, and from the east."

I gazed painfully up at the high ground. How, I thought, could my men, who are now stunned, dazed, and semiconscious, going to tackle a mountain climb that would be a major challenge for even fresh and rested troops? My men were loaded with heavy equipment. They were wet and sweaty, exhausted beyond imagination, and their means of locomotion, their feet, were blistered, torn, and macerated, with excruciating pain.

"Who else is in position around us?" I managed to ask numbly. "Who's on my flanks?"

"After all the troops withdrawing tonight have cleared this roadblock," Russell explained, "there will be no one ahead of you. There are no units on your right. Able Company will be on your left flank on the high ground to the north, across this road about a half-mile away as the crow flies—beyond contact. 2d and 3rd battalions will clear through shortly and will go into position somewhere down the road to our rear."

"And that was the extent of your instructions?" Ryan asked.

"Not quite. Russell also explained that the position was to be only temporary, until all forces then withdrawing had cleared through our roadblock, and that afterward, the order for our withdrawal, too, would be forthcoming."

"How long before all forces clear our block?" I asked Russell. "And how long afterwards must we stay here?" The anxiety in my voice must surely have been obvious to Russell and Shoemaker.

Shoemaker joined in. "Don't worry, Pratt," he tried to reassure me. "The last of the friendly troops should clear during the night, sometime after midnight. You should know when you no longer hear the noisy grind of traffic down here in the valley below you. Sound travels well in this cold night air. But we'll confirm by radio. How long we stay after that is anybody's guess. It has to be after all our people have gotten a safe distance down the road and some other unit has set up another block for us to pass through. My guess is, that would be early tomorrow morning, soon after daylight."

With that I had to be content. I ordered the company to move out. "Off and on," I announced—off their butts and on the road, in the military colloquial of the day—or night? The men struggled to their feet, many only half-conscious and certainly not wide awake, alert, or bushy-tailed, and we started to move off the road and up the steep slopes of the high ground. I was concerned that we were leaving men behind who had literally passed out in sleep and fatigue in the ditch or on road shoulders. I talked with two of my officers at hand. Groggy as I was, I urged them and the platoon leaders to be careful not to leave sleeping or punchy men behind.

Our column began its climb, slowly, cautiously, and with enormous effort. It was dark, cold, and windy, and we had no idea what the high hill had in store for us. If the troops felt anything like I did, and if anything they felt worse with heavier weapons and equipment they had been, and were, carrying, then I knew each step was a torturous challenge.

Our "hill" has no number at its peak on the military tactical maps to show its elevation, but there seem to be ten contour lines from its top down to the road and cut we were leaving. At twenty meters per contour line, or a total of 200 meters, or about 650 feet, this would place the hill height about midway between the Washington Monument in the nation's capital and the Empire State Building in New York City—not exactly a leisurely stroll, even for rested people in tip-top shape. It took my Baker Company somewhere between two and three hours to make the climb and reach the top. Totally exhausted, we paused for some moments and then I gave instructions to the platoons as to where they would go into position.

"Bob, take the right flank," I said to platoon leader 2d Lt. Robert Walker, and I told Lt. Floyd Darmer to take his platoon to the left front of the hill, so that he would have a field of fire toward the floodplain, bridge, and river we had just crossed. He would also be roughly above the cut and pass down below us on our left flank and could cover that zone with fire.

The remaining platoon, with no officer but under the command of Sfc. John L. Crawford, I ordered to take positions to our rear, looking backward. That platoon could serve as a reserve force, but also would round out a perimeter defense-arrangement in the event we were hit from behind.

I told 2d Lt. Jess Mendenhall to locate his weapons platoon as he deemed fit, somewhere in the middle of the company area. lst Lt. James G. Raney, the executive officer, and WOJG Ralph E. Dusseau, the company administrative officer, remained with me near the weapons platoon.

I passed on, as best I could in the dark on the windblown peak, such information as I had on the tactical situation and on our prospects for early departure. Above all, I tried to convey the uncertainty of what the enemy might be planning and the need for extraordinary vigilance.

I knew the men could not dig foxholes in the frozen ground, even if they had a mind to do so, but I urged the officers and NCOs to seek protected spots where possible, and to look for stones or large rocks to place around them so they would at least have a measure of protection in case the Chinese hit us.

"How do you remember all these details?" Ryan wondered aloud.

"I can understand why you would ask. I suppose the best answer is that with respect to the events that took place, they are not likely to be ever completely forgotten by anyone who took part in an occurrence as difficult, painful, costly, and spectacular as the major engagement during the Eighth Army's Korean withdrawal. I'm not sure that answer is completely responsive, but is the best I can manage." Ryan nodded in apparent understanding.

Actually, my memory has not been quite so photographic as might have appeared to Ryan at the time. Concerning the recollection of dates, times, places, names, and other such specifics, I confess that I have had additional help. I have been aided immeasurably by researching such records as the command reports and related files at the U.S. Federal Records Center at Suitland, Maryland. Also, there are numerous official or other published works at the Pentagon Library or elsewhere, to include, probably, Ryan's own historian's office or other sources at Eighth Army Headquarters.

"To what extent do you think official, or organized, repositories include the information that you are furnishing in this interview?" Ryan then asked me.

"Well, I think I am providing historical background that is not now recorded anywhere and that is of significant importance to anyone who would seek to better understand the events of those trying days. At least I hope that is the case."

"And you consider your experiences on the hilltop overlooking Kunu-ri and the Namdae River to be significant?"

"I do without a doubt, and in a most critical way."

"How so? Can't almost anyone from other units make the same claim?"

"Of course they can. But claiming something does not necessarily make it so. But hear me out and then you can draw your own conclusions. I contend, in light of the subsequent developments over the next few hours, as we shall see, that if the Chinese had occupied our dominant hill, the outcome of the action would have been reversed."

From our hill the enemy would overlook all the 2d Division CPs just to the rear. They also would have had thorough observation of the two routes of withdrawal to the southwest and directly to the south. With such critical and commanding terrain under CCF control, the blocking and withdrawal of the division would have been seriously impaired or impossible. Indeed, the whole operation likely would have turned into a disorganized rout and would have been even more disastrous than it turned out to be, especially for the division's other two regiments on the road south to Sunch'on. It is difficult to adequately emphasize the criticality of the terrain that we were on.

"So what then happened on the hill after you placed your platoons in position?"

"I guess the short answer is that everyone promptly went to sleep. At least I think everyone, except perhaps me. If anyone was later awake, I was not able to locate that person. Exhausted as I was, along with everyone else, I could not fall asleep, nor did I want to."

For some time after midnight up on our hill, I could continue to hear the constant grind of vehicles passing through the road cut below and to our left. If I stood up and walked forward a bit to the forward crest of the hill, I could hear the motor convoys and, I thought, dimly see them on the bridge out to our front.

My radio operator, Rodriguez, and I usually shared our foxhole, or substitute "living accommodation" so that, among other things, we could take turns on the radio. The radio was a must to maintain communications contact with the battalion commander, as I've stressed. We usually had another trooper in company headquarters to man the walkie-talkies or sound-powered telephones to the platoons.

Once on top of the hill and in position, I knew I must keep in touch with the battalion as a routine requirement. Of special importance on this occasion, I needed to be told when the friendly troops had all cleared through our roadblock. Anyone thereafter would be an enemy, and would constitute a danger to be met with and fired on—but we did not need to fire on our own troops as they withdrew.

"Rodriguez," I said in a low voice, "do you want me to take first shift of the radio?"

"Si, Capitano."

Whereupon I took the earphones from him and placed them on my own head, pulled the blanket a little tighter to try to keep from freezing to death, and Rodriguez audibly went promptly to sleep. I always marvelled at, and envied, his ability to sleep soundly no matter what the circumstances or how urgent the situation. The guy was a "sack artist" of the highest caliber. Nothing, it seemed to me, ever bothered that unflappable Mexican-American.

The minutes ticked mercilessly by. The wind howled, and the freezing cold penetrated deep into my shivering form. All around, the darkness attacked and intimidated us. Especially did my feet suffer, as well as every muscle and bone in my body. After what seemed a half-hour or more, and with only stillness in the air except for the motor columns inching by below, I decided to get up and circulate around. I needed movement for warmth and blood circulation, and I also was anxious about the state of alertness of the platoons.

"Rodriguez," I said, shaking him roughly. "Can you wake up?"

"Si, Capitano."

"Can you take the radio now for a bit?"

"Si, Capitano."

"But will you stay awake? The battalion CO may contact us at any minute."

"Si, Capitano."

I wasn't sure at all that he would. In fact, my bet was that he would not. Still, I had not much choice, so I handed over the earphones to him and struggled to my feet. I woke the first sergeant, or was it the exec—either way, I left word that I was going to roam around a bit and check the platoons.

I walked over to the forward slope of the rise overlooking the cut below. I could not see the cut because of a thrust of hillside out to my front, but I listened for motor noises. I heard none. I stood there a bit, gazing out into the partial moonlight, straining to see what I could see.

All around me the jagged horizon marked the end of the dark, star-filled sky. Out front there was nothing but stillness. Overhead the needles from the scattered scrub pines rustled in the wind. I decided to work my way along the ridge easterly through the left platoon and to the right platoon. I was hoping I would be challenged by my ever-alert and watchful troopers.

As I walked along the ridge, I found no one awake. Now and then I found an NCO, and when I did I cautioned him to maintain a sharp eye, that friendly forces had withdrawn, that we were on our own, and that if they detected movement out front, to shoot first and ask questions second. Mostly, I let the men alone. In some cases, I tried without success to rouse them.

I was increasingly worried. I did not at all like the situation. If I tried to wake the command then, long before daylight, and they remained alerted, would they be in any shape to fight off an attack if it came then? On the other hand, if I let them sleep on and an attack caught them off guard, would they all be bayonetted in their blankets while still asleep?

I roamed back to where I had left Rodriguez. Far off to the north and, I concluded, beyond the river in the outskirts of Kunu-ri, I dimly heard man-made noises. They sounded like some shouting and an occasional banging of metal of some kind.

Anxious thoughts and worries crossed my mind. *Were the Chinese setting up mortar or artillery positions out to our front in preparation for a river crossing and an attack on us?* I mused. Otherwise, all was yet quiet except for the alternating howl or whisper of the wind as it rose and fell in gusts. I made my way back to the place I considered my command post. I bent over and pulled back the blanket from Rodriguez's head. He was snoring like a logger—or a trooper.

"Rodriguez," I spoke to him softly. No response. Again I called his name and this time shook him by the shoulder. Still no answer. Finally, I called his name louder and practically with my mouth in his ear, and with both hands I gave him a violent shake on both shoulders. He then sat up with a jerk and looked around in some bewilderment.

"Are you staying awake, Rodriguez?" I asked him with some frustration but also, under different circumstances, with what could have been some amusement.

"Si, si, Capitano," he answered, in all seriousness and without hesitation. He even had the effrontery to pretend some indignation that I would even ask. With that I gave up. I concluded that Rodriguez would not change, that he would always be Rodriguez. But then I was not sure I would want him any other way.

"Let me have the earphones for a while. I think you need some rest." He mumbled something in agreement and, almost before I could get the earphones on my ears, he was enthusiastically snoring again.

I then called battalion. The operator said the CO had been trying to contact us to let us know that all friendly troops had completed their withdrawal through our lines. I asked for information on any enemy nearby. Capt. John King, the S-2, came on the radio and said they had no information on any nearby Chinese; that if we learned otherwise, to let them know. He sounded quite calm. I settled down to wait out the night.

The Predawn Attack on Baker Company

"So the night did eventually end?" Ryan said, almost as though he doubted it would.

"Yes. Most nights seem to do that. And when it did, that's when the scatological paraphernalia hit the rotating blades of the ventilation system—or, as my troops would have put it more bluntly, that's when the shit hit the fan." Ryan looked a bit surprised at my use of an expletive, even if mild by modern standards.

The first rosy fingers of dawn were barely making themselves faintly visible on the eastern horizon in the early gray daybreak. I was almost dozing with the earphones on, and had just completed an exchange with the battalion CP duty officer, who was, as I recall, lst Lt. Lynn Freeman, the S-1, or administrative staff officer.

I was prodding Freeman for any new information. He reiterated that he had none, that the situation remained the same. We may have had some light chatter. I continued to shake with cold and discomfort and closed my eyes for a brief moment.

As I drifted in a half-awake, half-snoozing state, I suddenly came alive with a jerk. I heard small-arms fire in my company sector from the right edge of our positions. I sat up with a start, waking Rodriguez and handing him the earphones so I could learn what was happening. The fire increased and rapidly spread across our front. I struggled to rise in my numbed condition and reached for my carbine. Rodriguez was doing about the same.

There was a rustle in the dry leaves and I looked up to see several human forms above me. Their pile caps, quilted uniforms, and general appearance told me they were not our guys, which meant they might very well be Chinese. Things were happening almost faster than one could keep track.

It seemed at first that the Chinese looming above Rodriguez and me had not seen us down below them, but as we tried to rise and made some noise, they spotted us and turned with their rifles pointed in our direction.

I quickly aimed my carbine to "fire from the hip" and heard the hammer move slowly forward and hit the firing pin in the bolt with a soft "click." Again I knew at once I had not cleaned off all the lubricant and the cold had frozen it into a near-solid, preventing normal firing and operation. I frantically worked the bolt by hand, little hoping that I could get the weapon to work before the Chinese trooper fired at me. "This is it," I thought. "Good-by world. My time has come."

A second later, the report of a rifle almost in my ear jolted me, and I felt the Chinaman fall squarely on me where I was kneeling. I glanced around and saw that it was Rodriguez who had fired the shot, and none too soon. He had clearly saved my life. But this was no time to undertake awards ceremonies. Rodriguez was firing like mad. He had shot the second Chinaman as I again tried to fire. This time my carbine worked. We saw several other Chinese on our right.

We continued firing. Some enemy soldiers were hit and fell down. Some seemed wounded and withdrew. Still others turned back as our fire increased. Troops all around me were by then heavily engaged and firing as the daylight increased.

Bit by bit, the enemy amidst our company disappeared or withdrew, but I could hear almost continuous heavy firing across the hilltop. Dead and dying Chinese were everywhere on all sides. I paused and told Ryan I would furnish him color slides of the carnage for his Eighth Army records.

Then back to the fighting, I told Ryan I had spotted several of my men who were either dead or wounded. Raney, Dusseau, and the first sergeant were already busy organizing litter bearers to evacuate the wounded. I was preoccupied with trying to assess the situation, and, above all, to establish contact with the forward platoons to determine their situations and whether they had stood their ground or needed assistance. The firing continued, sporadic, intermittent, and scattered. Small-arms fired was interlaced with explosions as hand grenades detonated throughout the positions.

An hour later, as the sun slowly rose over the eastern hills, the worst seemed all over. All the Chinese were either dead or withdrawn from the hilltop. An unknown number seemed to be just over the forward crest of our positions, partly downhill from us and just out of sight. They could not be seen because the hillside dropped rather abruptly. My men heard them talking and moving about, however, and spent their time during the morning throwing or rolling grenades down on them.

We had suffered about twenty-five casualties, all of which were evacuated to the battalion CP area, which we could now see in the full daylight down in the valley behind us.

As things calmed down, the troops became emboldened, got up, and walked around in the sunlight and cracked out their frozen C rations. I asked the platoon leaders to make a head-count of enemy dead. They came up with a figure of a little over 500. I think they duplicated their count, however, or overlapped somewhat. Later in the day, I made my own count and my total was about 325 dead. Of course, the platoon leaders might have gone further down the hillsides, or to places where I did not go. For sure we had experienced one hell of a fire fight although, fortunately, a relatively brief one.

As the morning wore on and relative calm returned to our hill, the center of action changed from our hilltop to the broad plain out in front of our positions. We busied ourselves in licking wounds, taking head-counts, evacuating wounded and dead, trying to grab a can of rations to eat, and occasionally firing or throwing the hand grenades at the enemy soldiers suspected to be still near the top of our hill.

Meanwhile, out front on the valley before us and in plain sight but just beyond small-arms range, all hell continued to unfold. Countless thousands of enemy troops covered the landscape, and artillery and aircraft were trying to interdict them. Shells, bombs, and napalm were dropping all across our front. Later, I would read that more air sorties were flown to the valley before us that day than at any other time in one spot in the Korean War.

But I did not have the impression that all that firepower had much effect. Troops dispersed in open fields are not especially good targets. They are hard to see or hit if moving around, at least by a jet pilot flying by or strafing at 500 or more miles per hour. Nor is it easy to hit moving troops with artillery fire from guns many miles away—that usually requires time to adjust by forward observers with frontline troops.

The heavy artillery fire and close air support during the morning was keeping the enemy occupied and away from us, although far out to the flanks we could see the long columns of troops steadily moving around us and toward our rear. It was clear that soon we would be surrounded if we remained in our existing positions much longer.

As we contemplated our situation and awaited further instructions, I surveyed the surrounding landscape and pondered. Down the hill to our rear, in the valley below, I could see the battalion and regimental CPs. I was like an eagle sitting on a limb looking down on its prey before swooping. The view was spectacular and commanding. It was a military commander's dream of a most advantageous tactical position for threatening and overpowering an enemy.

Gawd, I thought. Suppose Baker Company had not held tight, had been overrun, and the Chinese now stood on this ground and had this view and could bring devastating fire on the troops below? For sure the CPs below would have had to prematurely abandon their positions and retreat in complete disorder. Our lines would have collapsed without command direction. There then would be nothing to stop the Chinese from overtaking the whole Eighth Army, which was then strung out helplessly on the roads to the south.

But below me on my hilltop there was an almost pastoral scene of peacefulness as individuals moved about unaffected by the firing over the hills to their front, out of sight and sound. Only the guns of our field-artillery battalions seemed involved in the battle out front. From my exchanges by radio with them during the morning, it was clear that higher headquarters had little knowledge or appreciation of the severity of the Baker Company dawn engagement. For sure they did not realize, I thought, how near they had come to defeat and extermination.

I slowed down again while Ryan caught up in his note-taking and put a new cassette in his recorder. After a bit he asked me, "Did you have the feeling that the Chinese knew you were in position on the hill?"

"No, I think they did not. As on previous occasions, I feel the sudden and close contact was more by happenstance than by design. Events later that day would seem to bear out that assumption."

"What events?"

"Well, in a nutshell, the fact that after the Chinese hit us at dawn and then pulled back hastily as daylight increased, they then did not frontally assault us again. Rather, as I say, they fanned out to the flanks to go around us, far out to the east and west, where there were no UN forces."

"You seem to make quite a point repeatedly that the Chinese did not attempt to hit you head on and when they did it was by accident. Why do you stress that?" Ryan wondered aloud.

"I suppose the answer lies in my disagreement with much that was written and recorded about the initial Chinese entry into the war when we were far up north. The media at the time, and it seems many historians since, painted a picture of the UN forces being 'driven' back and out of North Korea. I've never agreed with that characterization. My experience was that we pulled back not because of frontal pressure, but when greatly outnumbered and in the process of being surrounded, because no friends were on our flanks—in short that we 'pulled' back and were not 'driven' back."

I explained to Ryan that I thought the difference was far more than mere semantics or academics. The point is that if the UN forces had stood their ground on a more narrow front, say across the peninsula in the P'yongyang area, where they could have manned a more solid front line, I think it probably would have been unnecessary to withdraw all the way to points below the parallel. In other words, I have wondered if MacArthur or others did not overreact in panic and gave up more territory than was necessary. I think the point is worth careful study by anyone attempting to place Korean matters into proper perspective. Some may disagree.

As the day dragged on our situation became one mainly of waiting anxiously for an order to withdraw, while watching the enemy constantly closing its ring around us, making withdrawal impossible.

Our situation looked more and more as though there would be no retreat from the Kunu-ri area by our rearguard regiment in spite of Baker Company's early-morning tenacious stand and the fact that our capture by the Chinese was inevitable.

I spent most of my time roaming around amongst the platoons trying to the extent possible to exhibit optimism and radiate encouragement. At one point I approached Warrant Officer Dusseau and Weapons Platoon Leader Jess Mendenhall.

Dusseau was one of the most unforgettable characters in my company or whom I met in Korea. He possessed an amazing degree of tolerance and capacity for punishment. He seldom ever complained, no matter how grueling the developments, and he would often go around quoting poetry. A favorite of his was Rudyard Kipling and he knew many of his works by heart.

Sometimes in the most unusual and unthinkable places, or moments, Dusseau could be heard, in the heaviest of Scottish or Irish accents, reciting extracts such as "'Tis bitter cold. 'Tis bitter cold, said Files on Parade. 'Tis Danny's soul, 'Tis Danny's soul, the color sergeant said." And Dusseau could continue on and on.

But above all, or perhaps with his poetry, Dusseau liked his beer, and it seemed, missed it along the front lines more than anything else. Not that he was a boozie by any means. It seemed he knew where to stop, but bliss to him was to sit leisurely and sip the suds. If I asked Dusseau what was on his mind or what he longed for at any given time, I knew the answer most often to expect.

I looked at Dusseau for a moment on this occasion. He, like the rest of us, was a pitiful picture to behold, a Mauldin GI "Willie" in every respect. Dirty, unshaven, glazed-over eyes deep in weary sockets, muddy, torn, and ragged clothing, and the epitome of defeat and despair.

"Mr. Dusseau," I said. Warrant officers in the army were addressed as "misters," as are officers of most ranks in the navy. "I'll bet I know what it would take to raise your spirits at a time like this."

Without a blink, but with a faint and affirming smile, he shot right back at me, "You got that one right, Captain. Find me a six-pack of cold ones and I'll lead this whole command out of here and on the road to escape alley."

We chuckled. Dusseau's droll humor was much needed at such a depressing time. I turned to Mendenhall. His personality contrasted sharply with Dusseau's. Mendenhall constantly griped and had an excessive fondness for the bottle that was to strain relations between us later on to the breaking point. But he was also a fearless and highly reliable combat officer on whom I could depend to perform faithfully in the worst times, when the chips were down. He too was stubborn, had an uncooperative mind of his own, and was sometimes outspoken to an abrasive degree.

"How's your morale, Jess?" I said, half jokingly. Well-disciplined troops are trained to have high spirits and unfaltering morale no matter how unbearable the circumstances. And conscientious commanders are supposed to exhibit concern always about their men's morale.

Mendenhall studied me for an almost indefinite period, spit out a wad of tobacco juice, and then slowly spoke.

"Well, Captain, let me think about that one for a moment. You ask how is my morale. We've been in almost constant contact with the enemy for over a week with practically no sleep other than sporadic dribbles. Most of the men are near starving. We've experienced some of the coldest weather that troops anywhere have lived through since Valley Forge. I was snatched away from my family almost without any notice or warning to a war that I have little or no interest in, in a country I had just about never heard of. Over half my men are dead or wounded from this morning's frivolities—we are down to our last few rounds of ammunition—and I've been sitting here watching those damned Chinks steadily close the ring around us that is going to seal us up and prevent us from hauling ass out of here. And you ask me how is my morale. My problem before answering is to figure out whether you are for real."

"Good ole" Jess—no mincer of words is he. Whether he meant disrespect or not, one could hardly quarrel with what he said. I attempted a smile, and turned away to leave him to his devices. I did not know what could be gained by further discourse at that time with my weapons platoon leader.

What Made Baker Fight?

"How do you account for such fierce and prompt resistance by your men, whom you had found such a short time before the arrival of the Chinese to be mostly fast asleep?" Ryan ventured.

"I'm not at all sure that I can give a dispositive answer to that question. It was much of a mystery to me then, and so remains to this day. I had been most apprehensive, to understate the case, about our wherewithal to defend our position, as stated, with the company so spent, and, I thought, passed out in sleep. I spent much of the day while we lolled around waiting impatiently and eagerly for orders to withdraw, quizzing anyone who might have answers."

I guess a better explanation lies in several areas. First, except for my radio operator Rodriguez, any sleep by a frontline soldier is not likely to be very deep or sound. On the contrary, it's mostly fitful, and is usually light dozing or napping. Many soldiers would not even admit to having been asleep at all. Others insisted they merely closed their eyes from time to time for rest.

Second, it seems that when a sleeping person is under great stress, and fearing a threat to his safety or well-being, the slightest sound or commotion is likely to bring him, or her, immediately to his or her senses and alertness. Every one of my men I questioned said that at the first sound of small-arms fire they were instantly wide awake and on guard.

"But were they in any kind of suitable condition to begin and maintain a successful defense of their positions?"

"That, of course, is a different question. It is also a hard one to answer. I guess the short answer is a qualified yes."

At least my men did fight off large numbers of Chinese. We were not dislodged from our hill. We don't have very accurate numbers of how many Chinese were there. From the dead count of somewhere between 150 and 300, I think we could assume there must have been at least several times that number involved in the attack. But we can't say with any certainty, either, whether our success was because of a superior defense, or whether, upon finding us there, the enemy simply withdrew voluntarily as opposed to being forcefully thrown back. Perhaps it was some of both.

We do know for certain that: we were there; the Chinese came in waves and masses; there was one hell of a fire fight; when it was over we remained and the Chinese did not; they paid a far heavier price than we did; and finally, to repeat, and most critical of all, by holding the hill, the most dominant terrain in the nearby area, we denied its use to the enemy and prevented observation of, and chaos for, our forces still withdrawing on the roads leading from the area, or who still had CPs or gun or other positions just behind us.

"How did your battalion or regimental commanders react to your dawn fire fight?" Ryan queried.

"That's the rather galling and ironic aspect of the whole matter. No one seemed to understand just what had happened, on what scale, and how indebted the command was for our contribution to the success of the withdrawal."

It's possible that the people in the valley to our rear did not even hear the small-arms fire in our fire fight. Most of it was on the forward slope of our hill, out of sight, and seemingly out of hearing of anyone far down the slope to the rear. There were no explosions, other than grenades, from our fire fight, and most of the grenades exploded even farther down the forward slope as they were thrown or rolled onto the withdrawing enemy by our men.

For sure, almost no one not on our hill with Baker Company could have fully appreciated what was going on, and especially the severity of the engagement. The 23rd Regiment's command report for the month of November 1950 contains only a brief entry: "0500: lst Battalion attacked by small enemy force which were repelled by 0700." I have always concluded that the regimental unawareness of our predicament and fight was caused not only by the above, but also by numerous distractions going on all about them below.

Just to the south of our regiment, all hell was breaking loose with the 38th and 9th in the passes on the road to Sunch'on. All around the higher headquarters' CPs to the rear, there were noisy motor- and armored-vehicle movements that could easily have drowned out any faint sound of small-arms fire over the crests of the distant hill to the front. Added to this was the almost continuous deafening roar of 105-mm artillery in positions in the valley near the infantry CPs.

Daylight that fateful day revealed that the enemy forces were all around the regiment, and in great numbers. Artillery targets of moving troops were everywhere, and they kept the artillery busy. With withdrawal imminent, it seems that Lt. Col. John Keith, with his 15th Field Artillery Battalion, was not interested in filling his weapons carriers with unspent ammo. He and Colonel Freeman much preferred that it be used on the Chinese rather than hauled back on trucks that could be used to carry our infantryman.

So the guns of the 15th stayed busy all day. Late in the day, they undertook the well-recorded event of firing up all their ammo before leaving when they concluded it was impracticable to tow out the howitzers. Using all available artillerymen, including cooks, as ammo bearers, the battalion is known to have fired over 3,000 rounds in only about twenty minutes. That firing may have diverted our commanders' attention from us.

"During the early-morning fire fight, how did your weapons perform?" my historian visitor inquired.

"I spent some time during the day investigating and exploring that point. I found few men who said they had had no problems with their weapons, especially any that were automatic or semiautomatic. The same old story; the lubricant congealed so stiffly in the cold that it acted like glue and prevented the movement of parts.

"Many men told me their weapons would not fire at all, and that resulted in a considerable amount of man-to-man fighting. Soldiers told me that when they aimed weapons and they did not fire, they would physically attack the Chinese and in some cases grabbed the enemies' weapons and either fired them back or beat them with their own weapons. Those who told of personal confrontations did not report that the Chinese had put up much of a struggle."

I've heard many stories of veterans who tell tales of personal contact with the enemy. Most of these, other than the Vietnam War, where I had no personal experience, I take with a grain of salt. I think the natural human inclination is to use weapons, rather than engage in physical contact, no matter how many Hollywood movies we see to the contrary. Of course if there is no weapon, or ammo, there may be no other recourse but hand-to-hand fighting. That seems to be what many of my men did at Kunu-ri.

"So all day you waited for permission to withdraw?"

"Yes, with steady and increasing alarm. The river floodplain to our front, short of the Namdae River, had been filled with Chinese from the time of sunup when we could see them. We watched them, and some men took occasional shots at them, including Jess Mendenhall with his mortars. But they were simply beyond small-arms range, and very difficult to hit while moving around with indirect-fire weapons such as mortars."

Several artillery missions were undertaken during the day, also on those Chinese in the valley, in plain sight. But the results were not very effective. The fighter pilots were strafing and napalming the Chinese in the valley to our front, but we couldn't see that the pilots caused much harm to an enemy so well dispersed. But the air strikes did probably delay the enemy and to that extent gave the withdrawing ground troops valuable time.

Our main cause for alarm, as stated, centered around the masses of Chinese we could well see from our high hilltop that during the day were constantly moving around our flanks and to our rear. Most could not be seen with the naked eye, since they were some two or three miles off in the distance. But with binocs, I could see long, dark lines of troops moving ever along, and deeper and deeper to our rear.

By midafternoon I could see them on each of the two roads that were being used by other friendly forces for withdrawal, and the only roads that we could use when it came time for us to withdraw. I wondered if my commanders below realized just how precarious, and perhaps hopeless, was our predicament.

Excitement on Baker's Kunu-ri Hilltop

"So, Sherm Pratt, while you were waiting for the order to withdraw, as the day wore on, how was this fire support you mentioned used? Or perhaps I should say, what limitations were there on the normal fire support for frontline units?"

"There was no significant artillery or mortar support other than our own regimental weapons, and our own normal artillery support battalion, the 15th Field Artillery. I think most of the remainder of the division or corps fire-support units were probably mobile and on the road and on the way out, and thus not in firing positions."

We did have, however, close air support on a scale that I suspect was unequalled elsewhere for most of the Korean War. Fighters were overhead for most of the day. They were busy, as I've described, dropping napalm in the valley out front and on the town of Kunu-ri at, we assumed, targets of opportunity.

Sometimes we could not see what the aircraft targets were, except in the closest areas, where we knew there were masses of Chinese troops. Some we could see them moving or crawling around, but many remained hidden from view, waiting for darkness. The aircraft must have returned to their bases repeatedly for reloads of fuel and ordnance, but there was seldom a time when we could not see planes somewhere over and diving at the combat areas.

Blair, in his *The Forgotten War*, writes that Freeman was helped immensely by the Far East Air Force, "which flew an astonishing 287 close air support missions over Kunu that day, attacking the advancing CCF troops with bombs and napalm and strafing them with machine guns." I think there can be no doubt of the value of the air force help, although it is generally recognized, reluctantly by ground troops, that such air activity is the least efficient use of military combat aircraft.

Rather than closely supporting ground troops, air force people would much prefer to use their expensive planes and skilled pilots to attack concentrations of supplies, or bridges or lines of communications, where their bombs will be the most effective. I have always fully understood that. I've seen too many instances where we have called for an air strike on frontline enemy positions, and the fly guys dropped all heaven and earth in a virtual inferno of fire, only to have the enemy as well entrenched afterward as they were before.

But the air-force help at Kunu clearly disorganized and slowed down the enemy at a time when hours and minutes were critical. Most of our division was on the way out at that very time, and we were about to be. Even so, much of the division was to pay a ghastly price during the withdrawal. One can well wonder, though, whether there would have been any survivors at all from the 2d Division if the CCF had not been delayed in and around the Kunu area by our regimental combat team with the help of the air force.

"Just how close was the 'close' air support that day?"

"When the air support first began arriving about midmorning, it was as close as the bottom of the hill that we were on. The hill was very steep on its forward slope, as many hills are along a river, so we could almost spot the rank of the pilots, or could have if they were not traveling at such a spectacular speed. They were jets, of course, and in or coming out of dives could have been moving at around the sonic barrier. But then late in the morning a development occurred that caused the planes to almost cease their attacks on the valley."

I was sticking pretty close to the radio and Rodriguez to make sure I did not fail to receive permission to withdraw. That was a word I did not want to miss. At the same time I tried to keep tabs on what was going on around me. Shortly before noon a runner from one of the forward platoons came rushing up and said, "Captain, it seems the Chinese are attacking again!"

"How so?" I asked.

"We can see mobs of them running through the fields toward our positions. All morning they have been either holding their own and staying concealed or trying to pull back. The lieutenant wants to know if you have any instructions."

"Tell him to hang on. I'll be right up to see what to make of this."

I unlimbered myself from my abode, grabbed my sometimes trusty carbine and binocs, and followed the trooper back to his platoon. I found Lieutenant Walker and Warrant Officer Dusseau huddled together and peering intently down into the valley. They heard me coming and looked up.

"Captain, this is real weird," Walker said. "We can't make heads or tails of this. You can see dozens, or hundreds, of the rascals, down mostly on the left bank of the road, there," as he pointed in the direction of the spotted movements. "It's hard to believe they would try to advance in broad daylight directly into our positions. They haven't been doing that for the past week, and especially today."

"And they don't seem to be very organized," added Dusseau. "They're darting along like a bunch of chickens. Should we get Mendenhall on them with his 60s [mortars]—that is if he has any ammo left?"

"By all means, get Jess alerted for a fire mission and also see if you can get word to the artillery FO [forward observer] to stand by for a fire mission by the 15th."

The mysterious troops in the valley were still rather far away, a least a mile or so, and beyond small-arms fire. All three of us watched intently for some moments.

"Jess wants to know if he should open fire?" Dusseau pressed me. True to form, Mendenhall was always eager for a fire mission.

"Tell him to stand by for a bit yet, but be fully ready on short notice."

By now, the advancing horde was much closer and almost within small-arms fire. They were only three or four hundred yards from the base of our hill. I had already passed the word along to all the forward machine gunners and rifle platoons to stand by to commence firing when the targets got just a little closer.

Suddenly, as we continued to observe with our binocs, Walker blurted out excitedly, "My God, Captain, I don't think those are Chinks! I think they are GIs!"

"I was about to say the same thing!" Dusseau and I said almost with one voice.

The forward men were now quite close and some could even be identified with the naked eye. We could recognize their American uniforms, but most had no helmets, and few had any weapons. Some were barefooted. Others looked wet and all appeared, even at that distance, to be thoroughly disoriented and terrorized.

As the fleeing men ran and stumbled along over the frozen and patchy snow-covered ground, many fell. Some did not get back up as best we could determine. Here and there we could see a trooper halt, look back, and fire.

We then noticed that mixed amongst the GIs were Chinese. They did not seem to be firing much, but they would run after the GIs and, when they overtook them, several Chinese would grab the GIs and try to pull them to the ground. We could see fistfights as the GIs attempted to throw off the Chinese. We saw other GIs hitting their Chinese tormenters with their rifles, or with what appeared to us to be rifles, or perhaps clubs or sticks.

The wild melee continued for almost two or three hours off and on. As the GIs that succeeded in evading the Chinese neared our lines and entered the road gap down below, the Chinese would abandon the chase and fall back and try to capture or otherwise eliminate other GIs coming along to their rear.

Watching the frantic GIs and the events below, we felt helpless and frustrated. It was too far below to go out and help and we could not fire on the Chinese without risking the GIs. We could do little else than sit and watch and root for our guys. We noted that most of them were black troops.

As the escaping GIs made their way into our lines, they entered along the road stretching from our front to the rear and through the gap, to our left flank. We could not see them as they disappeared into the gap, but we could as they emerged and were collected into the battalion and other CP areas.

We learned that day by radio, and when assembling below near sundown for motorized withdrawal, that the pathetic and heartrending collection of troopers we had been witnessing most of the day was what was left of the 3rd Battalion of the 24th Regiment of the 25th Division. They had been overrun and bypassed in their positions northwest of Kunu-ri on our left and on the west bank of the Ch'ongch'on River.

There is no question that the fleeing troops were overwhelmed and had fled in desperation and panic. The troops from the 24th's 3rd Battalion that did not pass through our lines on that last day at Kunu-ri were either taken prisoner or experienced a sad fate that to this day is not fully known.

As a post-Ryan-interview note, it should perhaps be pointed out that the 3rd Battalion of the 24th Infantry Regiment was one of the last all-black battalions of the army, except for officers, who were both black and white. Its performance in combat in those closing days of November in and around Kunu-ri has been the source of much controversy.

The problems of the 3rd Battalion were well known around the frontline units at the time, and it was generally believed that the battalion had "bugged out."

The pejorative term *bugout* came into use about that time in the Korean War and was applied, at least as long as I was there, to a unit, or action, in which the men would panic under attack and flee to the rear without putting up any, or enough, resistance. In short, it stood for disgrace and cowardice, although the term was sometimes used by troops with an air of expectancy and almost hopefulness as a means of ending one's participation in an undesired conflict. There was no shortage of units, or parts of units, in the Korean War who were accused of "bugging out," white as well as black.

We shall probably never know with certainty to what extent the men of the 24th's 3rd Battalion can be held accountable for their performance in Korea. Versions differ sharply, and, I notice, along racial lines, to a large extent.

Shortly after the Kunu-ri fighting, the *Saturday Evening Post* carried an article by correspondent Harold Martin about the 3rd Battalion of the 24th. The piece is in the files in the Pentagon Library. The article was far from complimentary. It painted a picture of a battalion that had "bugged out." Martin wrote that the battalion commander, Lt. Col. Melvin Blair, had put his security guard to flight "without firing a shot." He said that "men fled like rabbits" and, "As the Chinese came running, all three [rifle] companies broke at once."

Some survivors of the battalion are on record as taking a sharply different view of the incident, or at least the cause of the 3rd Battalion's flight. A black warrant officer, Thomas Pettigrew, who was decorated and promoted to lieutenant for action at Kunu-ri, asserts the disaster was caused by inept and erratic leadership, and especially by the white battalion CO, Blair. Pettigrew wrote in a short book titled *The Kunu-ri (Kumori) Incident* (Vantage Press, 1963), also on file in the Pentagon Library, that Blair had placed his troops so that they stuck out like a sore thumb and they were vulnerable to being attacked. He wrote that Blair was "hysterically and incoherently giving orders." He charged that Blair's staff panicked, and as the enemy closed in Blair became more hysterical and finally pleaded, "Someone take me out of here."

In a footnote, author Pettigrew points out that battalion CO Blair was highly decorated, including two Distinguished Service Crosses and four Silver Stars, but that later, when out of the service, he destroyed his image by attempting a bank robbery in 1958 at the Bing Crosby Golf Tournament, for which he drew five years and served fourteen months.

Long Awaited Permission to Withdraw from Kunu-ri

At long last, late in the afternoon of that unforgettable last day of November in 1950 at Kunu-ri in far North Korea, on a desolate and isolated hilltop, we got the word to withdraw.

The sun was low on the western horizon. Chinese were still infiltrating around our flanks. We could see them on the escape road some three to five miles to our rear. Now that we had heard the word to withdraw, I wondered how we were going to be able to do so.

But start we did. During the day we had carried down all our wounded, Chinese and American and ROK. Everyone was more than ready to pull out. We had been ready for hours, for that matter. When the word came, we practically flowed down the hill to the area of the battalion command post, probably 600 to 800 yards below and away.

As we started down, the 15th Field Artillery Battalion began a barrage the likes of which I had never seen or heard before. It seemed their l05-mm "hows" must have been belt-fed. By the time we reached the low ground, they had completely fired up all their ammo. I learned that all this was to expend the ammo to the last round, since they would not try to take out their weapons. The 15th's battalion commander and Colonel Freeman had decided to remove firing pins and otherwise disable the guns, and leave them behind rather than risk overturning guns in the dark, blocking the road, and trapping all the rest of the combat team on the only existing escape road.

Far from Korea back in my Arlington, Virginia, rec room Ryan interrupted me at this point with another question. "Lets return for a moment to your revelations concerning the flight of the 3rd Battalion of the 24th Infantry. There has been disagreement over the years as to the cause; whether it was cowardice by the men, mostly, or all, black soldiers, or poor leadership by white officers. Based on your own presence there at the time, do you have any opinions or conclusions as to where the blame should lie?"

"I think a fair and objective answer, to elaborate on what I've just said, would have to be that both are to blame, assuming that there is blame, or fault. And I include the 'if' because I don't think all disasters on the battlefield, or on the football field, are necessarily anyone's fault."

It's easy to be a Monday-morning quarterback. The test for

determining fault, not necessarily competence or wisdom, is not what one would do calmly and without haste or pressure on Monday, but rather what one would do under great pressure and urgency and instantaneously in the middle of the game, with no time for delays or drawn-out contemplation. Additionally, on the battlefield you have the added element of life and death for perhaps a great number of people.

I think that no one has any way of correctly judging the performance of the battalion commanding officer and his staff. Blair is described by Pettigrew as out of control, but that seems to fly in the face of a remarkably courageous and productive combat record. His later bank robbery sounds like the act of a veteran who fell apart. We've seen lots of that after every war, and especially since the Vietnam War.

Society seems to recognize that human collapses are not necessarily attributable to weaknesses of character. In war, breakdowns might be caused unavoidably by the severity of the strain that a person is or was under. Even the strongest of men can break at some point. There are few who have no breaking point, ever. But some are stronger than others. Accordingly, I would be especially careful in faulting Blair. Nor do I want very much to defend him. I suppose I lean mostly toward compassionate detachment. Let he and his Maker work it out.

With respect to the troops who fled, here again I hesitate to throw the first stone. Fortunately the battalion involved was one of the last all-black combat units. I have read studies that point up the inadvisability of having all-black combat units. My experience and observations support that finding. Aside from racial or sociological considerations, such segregated units were simply not militarily wise. They do not fight well, nor is it reasonable to expect them to do so.

Nowadays, there would be understandable resentment by black troops, or those of any other minority, for such discriminatory treatment, and it would surely rob them of their motivation to fight. Earlier, during the transitional period in the Korean War, I think there was fear and lack of confidence in each other among the blacks themselves.

Blacks as a class had never occupied the higher-level management and control positions in our society and, through no fault of their own, they had not developed forceful, reliable, and dynamic leadership ability. Under those conditions, to expect inspiring performance and tenacious resistance might have been quite unrealistic, as well as unfair.

I have always doubted that white units under the same or similar circumstances and with the same backgrounds as the men of the black segregated battalion would have performed any better. We'll never know, since whites in our society have not existed under the same conditions. At any rate, it was soon after the Kunu-ri rout that segregated units such as the 24th Regiment became a thing of the past. I heard much praise for the performance of the 24th earlier on the Naktong River in the Pusan perimeter.

"Were you off your hill before dark?" Ryan continued, returning to the activities of Baker Company at the critical engagement at Kunu-ri.

"Just barely. The sun was almost on the western horizon. Still it was biting and painfully cold, and getting much colder as dusk approached. Hustle, bustle, and near-pandemonium reigned supreme all around. Officers and NCOs were barking out orders and trying to organize the loading of men and equipment. It seemed to me that more people were running around in circles than not."

I spotted Capt. John King, the lst Battalion S-2, and Capt. Joseph Power, who I think was the communications officer at that time.

"Hey, guys," I said, walking up to them, "can anyone give me some scoop on what is going on? Are we going to get out of here, and when?"

I had never seen John King so wretched looking. He was usually the ever-cheerful and optimistic intelligence officer. To him the glass was always half-full, not half-empty. At that moment, King looked as though he had just lost all his blue chips on Wall Street, plus about every other priceless possession he owned.

"Boy, we wished we knew, Pratt," King answered. "We're starting out. Our RCT is the only troops here. 2d Battalion is already road bound. 3rd Battalion is a short piece down the road in position to cover our withdrawal through them, and then they will pull out and be the last."

I looked around and then back at King.

Which Escape Route for the 23rd?

"Which road are we using?" I asked, my nervousness showing. King pointed to the west. We were standing almost at the fork in the road from Kunu-ri where it splits with one leg going west and one almost due south.

"You mean the Anju–Sukch'on road?" I asked in disbelief. "Keyrist, John, we can't get out that road. All day I've been watching the Chinks and they are all up and down it as far as the eye can see. There are simply thousands of the enemy. From the early afternoon they have been moving south and crossing the road. By now they must be well dug in and waiting for us to come down."

"Yeah, we got your radio reports, Pratt, and there's a chance that they have moved across the road and, instead of blocking it, may be working their way on further south. We have to hope so. Otherwise, we will have to fight our way out, if indeed we can get out at all."

"But why the hell don't we go south out the Sunch'on road? Wasn't that the plan?"

Just then, Maj. George Russell, the battalion executive officer, and soon to be commander, rushed up and frantically began dispensing orders. He had heard my protests about going out the western road.

"Pratt," Russell said, "there's no time to give you all the details, but just believe that much has been happening on this ole ball field today, hour by hour. You're right about the road south. That's the route Walker wanted General Keiser to take us out after holding 'til the rest of the army cleared. The western route is the main highway to P'yongyang and all points south. But it has been carrying the entire Eighth Army for the past hours and is jammed beyond description. Tens of thousands of vehicles, bumper to bumper, for miles and miles. So army ordered us to take the southern route when we got the green light to scram out."

"Then why don't we?" I innocently asked.

"Because the rest of the division took it starting early this morning, and they are at this minute in the damndest fire fight over a several-mile stretch just down the road, not far from here. They are ambushed, mostly at a standstill, with dark coming on rapidly. They are literally being slaughtered. Status reports are quite sketchy but tragic.

Artillery fire and aerial bombing smoke in Kunu-ri and Namdae River valley in front of Baker Co./23rd Reg. positions in early days of Chinese intervention.

Dead Chinese communists in Baker Co./23rd Reg. positions at Kunu-ri with distinctive quilted uniforms with canvas shoes.

Some of 300–500 enemy killed by Baker Co./23rd Reg. in fierce predawn fire
fight on hills overlooking Kunu-ri and Namdae River on November 30, 1950.

View of the west of Baker Co. positions after fierce predawn fire fight on high
ground overlooking Kunu-ri and Namdae River on Korean west coast.

Korean members of Baker Co./23rd Reg. awaiting permission to withdraw after critical dawn fire fight on high ground at Kunu-ri on November 29, 1950.

Chinese dead in standard quilted uniforms after Baker Co. fire fight on high ground south of Kunu-ri in closing days of November 1950.

"Colonel Freeman has been working feverishly all afternoon to get permission to withdraw westward instead of into that inferno on the south road. Just moments ago, he got permission by an air-dropped message. So now we are going out the west and south route."

Here, another post-interview note is needed. The question of whether Colonel Freeman had in fact gotten permission from the division commander to use the western road, instead of following the rest of the division down the southern, and inland, road was later the subject of much dispute, which has never apparently been completely resolved. Also, whether the movement was the wisest course of action has also been much debated. Freeman is reported to have felt that to follow the rest of the division south would be nothing less than suicidal. Others insisted that in not doing so, he improperly uncovered the hindmost elements of the division under murderous assault on the Sunch'on road. This matter too is treated in some depth by Blair in his *The Forgotten War* on pages 490–493.

"But how do we know we can get out on the western road?" I persisted.

"Short answer to that one, my anxious Captain, is that we don't. In fact, to be brutally candid, the odds are that we won't. But small as our chances are, Colonel Freeman is convinced they are better than no chance at all, which would be the case if we go south and follow the rest of the division into the cauldron. We won't know until we try, and we sure as hell can't just sit here. We might well wind up by tomorrow morning all slaughtered along the road, or in a Chinese POW camp. I'm not sure which is to be preferred."

George Russell was not one to pull his punches. He was not doing so now. He was to show himself at his best a few weeks later, when he took over the battalion from Hutchin, who was to assume higher duties at division. Russell would be known as a cool, deliberate, highly dependable and respected leader. He would earn an image as a commander who knew his tactics and gained respect and loyalty from his staff and lower commanders. At least he surely did from me.

Russell had hardly finished his diatribe when Hutchin rushed up. By then, Capt. Mel Stai of Able Company had joined us. Hutchin looked at Stai and me and said to us both, "Fellers, we've got the OK from Colonel Freeman—we are to move and move fast, or we'll not get out of here. The 2d Battalion is already on the road and moving.

The 3rd is in position just down the road. We'll pass through the 3rd and then they will pull up and bring up the rear. You two," looking at Stai and me, "spread what troops of your companies you have left, and load up on the tanks of the 72d and trucks of the 15th Field Artillery. Crowd in tight. We don't have any extra vehicles, and we don't want to leave anyone behind. We also must make room for some remnants of the 9th. Now move!"

We did. No prodding was needed. The last faint glimmers of daylight were rapidly fading away. As the convoy moved out with the angry roar of dozens of heavy armored and truck engines, I glanced back and up on our hill above that we had just left. I saw a line of enemy troops on the skyline watching us, and some were already running down the hill toward our convoy. Chills ran up and down my spine as I clung to the side of my tank with a dozen or more of my wretched troops.

What, oh what, was in store for us as our motley group rode off into the night? Would it be our last night? At such times I could get nostalgic and wonder what was happening back in the States or at other places I had been. I studied the gaunt and haggard faces of my men and wondered what their families back home would say if they could see them at that moment.

CHAPTER SEVEN

The Escape from North Korea—Jaws of Death

Thus, in the early hours of darkness in the evening of November 30, 1950, the remnants of the 23rd Infantry Regimental Combat Team began feeling their way cautiously, desperately, and with unbounded uncertainty southward from their rearguard Kunu-ri positions. The goal was to follow, if possible, the rest of the Eighth Army to positions again somewhere around the 38th parallel.

A more weary, disoriented, untidy, confused, worried, and distraught military force could hardly be imagined. Shades of Bataan, Dunkirk, Gallipoli, Khartoum, and other historical evacuations hung in the air like curtains of doom.

The road for the 23rd ran west-southwest for about twelve miles to Anju; thence another four miles to Sinanju; after which the road turns almost due south along the western coast of Korea but slightly inland for about sixteen miles to Sukch'on, and finally on to P'yongyang.

The road south from Kunu-ri was reasonably good, by Korean standards, although narrow. It certainly was not an American interstate or a German *Autobahn*. It was asphalt most of the way except for many chuckholes and other damages caused by heavy military traffic, bad weather, and lack of proper maintenance.

We had gone not more than three or four miles when suddenly, but not entirely unexpectedly, we began to receive burp-gun and machine-gun fire from the fields and paddies along the road, especially when we passed through rolling terrain where the hills were very close to the road. We were to learn through the night that we, too, were to experience our own "mini" gauntlet in the 23rd Regiment, albeit not nearly so devastating overall as that imposed on the rest of the division on the Kunu-ri-to-Sunch'on road to our east.

At this point, I think some additional "post-interview" comments are in order.

I have noted that there are some discrepancies among writers as to the exact date of the final withdrawal of the last elements of the 2d Division from the Kunu-ri rearguard blocking positions of the Eighth Army. In his *Compact History of the Korean War*, Harry J. Middleton writes, in part, concerning the Kunu-ri withdrawal: "Keiser was given the order to withdraw, and on December l, the Division began to move back to Sunchon" (p. 147). Most other accounts, including the 23rd Regiment's command report, show the date as November 30, a day earlier, which I believe to be correct.

Concerning our own difficulties in our "gauntlet" on the road out of Kunu-ri, veterans of the 23rd's withdrawal on the road southwest and south have every right to be chagrined that there has been so little recorded, or perhaps even known, of their struggles with the enemy on that occasion. The 23rd's trials and hardships seem to have almost completely escaped recognition. Even the command report is all but silent, reading only that the regiment withdrew with "relatively little difficulty."

One of the few, if not the only, narrative in contrast with other terse or missing accounts of the 23rd's ordeal is contained in Blair's *The Forgotten War* on pages 493-94:

The column proceeded west in haste . . . Almost immediately, the column stalled for an hour and a half, blocked by a massive traffic jam. During the stop some CCF troops worked in close and attacked . . . with machine guns . . . Trucks were shot up . . . men scrambled aboard other vehicles. . . . The column began to move . . . and proceeded . . . three miles . . . before it stopped . . . again. In this halting fashion the 23rd Infantry and 15th FAB . . . got away. . . .

The reader may find it interesting to compare those words with my own following account, and draw his or her own conclusions. Only my account, of course, is based on the actual experience of the narrator. Most other writers, not having been there, had no choice but to rely on the recollections of others or whatever records they could locate.

As our command crawled down the road in the darkness, the Chinese bullets very soon, as reported by Blair, began ricocheting off our tank. Terror quickly spread amongst my men. There are few places where a trooper feels less secure under enemy fire than when high from the ground on the exterior of a vehicle. There is a feeling of utter helplessness. When afoot, one can always "hit the dust" and take up the well known prone position, or ditches or rocks can be used for protection. But on a vehicle one can only cling and hope he is missed, in dread that he will be hit.

In the second or third volley of fire from the Chinese, whom we could hardly see from our rolling and bouncing perches, two of my men were hit. Most men were trying to fire back, but at elusive and baffling targets. The night was exceptionally dark, either because the moon had not yet risen or because it was behind clouds. I don't remember precisely. In a way we were lucky the Chinese must have also had difficulty seeing us, although they had the advantage of simply firing in the direction of noisy vehicles passing by them on the road.

The Chinese seemed to be everywhere in great numbers. Manpower in abundance was certainly one of the areas in which the enemy outdistanced the UN forces. Many of the Chinese were massing around our slow-moving vehicles and reaching up to grab the troops by the legs or feet to pull them off the vehicles and onto the ground.

No one in our column, it seemed, had any inclination to halt. To do so would certainly be pointless and, in fact, suicidal. You could hardly engage an enemy you couldn't see in the dark, and for certain, if one dismounted into the darkness and the swarms of Chinese, he would be instantly outnumbered and overpowered. Furthermore, the safety and security of the entire column behind would be thrown into serious jeopardy. Halted vehicles and troops in or on them would be easy prey for the circling swarms of Chinese foot soldiers eagerly awaiting an opportunity to get their hands on us.

Perhaps the most agonizing and heart-wrenching moments were when we were unable to help men who had been shot off or fallen from vehicles ahead, or pulled from them, and were lying out in the darkness as we passed by, screaming for help. I can hear their voices to this day pleading: "Don't leave us behind"; "Help me, I'm shot in the shoulder!"; "Please take us with you!" To not respond to such pleas from our own men was one of the war's cruelest burdens.

These conditions continued through much of the night. At times we all were firing into the shadowy figures milling around our vehicles. On several occasions, vehicles were blown up or destroyed by gunfire and had to be abandoned, and men reloaded.

Down and Almost Out

The night withdrawal from Kunu-ri was to be one long, bloody, and terrifying nightmare.

Off and on during the night the motor column would come to a complete stop. When it did, the Chinese troops rushed up and tried to grab our men by the legs or shoes and pull them off the vehicles. Surprisingly, there was very little gunfire at those times. I suppose that in the dark both the enemy and our men were hesitant to fire small arms at such close range for fear of hitting their own friendly troops.

My recollections of the ordeal are not without their more poignant segments. I recall so clearly halting at one point shortly after dark and hearing an American soldier in the ditch alongside the road, crying out for help. He was pleading not to be left behind and said he could not move because he was wounded.

I was aware it might be a trick, but I could not completely turn a deaf ear to such a heartrending call. In a moment of impetuosity, and perhaps imprudence, I grabbed a couple men from alongside me on the tank turret and told them to jump off with me to see if we could get the guy up on the tank before the column moved out and perhaps we too were left behind.

I located the wounded man and said something encouraging to him. The two men and I then proceeded to carry him out of the ditch and up on the road shoulder. As we were struggling to lift him, with the help of some men on the tank, I suddenly felt a stinging, heavy, and near-paralyzing blow on my back. I collapsed in pain with my head spinning, fighting all the while to retain consciousness. From the road where I lay I looked up and saw shadowy figures that I knew must be Chinese soldiers. One of them had apparently struck me between the shoulders with his rifle butt, knocking the wind out of me and sending me down.

As my men were trying to push the wounded soldier onto the tank, the Chinese were trying to pull him off. It was, in essence, a tug of war. By then I began to regain my composure and I came up fighting mad. I laced into the Chinese furiously, jabbing my carbine butt with side strokes and any kind of blow that comes to mind in such a frantic moment. Some more chaps leaped down off the tank and we soon had a regular free-for-all in one of the rare instances of close hand-to-hand fighting with the enemy in that, or any, modern war.

Almost as fast as it started, it was all over. At least for that halt. The Chinese must have concluded they were outmanned and over-powered. They began to fall back into the fields from whence they had come and into the protection of the darkness.

We proceeded to get our guy on board and soon afterward the column again started moving. I learned later that similar incidents had occurred all up and down the column during the early night hours. Sometimes wounded or straggling troops along the road were loaded, but many were not and had to be left behind.

"So these were the painful ingredients of the 23rd's own 'mini' gauntlet that night?" Ryan mused as he paused again in his note-taking.

"I think one can safely say that, Tom," I answered. "Overall and on a larger scale, I think we must concede that our 'mini' bore little resemblance to the big brother being experienced by the 38th and 9th some miles away to the east. But to the individual soldier, in a particular location, the severity of the experience, I am sure, was little different. All can be quiet on the western front, but it is not so in a small area if the enemy has you pinned down with machine-gun fire."

So our withdrawal was far from uneventful, as we can see. Some of the smaller units in our column, such as squads or platoons, had casualties as heavy as similar-sized units of the other regiments, even if the total losses were much less.

Strangely, it seems that the regimental commander and his staff were mostly unaware that any significant problems were occurring at all. At one control point along the way during the night, we halted briefly while the tankers refueled. We had left behind the area where the roughest of the earlier encounters with the Chinese had taken place. The fear of imminent enemy attacks had largely abated.

While the refueling was taking place, troops dismounted to limber up, for toilet breaks, or other reasons, and many were tense and weary beyond the breaking point. I came upon some individuals clustered and talking and recognized Shoemaker, King, and Freeman, the regimental and battalion staff officers.

"Do you think we are out of the danger area, Hal?" I asked Shoemaker.

"What danger area?" he answered, somewhat surprised.

"Back down the road where the Chinks were attacking the column—just after dark!"

"Oh yes," Shoemaker admitted, it seemed to me grudgingly, "we did hear something was going on behind us in the column. But we didn't have any big trouble where we were. Must not have amounted to much. We don't think there is anything to worry about from here on."

"Well, 'not amounting to much' or not, I can tell you it sure ruins a feller's day—or night. I've lost as many as a dozen men, and when the reports come in I suspect you are going to find that other companies are hurting, too." Our exchange ended abruptly when the column movement resumed and all had to scramble back onto the tanks and trucks.

Shoemaker's mild interest in our earlier problems annoyed me, but I also could understand. It is very common for battlefield people to be not overly concerned about things, no matter how active, if they are not happening under their noses. There is always the tendency to feel justified in being preoccupied with your own problems, which are immediately at hand.

The 23rd's Unwritten Record

"How do you account for the fact that there is so little known, or recorded, about the 23rd Regiment's difficulties with the CCF on its withdrawal from Kunu-ri?" Ryan wanted next to know.

"That too, has always been a mystery to me. I have groped often for some reasonable explanation. I'm not sure what the answer is."

Insofar as historian Marshall is concerned, we can never approach him for elaboration on his omissions because he is no longer around. I can, to some extent, understand his slighting of the 23rd, though. After all, his work, *The River and the Gauntlet,* to which we repeatedly allude, focuses primarily, almost exclusively, on the gauntlet, i.e., that section of the Kunu-ri-to-Sunch'on road where the main 2d Division column was ambushed and nearly wiped out.

The 2d Division regiments in the main column were the 9th and 38th, not our 23rd. Therefore, Marshall handled in depth the events and tragedies of those two regiments in the gauntlet and the days immediately preceding it, north of Kunu-ri along the Ch'ongch'on. I'm sure we must conclude that Marshall considered the experiences of our regiment somewhat incidental as compared to those of the other two regiments directly in the gauntlet. If he learned of our problems, I imagine he felt they were minor in comparison, and overshadowed.

Harder to explain is the relative silence of our own regimental report writers with respect to our harassment and losses at the hands of the CCF on our westerly and southerly withdrawal. I can only assume that in those hectic hours, with confusion and desperation taking the upper hand, with so many things happening all around, and with the division sorely crippled, reeling and devastated in the following days, coupled with major personnel shakeups, no one got around to recording in detail that part of the regimental experience.

It is also possible, I have thought, that people in the regimental command-group may simply not have fully known what was going on, as reflected by the reaction of Major Shoemaker, the S-2 at the refueling stop. Or at least they did not realize the extent of the confrontations at other places in the motor column.

The withdrawal columns on the road from Kunu-ri stretched at times all the way to P'yongyang, a distance of about a hundred miles. Three battalions, or what was left of them, and numerous support and service units were strung out for this distance. The line of vehicles wound up hills and down into valleys, through twisting turns on a winding, mountainous road and through desolate, rubble-strewn villages. Under such conditions it is easy to see how a command group near the head of a column may be oblivious of developments far back, and unaware of the intensity of a fire fight in progress well back behind them.

Of course there were radio communications, but many of the sets had, by then, very weak and rundown batteries. Loss of power, weary operators, and adverse terrain conditions can all severely curtail the range of radio signals and prevent continuous contact by all of the elements of a moving military force.

The recording of significant events in warfare is always a worthwhile objective and can be essential to historical and scholarly accuracy. But it is seldom very complete or infallible in every detail. Such was the case, I conclude, with the sketchy record of my regiment's pullback from northernmost Korea upon Chinese intervention.

All through the night the column moved on. Surviving men were nearly frozen to death. Some, perhaps, were. For sure their feet and hands froze. Always that cruel cold was with us. The temperatures were recorded at just above or below the zero mark, but with high winds the chill factor, as on earlier nights, must have pushed them well into the subzero ranges.

Ryan shuffled in his chair and apparently felt it was time for a question. "Surviving elements of the 2d Division continued on through P'yongyang to Munsan, did they not?"

"Yes. By December 3, most of the 23rd was through its gauntlet and in bivouac around Munsan just below the Imjin River, south again of the parallel and some twenty-five to thirty miles north of Seoul."

If ever there was a case of an outfit licking its wounds and trying to recover, it was us. We were told that the 2d had suffered more than 50 percent casualties in its Eighth Army rearguard action and was designated officially as "combat inoperable."

Troops of Baker Co./23rd Reg. "take ten" while en route to roadblocking positions in central Korea in late December 1950.

The author's command post and foxhole near Munsan, just south of the 38th parallel, after withdrawal of UN forces from North Korea in December 1950.

The three regiments of the 2d Division had incurred over 3,000 casualties, the heaviest of which were by the 9th and 38th regiments on the Kunu-ri-to-Sunch'on road with its "gauntlet" and "pass" debacles. Numerous records establish that casualties on that road by those regiments would probably have been even higher, or perhaps total, had they not been helped by the 1st Cavalry Division's roadblocks out to the east, which tied up and delayed the Chinese forces who were hounding the 2d's regiments, including our own.

"And, of course, the 2d was not the only division to be hurt badly in those actions. The 24th Division in particular also had extremely heavy casualties," Ryan hastened to point out, to which I agreed.

"Our records also show that following the withdrawal with its period of heavy casualties, there was quite a shake-up of command. Do you recall that?" Ryan asked.

"Yes, we were aware of big changes, although some of them were not so profound to us down at the lower echelons of command. In December we lost our division commander, General Keiser. We heard that he, and some of his staff were, in effect, fired. But I have no personal knowledge of the circumstances from my lowly perspective as a captain of infantry. There were several levels of command between us. I note that many writers have devoted space to those changes of command."

I do remember getting the word that the new division commander was to be Maj. Gen. Robert McClure, whom I did not know at the time. A few years later, however, I was to serve directly under General McClure at a time when he headed up the military advisory group in Iran, where I was stationed as an advisor with several hats.

After Withdrawal: What Next?

By the time the withdrawal of UN forces from their farthest north positions in Korea had been completed, the first days of December 1950 had arrived; so had the full force and brutality of the Korean winter and so had a period of uncertainty and apprehension. Gloom prevailed everywhere and unanswered questions abounded.

Were the Chinese going to continue their advance and catch up with the hastily repositioned UN forces? How successfully could they do so? Did they have the transport and logistical wherewithal "to maintain the momentum of the advance," as military people put it? Just what were their objectives—political and military? Peking had us away from their Manchurian borders. More than that, they even had us out of North Korea and south of the 38th parallel. Would China now be content with that?

If the Chinese, on the other hand, were not yet satisfied with their accomplishments and decided to push on, perhaps with an asserted goal of driving the U.S. and the UN completely out of Korea and off the central Asiatic mainland, could they, as a practical matter, do it? Were they as invincible as they seemed at the moment? Could the UN prevail against them on a more withdrawn, narrow, and defendable line?

Or still, more pertinent yet, if the Chinese desired to continue their assault, or the UN to defend as best they could in place, was either side willing to pay the resultant costs? These questions were on just about everyone's lips in Korea and elsewhere as the world awaited further developments.

I had tried, with those burdensome and startling developments in Korea, to keep abreast of the changing events. This was not easy for a lower-level combat commander. In the ranks, we did not have access to the daily network newscasts, or voluminous written words from reporters or columnists, or even from military sources. We also wondered to what extent our own senior leaders understood the seriousness of our situation.

It was understood that MacArthur wanted to step up the combat efforts, to expand the air war into Manchuria, to bring up the Nationalist Chinese from Formosa, and even to blockade China. News sources reported that President Truman had managed to alarm other major powers with suggestions that we might resort to the use of atomic weapons. For every hawk who urged the expansion of the war, it seemed to me there were more doves, domestically and among our allies, who insisted upon restraint.

As one on the ground at the scene, where it seemed we had more than we could handle, I remember listing myself amongst those who hoped that someone with authority would not be rash. It seemed to me that we were already overcommitted, and to a higher degree than the American public would much longer support.

I knew of high-level military leaders, especially in the army and navy, who had said for years that the worst possible scenario for American overseas military involvement would be large-scale operations on the Asiatic mainland. They insisted that we would be swallowed up by vast lands and countless people. Decades later we were to see proof of that in Vietnam where we were to go down in defeat.

The fly guys of the U.S. Air Force in the Far East had been operating up to the Manchurian border from bases in Japan and southern Korea, and the navy flew from carriers offshore. Both were flying at, or near, the absolute outer edge of their operational range and could spend only minutes over their aerial combat zones. Except in the MIG alley locality at the border, our side did not have enemy planes with which to contend. I don't ever remember being subjected to an enemy air-raid. Only once did we think we heard a plane, and it was at night and probably on a reconnaissance mission.

In those anxious days of December 1950, I was clearly a "dove." I looked with not a little skepticism on the advisability of extending the war, and if it were done I preferred it would be without me. On the ground we were in tatters. In the air, I thought it ludicrous to send the pilots even further across the border into Manchuria and into enemy territory, where greatly increased air opposition must be expected.

I was worried particularly about the reported large numbers of enemy fighters in Manchuria that thus far had not been thrown against us either on the ground, or against our flyers above who were trying to support us. I never felt particularly qualified to pass judgment on these matters, but they were thoughts that dominated my nervous thinking in those critical days of uncertainty.

Reconditioning the "Indianhead" Division

"So what happened to the Second Division and the rest of the Eighth Army in those days immediately after the withdrawal from the far north?" Ryan next asked.

"The Eighth Army, as I'm sure you must know, pulled back deeply all along the front and came to rest along a line roughly south of the parallel and north of Seoul on the western side of the peninsula.

Up to the east the line ran closer, at first, to the parallel, and perhaps in spots actually crossed over. Research might clarify that somewhat.

"The mobility of the UN was much better than that of the CCF, which was lacking in motorized transport. When we pulled back so far and so rapidly, the enemy was unable to keep up. So there developed a several-week period of limited contact with the enemy where we were positioned."

The immediate task was to try to recover as rapidly as possible from the disabling beating we had taken up north. Priority was given to weapons and equipment repair and maintenance. Also replacements began to pour in to round out our severely depleted ranks of personnel—and supplies of arms.

In the second week in December, we moved to the Angang-ni area and then to the south bank of the Han River near Yongdungp'o. Winter continued to move in with all its fury. We stayed constantly outdoors and were miserable.

For several days we remained in riverbank defensive positions waiting for something to happen. We knew the Chinese had reoccupied Seoul across the river, but no one seemed to know in what strength, or with what intentions.

Each day the air around us was filled with smoke and the sound of explosions as dumps and depots of military supplies were burned and destroyed to prevent them from falling into enemy hands if we fell back further.

The prevailing talk in bull sessions and at briefings was of evacuation from Korea or, at the very least, a pullback to something resembling the old Pusan perimeter of months earlier.

While we sat and waited in the Han riverbank and certain other defensive positions, the X Corps of Gen. Edward Almond over the mountains to the northeast was struggling to disengage itself from the Chosin Reservoir and withdraw through the port of Hungnam.

As we know, the X Corps and its Marine Division and the army's 3rd and 7th Divisions in their withdrawal efforts, were also having their version of "gauntlets" to contend with. They had advanced deeply within that rough, mountainous and remote section of northern Korea. Their route out, as recorded in many places, was long, and hazardous with the Chinese tormentors constantly nipping at their rear and ambushing them at almost every curve or pass in the roads.

The evacuation of the X Corps at Hungnam and the magnificent role of the navy in making their escape possible has been well reported by others who were there and needs no attempt at elaboration by me, who was not there. The action stands as a monument to the heroism and achievements of the many who participated in that sad operation. I mention it here because the units from there were soon to appear as our comrades in arms on the main frontline positions in our areas.

Ridgway Replaces Walker

"Following the withdrawal of the X Corps from northeast Korea, it was relocated and consolidated with and became a part of the Eighth Army. Right, Mr. Sherm Pratt?"

"Yes, and in due course our 2d 'Indianhead' Division was to be transferred to the X Corps from the IX Corps. Other things were happening, too, in December."

December was the month in which the army commander, Walker, was killed in the vehicle accident near Seoul. As we know, he was replaced by the more dashing and colorful paratrooper Matthew Ridgway. While Walker had been described as the "bulldog," he also was reputed to be quite subservient to MacArthur for fear of losing his job.

I think no one would quarrel with our impression that Ridgway was by far the more warm and imposing leader. At least I recall that with his arrival, talk of bugging out of Korea completely, or significantly, began to subside, or at least took the back burner.

Ridgway visited us one morning soon after his arrival and walked and talked amongst the troops. With his erect, youthful, commanding, and energetic bearing he was inspirational and generated confidence. His grenades ever hung from his shoulder straps, which I thought a bit showy and corny, but otherwise he looked the part of the dedicated and purposeful combat soldier. He did not look the part of one about to retreat further.

French Battalion Arrives

Around the middle of the month, the French Battalion arrived and became a part of the 23rd Regiment as our "fourth" battalion. Other UN battalions from the Netherlands, Brazil, Greece, Belgium, and several other countries were arriving about that time, and were attached as "fourth" battalions to various regiments in the various divisions.

The way the foreign battalions were used turned out to be a splendid arrangement. The help of a fourth battalion was much appreciated by the hard-pressed battalions organic to the regiments, and since the foreign battalions arrived without logistical support, we provided it through the existing service units of our American structure without any great burden. Someone in the UN or American command deserved orchids for that approach.

As we steadily healed our wounds through the month, we were assigned patrol missions along the main Suwon-Wonju-Chech'on-Ch'ungyu roadnet east of Seoul. These were the suspected avenues of approach for the enemy.

Christmas Roadblocks

On December 21 we moved to the vicinity of Ch'ungyu and on Christmas Day we took up blocking positions in the area of Mok-haeng-Ni, not far from the central major communications center of Wonju.

From our perspective in the rifle companies of the 2d Division, I would describe the month of December as a period of reassessment and pause. We tended to our needs, patched our sores, rehabilitated our equipment and ourselves, and aggressively patrolled so as not to be caught napping when and if the enemy closed the gap and resumed his attack. As we did so, the Korean winter continued it move in. The hardships and desolation increased and the Korean people suffered in strange, pathetic, and admirable silence, waiting out their fate.

Suffering of Korean People

These were the days when we would pass through or occupy Korean villages that were usually burned out with most of the former residents gone. Some might still be hanging around, not knowing quite what to do or where to go for warmth, sustenance, or survival.

Sometimes we would find groups of Koreans, usually the old, the invalid, or children, huddled in clusters on some kind of rice-stalk mats or in other makeshift lean-tos or in some partially remaining structure.

If some house or school or other public building happened to be standing, the Korean refugees would ordinarily have to compete with us for its use and we would more often win out, leaving the local people to root for themselves.

Korean houses in the rural areas and small villages were most often constructed partly from adobe and partly from straw mats, with sliding doors. They had earthen floors with ceramic pipes running underneath that served as exhausts from their ovens at one end of a room. In this way the floors and houses were heated. We found the arrangement to be useful, but too hot at night.

The deprivations, displacement, and hardships of the Koreans during those days of the war seem to be almost beyond description. Most of the young men who could better survive displacement were off somewhere in the war or were casualties from previous fighting. Those left behind, the civilian and noncombatant population, were the ones least able to bear the hardships being inflicted on them. They starved and froze by the dozens and hundreds. The roads would be filled with fleeing people, without means of support, only packs on their backs, and not knowing where they were going.

All the normal problems and routine daily experiences of any people in nonwar situations were borne also by these people in the open, on the roads, in the fields, or elsewhere. The sicknesses, deaths, hunger, pregnancies, births, and other troubles did not end just because the people were forced from their homes. They continued, but under the distressing conditions where the afflicted were without any adequate means of coping with their burdens.

In those hard and cruel winter spans, the Korean people could only suffer and die. We lost count of the bodies of adults, children, and even newborns who were delivered before our eyes in the ditches along the roads or in the rice paddies and left to freeze and die by new mothers unable to care for them. These were the pictures and the prices of war that were unknown and unseen by those on home fronts in countries throughout the world.

CHAPTER EIGHT

1951 OLYMPICS?

Midwinter—Rolling with the Punches

Historian Ryan and I, in the quiet and relative luxury of my Arlington, Virginia, home in the late 1980s, were finding it ever more difficult to envision the hardships and realities of a war almost half-a-century earlier and halfway around the world.

Ryan was much younger than I and in his early forties. He had not experienced the Korean War at all. He knew modern Korea thoroughly as a recovered, prosperous, and incredibly beautiful and breathtakingly lovely land. For him it was hard to visualize his Korea of today as the torn country I was describing.

For me, Korea was an event and a greatly contrasting country of long, long ago. I had thought less and less about the war as the years passed, and my life had become preoccupied with different interests, problems, and challenges, not the least of which was caring for my family and meeting the routine requirements of work and community responsibilities. Now came this Eighth Army historian with a mission of gathering and recording my long-dormant thoughts for his official records.

Ryan must have thought he detected a degree of weariness, or impatience, about me. He asked, "Have you had enough of this wartime recollecting for now, or do you feel up to continuing?"

I glanced up from my own notes and studied Ryan's face for a bit. I didn't know whether he was pulling my leg or wanting a break himself, or just what.

"No," I answered Ryan. "Let's keep going. There is much to cover yet, in the event that someone is around some day who wants to know the details of the war as I saw it. We haven't even gotten to Chipyong—one of the most critical battles of the entire war."

"OK," piped up Ryan. "Then on we go to my next inquiry. Eventually, your division had to return to more active combat than roadblocks and patrols, did it not?"

"Yes indeed," I said, taking a new breath and continuing. "On the last day of 1950, we are recorded as having returned to combat by eliminating some enemy roadblocks north of Hoengsong, which is about fifteen miles north of Wonju in central Korea. It's heavy in the mountains.

"With this mission we were leaving behind the old year and embarking upon the new year of 1951."

If one could think of December 1950 as being a period of recouping, breath-catching, and repositioning after the big withdrawal, then January and early February, when the CCF caught up to us could be said to be a time of testing and "rolling with the punch."

No one was yet sure just how strong the Chinese were or how effectively we could defend ourselves against their assaults. The UN forces now had a much shorter line to defend. It was also being strengthened organizationally by a single unified command and augmented with the considerable strength of the X Corps arriving on the main front from the northeast region of the country.

It was concluded, in the intelligence reports of the day to which I had access, that the Chinese, with a population of almost a billion, were clearly superior to the UN in manpower, but perhaps not necessarily in military strength.

If MacArthur's intelligence officer, General Willoughby, could be

Korean Army soldiers serving with Baker Co./23rd Reg. as "fillers." Often 75 percent of American infantry troop strength in the early days of the Korean War consisted of KATUSAs (Korean Army Troops with the U.S. Army).

1st Lt. Maurice "Fendy" Fenderson (left) with gunner at recoilless rifle position of Baker Co./23rd Reg. in central Korea, midwinter 1950–51.

believed, the Chinese forces in Korea probably greatly outnumbered the UN forces. In most other respects we were clearly superior. Our firepower, armored, artillery, air, and otherwise, was far greater. Our motorization made us far more mobile, and there was virtually no limit to our logistical support capabilities.

Still, on both sides, there was the question, as there is in most conflicts, not merely of what a side can do, but also at what price it is willing to do so. Communist China could certainly have thrown in a couple million troops in Korea in that first winter, and had it done so, surely we would have been forced to withdraw, unless there was a massive counter-buildup on our side. Such an escalation would have likely had severe political repercussions on the home front and worldwide.

Also very uncertain at the time was whether the Chinese Communist government was willing to commit large numbers of additional troops to their war effort in Korea. There was always the matter of the Soviet Union on their borders; they were barely getting the organization and consolidation of their new and young Communist government underway, and there was no shortage of domestic programs to which to devote their attention.

While these questions were pondered at the highest levels, we settled down into a period of flexibility with the enemy, which, it seemed to me was designed as a time to feel each other out—to test both intentions and capabilities.

"How did you go about doing that?"

"I guess we could say it started on New Year's Day 1951. By then the Chinese had caught up with the UN forces. They had closed the gap created by our rapid withdrawal when we broke contact almost a month earlier. Presumably, they had stockpiled supplies well forward and were in a position to resume the assault.

"At any rate, it's recorded that the Chinese crossed the parallel on January 1, and launched what is officially designated as the Third Chinese Offensive."

"The first being in October, and the second the all-out drive in late November that caused your withdrawal?" Ryan asked.

"Precisely. The first offensive was at a time when UN troops were still congregating in northernmost Korea and before the launch of the final drive in the west to reach the Yalu. That offensive apparently had only a limited objective: to halt or slow the UN advance until sufficient CCF combat units could reach the area to undertake a general offensive."

The second offensive was the withdrawal and loss of contact, and the third offensive was a month later on New Year's Day when the gap was closed.

The Purpose of "Rolling with the Punches"

"And how did this 'rolling with the punch' work out from the standpoint of the small-infantry unit?"

"The command began to place us on roadblocks, in depth, or on a string of prominent and dominant terrain features. Mostly, for our 2d Division, this took place in the mountains and roadnets in the north-south axis around Wonju, Hoengsong and Chech'on; and a bit east and west."

Our instructions were to hold as long as possible when the Chinese attacked, exact the maximum damage on the enemy, and not get overrun or surrounded, but, rather, to withdraw at the last minute through a sister unit in a similar position to our rear.

After such a withdrawal, we were then to go into position behind that unit, in a leapfrog, retrograde operation, so the unit covering our withdrawal could withdraw in turn while we covered its withdrawal.

Mountaintop Warfare in a Korean Winter

Something should be said in detail about the weather, tactical, and other conditions under which UN troops operated in Korea in that first, very fluid, and precarious winter of the war. Very little has been written about this facet of the fighting insofar as I have determined in my research. I think it needs to be more fully understood if the observer really wants to have a meaningful grasp of that struggle.

If December was the month of pause and reassessment, then, as stated, the following weeks in the new year were times of testing the will and ability on both sides as the Chinese punched and we resisted briefly, then recoiled.

In our area, this occurred along the main roads, at passes in the mountains, or at other critical stretches. It was a time when the enemy was hurt more than we were. From prepared, defensive positions with at least some cover and concealment, a soldier can fight from strength with minimum danger. The attacking enemy is up and exposed and far more vulnerable.

We took every advantage of our odds through innumerable lesser engagements. Also, in road defenses, the danger of encirclement was more remote. Troops could always, at the very last minute, before possible overrun, pull up, load on waiting vehicles just behind, and be gone as the attackers' momentum was slowing.

Such "punch and roll" activities in the mountains of central Korea around Wonju were quite another matter. The memory of blocking positions and engagements on remote mountaintops during those cold and snowy winter months is most vivid for most any veteran of the Korean War, although most of the precise locations are unnamed and unknown.

In our mountaintop positions we had the problem of isolation. They were usually reached only with extreme difficulty and after long hours of climbing up desolate or nonexistent trails. Once on position, it was as though we had withdrawn from all contacts with our fellow troops and units. Rarely, in combat, is an infantry rifle-unit so "all alone" on this planet as when in position on a high and remote mountaintop in a country like Korea.

Perimeter Defense—No Front Lines

There was nothing in the fighting in the Korean winter of 1950–51 that resembled a front line, implying a solid disposition of troops over a designated area. Instead, there was a series of small islands of defense, each operating independently as a perimeter on its own. Under such circumstances, the unit operates with little expectation of assistance from other units in the event of an attack or other trouble.

The resupply of a combat unit on a remote mountaintop in Korea in that winter was, in itself, an operation of major magnitude. Usually, the unit would have to send down a team to a battalion, or other, supply dump for cases of rations, ammo, or other necessary items. Depending on distance, the trip down could require at least a couple of hours or more. Dragging the heavy cases back up the steep mountainsides could be slow and tedious, require twice as much time as the descent, and challenge the party to return to the unit perimeter before dark—an absolute must.

Once dark settled, an inflexible rule was that no one moved outside the perimeter. To do so, even if one could find his way in the dark, was to invite almost sure and deadly fire from within the perimeter.

Initial arrival on a high mountaintop for a blocking mission was usually preceded by perhaps hours of struggle over rocks or through dense underbrush, and constant tension, even if no enemy had been encountered on the way up, which was by no means always the case.

Once in position on a mountaintop, unit commanders had to undertake, hastily if it were getting dark, a survey of the terrain for possible fields of fire for automatic and other weapons, and for probable enemy routes of advance. Laymen and others without such combat experience may well be quite unaware of these essential requirements for survival under such conditions.

Having determined the most advantageous fields of fire and likely avenues of enemy approach, we then had to assign sectors to the various platoons and squads, and follow through to see that the men placed themselves properly in position. We tried to encourage them to dig in, but that often was not very easy, due to frozen ground.

"Did the Chinese attack you in these high mountain positions?" Ryan next wanted to learn.

"Oh yes. On occasion, but not as constantly as one might think. Repeatedly, with monumental effort, we would occupy and lay out a defense in a difficult spot, then wait for the enemy, and then they might not show up. This was inconsiderate, perhaps, but we did not complain. There were ample other times when we were hit, and rather hard, on other mountaintops."

"What were your main worries on those occasions, other than the enemy?"

"As always, the bitter and disabling cold must come near the head of the list. If every description of, or development in, the Korean winter warfare were preceded with a reminder of the detrimental impact of the cold weather, I don't think the point would be overemphasized."

Ryan nodded his head in clear agreement. Undoubtedly his records contained evidence of the debilitating impact of the intense cold. It constantly hung around the troops' shoulders like the heaviest of stones, limiting activity, making bones ache, stiffening fingers and other joints, slowing mental reactions, numbing bodies throughout, and disabling equipment.

History books are bulging with tales of other armies that have experienced similar hardships from weather extremes, and the cold weather's impact on us should be kept ever in mind by anyone who seeks to understand the Korean War with any degree of knowledgeability. Napoleon's invasion of Russia in 1812 and that of the German army's at Stalingrad in World War II are but two of the many disasters in which troops have endured unbearable winter weather.

Contagious Firing—Depletion of Ammo

"Then having established that cold is an ever-present problem for troops outside in the middle of a Korean winter, what next worried you most in your mountaintop defensive positions?" Ryan pressed me.

"I think I would have to say that the, or at least a, main worry that I clearly recall is the fear of troops firing up all, or most, of their ammunition at imaginary threats in the middle of the nights, and then having nothing left to use when a real attack later came."

"Why would they do that?"

"Because they get nervous through the long nights and the lonesome hours. Sitting in the dark, shivering from the cold, and not knowing from moment to moment what might suddenly hit them in full fury, their minds worked terrifyingly and created all sorts of evils and perils—sometimes real, sometimes imaginary. Finally, a sentry on watch lets go at what might, or might not be, an enemy in the dark."

"And why is that so bad?"

"Because small-arms fire is contagious and usually will spread rapidly and insanely, like a forest fire in a high wind. When they hear firing they get panicky. They assume it's an attack, so they join in

The author (right background) observes digging of company command post and bunker in central Korea in midwinter 1950–51 at roadblocking positions.

Cpl. Domingo Rodriguez, the author's faithful radio operator, at the company command dugout on a remote central Korea mountain in the winter of 1950–51.

spontaneously. I remember when half the 82d Airborne Battalions were shot out of the skies by friendly fire in the Sicilian landings in World War II when a couple of gunners thought the troop transports were German planes in the night. The ground gunners opened up and everyone within miles joined in."

"So? All you've lost is some ammunition?"

"Yes, but on a mountaintop in the middle of a night, when no one moves outside the perimeter, it is irreplaceable ammunition. There is no resupply until daylight, and even then it involves long hauls from below, which may or may not be feasible if there are enemy troops bouncing all around." I felt confident that historian Ryan well knew this, but he wanted to hear me say it for his records.

Admittedly, controlling, or limiting infantrymen in their firing requires very delicate balance for a small-unit leader such as a platoon or company commander. The last thing he wants to do is to discourage his troops from firing at a real threat. The object of the whole affair is to resist, overpower, and kill, if necessary, the enemy. On the other hand, how can that be done if troops have frittered away their ammo on imaginary threats and then are defenseless when the real attack arrives?

Ghosts in the Night

"And you found needless firing a real and ever-present problem?"

"I did indeed. To better understand it, I suppose one must try to recognize what fantastic tricks the human mind can concoct when left to its devices in times of great stress, fear, duress, and hardship. Its powers of creation and imagination seem almost limitless."

I then told Ryan of an incident, typical of many, that occurred one night on a Korean hilltop under precisely the circumstances I had been describing. Night attacks were no strangers to us, and we had had several over the weeks, so the men were probably more alert than usual. It was sometime well after midnight when Cpl. Ben Rubio, one of my men on watch in a wooded area I called our CP, nudged me.

"Are you awake, Captain?" he asked me in the usual low voice.

"More or less, I guess," I answered him. "What's up?" Things had been quiet in that location and we had not had any enemy contact since we had arrived.

"It's the first platoon on the sound power—they say they're about to be hit with a Chink attack." The "sound power" was the magnetic, rather primitive, and marginally effective telephone equipment used in the infantry platoons in World War II and in Korea.

"Is it the platoon sergeant or leader?"

"No, Sir, I think it's one of the men on watch."

"Let me talk with him," I told Rubio as I reached for the phone.

"This is the company commander," I spoke softly. "Who is this?"

"Woods, Sir. Cpl. Earl Woods, First Platoon."

I could detect the tremor in his voice, and knew he must be scared as could be. He obviously needed all the encouragement and support he could get.

"You say there is enemy movement in your sector?"

"That's for sure, Captain," in a voice barely above a whisper.

"How can you be sure?"

"I can see them—just in front of my position."

"How can you see them in the dark?" I pressed him.

"They have on their light uniforms and I can make out their outlines easily."

"About how many of them do you see?"

"There must be at least a couple of platoons—thirty to forty men."

"How long have they been out there?"

"Ever since I came on duty—about half an hour, I guess."

"What have they been doing?" I could tell that Woods was getting increasingly impatient with me. Anyone forward in combat is usually disdainful of the "rear echelons" behind, who do not appreciate the full seriousness of a threatening situation with which the forward troops are confronted, whether real or not.

"I'm not sure. They seem to be marching up and down across my front. Some of them are carrying something heavy like a mortar or small pack-artillery."

"Do you think they are going to attack?" I was not yet convinced the threat was real, but I did not want to convey any impression that the trooper's commander took the situation lightly and was not solidly supportive.

"I can't tell for sure. They don't seem to be getting any closer. I think they might be building bunkers or gun positions."

"And you can't hear anything they are saying, or what language they are speaking?"

"Oh, they're talking Chinese, all right. No mistake about that. But they talk in low voices."

"Have you let your platoon sergeant know about this? If not, do so. In the meantime, you just hang in there. You're doing a fine job . . . stay alert. I'm going to pass on your info the the other platoons, and also have the weapons platoon stand by to assist you with mortar fire the minute anything happens."

"Couldn't we have a little mortar fire out here now, Captain?"

"We could, but it might be smarter to wait a bit on the alert. If the enemy out there does not know we are here, fire might give away our position. Let's wait it out and see if we can catch them by surprise if they attack."

I tried to sound reassuring to Woods. I felt I knew just exactly how he felt. Troops in his forward position were usually the first casualties in the event of an attack, and he knew it all too well. He had no yearning for that clearly dubious distinction.

Before daylight there were several more exchanges with him until Rubio was replaced by his relief. During that time we were not hit. When daylight arrived, I worked my way to the platoon's positions and contacted Bob Walker, the platoon leader.

"Bob," I said to him as I slowly got his weary attention, "are you aware of all the enemy activity last night in front of your platoon?"

Walker looked like he was only about half with it, or less. It had been a cruel night out on a lonely mountaintop. Walker was dirty, unshaven, sunken-eyed, and haggard-looking.

"What enemy activity?" he answered blankly. "I thought we had a rather quiet night."

"Your outpost reported large numbers of enemy just to your front, marching up and down, busy as hell—preparing all kinds of positions and fortifications."

Walker studied my face for a bit to see if I was kidding. His skepticism showed. Finally, as he gathered himself together, he reached for his carbine and said, "It's news to me, but let's take a stroll to the squads and see what we can learn."

When we arrived at Walker's forward squad, we peered from the brush to the clearing ahead, beyond which would have been the enemy. The clearing was about two or three hundred yards across and along the saddle of a ridge. There was an unobstructed view of the whole area. The previous afternoon and early evening a slow snow had fallen and there were about two inches or so of fresh snow on the ground to our front.

"Can you see across the opening with your binocs, Captain?" Walker asked me. "I can see immediately ahead and I see no tracks of any kind. But what about those woods and brush across the draw?"

"No," I told him. "I see no tracks anywhere near our positions, nor do I see any fresh earth where some digging might have taken place."

"Let's walk out a bit and examine the snow closer."

"That's a bit risky, isn't it? What if there are Chinks across there watching us?"

"I just don't think there are," Walker insisted. "There weren't last evening when we sent a patrol across. And I don't see any signs of activity now. But come on. We won't go far. I'd like to settle this."

I agreed that I too would like to know whether our trooper had really seen and heard anything during the night or if it was just his mind playing tricks.

Walker and I eased out a little in front of his positions and looked for any signs of human activity since the snows of the night. There was none. The snow was undisturbed and there was not a shoe print of any kind. Had there been any activity of any nature during the night and after the snow stopped, it could not have escaped our notice. The evidence would have been there in the snow. It was clear beyond any dispute or doubt that the nighttime activities reported had been only a figment of the sentry's imagination.

"Do you think my guy was misleading us for some sneaky purpose, Captain?"

"No, I do not at all. I think he was as sincere as a person can be. He wasn't lying or guilty of any intentional or careless wrongdoing. For sure, don't take it out on him. Unbelievable and weird as it may seem, I feel sure that he really thought he was really seeing and hearing those things he reported."

Sentry Wood's experience was simply an example of what the mind will do under stress and strain in life-endangering situations when it is free to roam and "fantasize." I had similar experiences on numerous occasions, and so have many other combat veterans.

The fact that the mind does these things, and with such regularity and so convincingly, posing difficult problems for frontline commanders when trying to differentiate the real from the apparently threatening situation. The problem has long existed and is not likely to go away any time soon.

Praise the Lord and Pass the Ammo

All of our mountain positions in central Korea during that January were not so quiet. The month was not marked with any major engagements on the scale of what we had been through up north or were to see the following month in February. Mostly, there were patrolling and roadblocking and hilltop positioning on countless unmarked road passes or terrain features.

I continued to fear running out of ammunition in the middle of the night, all alone on a remote mountain and with no means of resupply. I became almost paranoid over this problem.

"Why?" Ryan asked.

"Because my nervous troops continued to waste ammunition firing at nothing. I can't count the times when at some lonesome hour of darkness, fire would break out in a platoon sector and rapidly spread. Precious moments would go by while we tried to determine whether we were truly under attack or not."

Even if there had been enemy activity in those agonizing times, there was a need in those remote and isolated locations to conserve ammo. If we just had ammo, I had great confidence in the will and ability of my men to hold their own against the heaviest of assaults. But without it any man will cave in or panic. Any time heavy fire occurred I always feared it was directed at nothing, and that when the firepower was needed for a real attack, we would not have it.

One day, when Baker Company was on its hilltop position after a night of nervous firing at nothing, the chaplain hiked up and offered to conduct field services. We welcomed him and he asked where and how he could carry out his mission without unduly endangering the men.

I showed the chaplain a spot near the company CP behind a rise where I thought a few men at a time could assemble and be relatively free from exposure and I suggested that he arrange for a dozen or so men at a time to rotate into his services from their platoons.

"Are you going to join us, Captain Pratt?" the chaplain said to me as he was about to begin his first service.

"At the moment I must contact the battalion commander," I replied. "We've got some logistical problems. I'll try to join you in a later service. But can you put in a word to the good Lord for me and my men in your prayers?"

"Of course," said the chaplain, "but I think he would rather hear it from you directly."

"OK," I shot back at him. "I'll do that, too, but I think we can use all the help we can get."

"Anything in particular you want me to say?"

"For sure we have a long list. But mention if you will our fire fights and ammo needs. Ask him to give my men patience so as not to shoot at nothing, determination to shoot when there is a need, and wisdom to know the difference between the two."

"Sounds like the Alcoholics Anonymous prayer," the chaplain laughed as he and I parted to carry out each of our objectives.

One incident related to the waste of precious ammo that especially infuriated me occurred on a high and remote and nameless hill in early January. The regiment was assigned to block on high ground to the north of Hoengsong, due north of Wonju. Matters had been rather quiet, except for some guerrilla units known to be operating in the area.

About midafternoon I received instructions from battalion on the radio to withdraw from position and relocate on another predesignated hilltop a few hundred yards to the east.

I told my helpers to put the word out to the platoons that we were to relocate as soon as possible and to let me know when they were ready. I wanted no delay, since dark was only a couple hours away. Most of the platoons had reported their readiness and I was about to give the order to start out when suddenly one hell of a barrage of high

" . . . forever, Amen. Hit the dirt."

Despite horrendous combat conditions in Korea, the commands usually made every effort to provide religious services for troops, even while in or near frontline positions. As indicated by cartoonist Bill Mauldin, such graces were not always easily available.

explosives rocked across the terrain, reverberating and echoing amongst the peaks and through the scrubby trees.

Our first reaction to the explosions was that we were under attack from an enemy we blissfully had thought to be nowhere around. Inquiry to the platoons revealed, however, that there was no enemy attack. On the contrary, the fire was generated by our own weapons platoon, under the command of lst Lt. Lee Brasswell.

I hurried over to the weapons platoon, a short distance from where I had established my company CP, and found Brasswell's gunners madly firing away with their 60-mm mortars.

"What are you firing at, Lee? Did someone give you a fire mission?" Mortar crews ordinarily place fire on targets in response to requests from their own forward observers, or from rifle-platoon leaders who need fire support. Heavy-weapons commanders, such as mortar or artillery leaders, seldom undertake fire missions on their own initiative.

"No, Captain, Sir, no one gave me a fire mission. I gave myself one." His voice was heavy with sarcasm when he said "Sir," and it rang with defiance.

Lee Brasswell had been a problem for me for some time. He was a thoroughly capable officer and knew his weapons and operations well. He never needed to be told by me or anyone else how to do his job. He also was the kind of guy who knew no fear. I had, in fact, recommended him for the Silver Star for gallantry in action. In short, when the chips were down, and peril prevailed, it was good to have "ole hot" Lee around to lean on. He would not let his commander down at times when others may be hysterical and unreliable.

But Lee had a drinking problem, and he and I had a conflict of personalities. I knew this and had for some time been hard-pressed to cope with it. On more than one occasion I had bitten my tongue and let an act of insubordination slide by rather than cause a disruptive incident, which I felt, in the stress of combat, I did not need.

In the back of my mind I suppose I knew that sooner or later there must be a day of accounting when Lee Brasswell and I would in some way have to part company. I also recognized that it might be handled by the tactical situation with one of us getting knocked off without a need for administrative action. That would be a pragmatic way of removing the conflict.

As I stood looking at Brasswell on this occasion, with my blood rapidly reaching the boiling point, I could see that he had been drinking. Somewhere he had gotten a bottle of spirits of some kind—not easy to do in those days of the Korean War, but possible.

Class VI supplies, as spirits were identified, were not the usual order of business in those early Korean War days, as best I can recall, although before I left, modest amount were available for purchase as a supplement to the PX supplies. In those early days a bottle or two would sometimes appear as hand luggage with new arrivals, or returnees, from Japan. If a bottle of booze was anywhere amidst the combat positions, Brasswell was just the chap who would find and secure it.

"Brasswell, I see no enemy where your shells are falling," I said with obvious displeasure.

"Nor do I, Captain," his clear sarcasm continuing.

"Then why are you firing, and especially just as we are preparing to relocate?"

"My men are weary and do not want to carry this ammo. It is heavy." He smirked as he burst forth with his insolent answer.

Somehow I kept my cool, but to this day I have never understood how. "If you have finished with your little project, do you think you might now be ready to join us in our new location? At your pleasure, of course." My attempt at returning his sarcasm probably failed because of his intoxicated condition.

I had concluded that my relationship with Brasswell could not continue in this way. His conduct was beyond the pale, and unacceptable to me. But I also knew that the moment there on the mountaintop with dark rapidly closing in and instructions to relocate was not the time to resolve the matter. I decided to take it up with the battalion commander when I could. The officer had to be either disciplined or reassigned, as a punitive matter and in the best interests of all concerned.

Was it satisfactorily resolved? Yes it was, but mostly to Brasswell's satisfaction, and not much to mine. As it turned out, the fellow got to the battalion commander before I did and managed to get in his pitch first. Colonel Hutchin had gone to division staff as G-3, and the battalion exec, Maj. George Russell, had taken over the battalion.

"Pratt," Russell told me a few days later, "Brasswell has told me about his confrontation with you up on the mountain. I tend to side with you, of course, but I think perhaps the least disruptive way to handle the matter is just to transfer Lee to another company." Russell did this, and the matter was closed, at least as far as Baker Company and I were concerned. I wasn't very happy, but I realized that I would probably have handled the matter in the same way. Personnel malperformances are always sticky matters to face.

Brasswell's departure from Baker Company did not end the unnecessary nervous expenditure of ammunition. It only stopped the waste in our company that could be attributed to misconduct or insolence. I never learned whether, or to what extent, he continued to be a problem for his new commander.

Enemy Mountain Tactics in Winter

Ryan seemed particularly interested in CCF tactics in the central Korean mountains during the first winter of the war. He asked about surprise attacks, and whether our forces had been caught off guard.

I told Ryan that sometimes on the high ground the CCF found us only half-alerted and that they hit us when we were a bit careless or off guard. Usually we recovered after an initial penetration. I don't recall that we were ever routed completely off a position, at least as far as my company was concerned.

The 2d Battalion of our regiment and the French took and retook several times some terrain known as Hill 247, just off the Wonju-Mokyedong road. That was more from design than enemy perseverance. As a battlefield tactic, our guys would take the hill, set up all kinds of booby traps, trip flares and other impediments, and then withdraw and place artillery fire on the area when the enemy forces entered.

But combat does not always mean constant contact with enemy forces. Times would slide by when no enemy soldiers were seen or heard for extended periods. Such periods were both a relaxing blessing and a nerve wracking uncertainty. Serious surprises of enemy action were, however, not the rule, at least in those initial days after the pullback from the far north.

UN forces were overall rather nervous and apprehensive from their recent contacts, and they usually knew when there were enemy troops in an area. Intelligence sources, aerial observations, and other surveillance means were usually flashing signposts of the enemy's presence or intentions.

When the enemy units started showing up opposite UN forces, our S-2s would plot them on the situation maps. If there was suddenly quite a concentration in a particular area, that was likely to be the place where the CCF would hit.

Pathetic Refugees

Another sign of an enemy buildup would be the sudden appearance of large numbers of Korean civilian refugees. On the roadblocks we would often be alerted to a probable enemy attack by the swarms of terrified and distraught people that would begin to flow toward us from the direction of the enemy. The greater the number of refugees, most likely the larger the enemy force.

The local Korean population would witness the growth of enemy-troop concentrations and know that an increase in fighting was in the offing. The Chinese would not let them escape to their rear areas and become problems, so the civilians had to flee toward our lines.

Clogged Roads

A common sight around UN positions in Korea during the first winter were the mountain and village roads clogged with thousands of those poor, wretched creatures fleeing their homes to avoid the fighting.

Few, if any, of the refugees had adequate clothing for bitter, midwinter weather, and the roadsides would be littered with their bodies where the old and sick and weak would collapse and die. Seldom was there much that we frontline troops could do to help. If they passed successfully through our lines, we assumed there were relief agencies in the rear areas to assist them. At least for us it was someone else's problem, so we could assuage our consciences over our inability to ease their suffering.

In our isolated positions there was no food, shelter, or medical assistance. We repeatedly stood by helplessly as the frail, the old, the invalid, and the afflicted died before our eyes and their bodies were left on the roads or in the fields to freeze or rot. Again and again we saw pregnant women give birth in the snow of a rice paddy and leave their newborns, living or dead, behind as they had no choice but to move on with their families to escape the war closing in behind.

Some of my troops were tempted to share, and did share, a ration or some edible item, but such a gesture was mostly pointless and meager among so many thousands.

The only salvaging feature of those masses of displaced humanity was that their presence served to alert us of the nearby presence of the enemy, and we stepped up our vigilance.

Personnel Changes

"January was a month of major personnel and command changes, was it not?" Ryan next inquired of me.

"Indeed it was. Not only had we seen high-level changes at the army and division and battalion levels, but at the company levels, too. Replacements for battle losses were pouring in. Baker Company received several dozen new men fresh from the States.

"Nearly all of Baker Company's replacements were recalled reservists from civilian life. Most were not overjoyed at being back on active duty to their shocking surprise, and especially in combat. The recall program, implemented in some desperation as a national policy, to which I previously alluded, produced some real hardships in some instances."

I made it a practice to interview personally every replacement who arrived in the company. I wanted each man to know his company commander knew he was there as a living, breathing individual and not just as an impersonal serial number.

With respect to our personnel replacements, there came the time in late January when a particularly tragic and heartbreaking event occurred, which I have never been able to erase from my memory. In one bivouac area where the battalion had assembled for a few hours between high-ground blocking and hopping, a batch of new men arrived late in the day.

I proceeded to talk with each as they were assigned to platoons. I tried to find out a bit about their backgrounds, experiences, and preferences.

One of these replacements was to meet a most underserved fate, almost before he got his gear off the jeep and his duffle bag channeled to the baggage trains. My better judgment, of course, tells me that I was not personally responsible for his cruel and most premature demise. Still, since I was directly involved, the matter has never ceased to bother me. I have always agonized over the incident and wondered if it could not have been prevented had I acted differently.

This sad story came about through a frustrated attempt to help that boomeranged. The young replacement here involved, perhaps in his midtwenties, seemed especially bright, but also innocent, and naive about combat. I gave him my usual questions about his homelife and background.

"Where do you come from, young fellow?" I asked him there at the CP.

"Minnesota, Sir. Saint Paul."

"What have you been doing for a living?"

"Insurance, Sir. Just started recently from the university."

"Do you have a family?"

"Oh, yes, Sir. Sure do. Wife and two small children. Would you like to see their picture?"

"Of course," I told him, sure that he was going to show it anyway as I saw him reaching toward his rear pocket. He took out and opened his billfold and showed me a snap of his most pretty wife and a little boy toddler and a girl about five or so.

I studied the soldier's picture for a moment or so and then looked back at him. He was a sandy-haired youth, perhaps in his mid- to late twenties, clean-cut, and his face beamed with pride at showing his family to me. It was a very touching family snapshot.

The thought of sending this trooper off to a platoon and perhaps soon having his wife receive that morbid "We regret to inform you" letter especially did not appeal to me. It didn't with any of my men, but somehow with him it seemed more distasteful than usual.

"Look, fellow," I told the young man, "my jeep driver has just been evacuated with the flu, or tired butt, or some such. If you can drive, why don't you slide that jeep right under your cheeks and serve as my driver for a bit until we can find the right assignment for you?"

Of course the lad was delighted. Not a bad development for him at all—arriving at a combat unit and being given right off one of the more plushy slots as the "ole man's" driver.

Even though the soldier was most elated, I doubted that he fully appreciated just how cherished was the assignment I had just given him, even if only temporarily. He thanked me, saluted, and made his way to the topkick to get squared away. I felt rather good about the matter.

The following morning I received word to report to Major Russell on the double—something hot was up. I called for my new jeep driver and told him to saddle up, as the expression went, that we had to go to the battalion CP. He cheerfully complied and forthwith we were on our way. Battalion was several hundred yards away in some burned-out Korean village huts where recent fighting had taken place.

As we pulled up in front of the battalion CP, he stopped the jeep and I jumped out. My new driver awaited my further instructions.

"Just pull ahead there, somewhere," I told him, "and stand by till I'm finished here." I motioned to a paddy a short distance away, where some other jeeps and drivers had collected.

As I walked up to where Maj. Sammy Radow and some battalion staff officers and company commanders were assembled, I suddenly heard a tremendous explosion. We all instinctively ducked, but knew right away from the sound that it was no incoming artillery round. There was no whistle or scream before or after the explosion, as is common with artillery or mortar rounds.

Glancing over my shoulder I saw a rising column of dirt and smoke in the paddy where I had sent my driver only seconds before. As the smoke cleared, there was shouting from the area, and a trooper came running up to us, yelling to anyone who would hear.

"It's Captain Pratt's driver." His voice was breaking and almost a sob. "He drove onto a mine. It could have been any of us."

I heard someone give orders for the rest of the drivers to be gotten out of the field. I ran to my jeep. Sure enough, it was blown almost to hell and back. The right-front end, where I would have been sitting, was laid open. My new driver's body was almost twenty yards or more away and mangled and bloody. One look showed that he was most

Elder Korean "Papa-san" in typical dress of war-damaged village in central Korea in winter of 1950–51.

The author's jeep, blown apart by a land mine moments after the author stepped out. The driver was blown from the vehicle and killed.

obviously lifeless, if indeed even in one piece. He had lasted only two days in combat.

I've never really ever gotten over that tragic development. Of course, had I sent him to a platoon he might well have perished there as well, considering the casualties we were to have in the next few days. Still, my heart was, and to this day remains, heavy over the incident. I would have preferred to have played no part in the drama. Nor would I have liked to face his young wife with two small orphans and break the news to them that they had no husband or father. Truly, oh so truly, as my Civil War namesake general said, "War is hell!"

When the author's jeep was destroyed by a land mine and his driver killed in February 1951 near Wonju in central Korea, he was reminded of the above classic cartoon by Bill Mauldin. When asked by a member of the audience at the Korean War Veterans Association annual convention in Arlington, Virginia, in July 1990 whether he had a favorite of all his cartoons, Mauldin, after a moment of thought, replied that it was the above drawing of a cavalry sergeant about to put his wounded vehicle out of its misery.

CHAPTER NINE

Slaughter at the Twin Tunnels

January was nearing its end when Sammy Radow, the battalion S-3, briefed me one day that Baker Company would participate in a scouting operation several miles to the south of the area where we were in position.

"Ole" Sammy was one of the most enthusiastic and energetic officers I encountered in those days. He was in his late twenties, like me, but taller, slimmer, and perhaps more agile. He was precise and clear-cut in his actions and manners.

As the battalion operations officer, Sammy Radow served his commander by assigning missions to the platoons and carrying out the overall planning of attacks or missions, either on the battalion's own initiative or as a result of instructions from regiment. His fellow officers used to ask, approvingly, "What makes Sammy run so?"

But no one knew why Sammy ran—he just did—up and down the ridges and in and out of CPs.

"Pratt," Sammy began, on this occasion, "division is under pressure to find the enemy around here, and it seems they are somewhat scarce and evasive. Word is that General Ridgway wants to take more of the initiative. We're going to send a patrol down into this area," he explained, pointing to his map at Sinch'on, "into some hills where there are some railroad tunnels. There are reports of CCF there and we need to know for sure."

The area pinpointed by Sammy was about four miles from our Baker Company position at Iho-ri where we had been guarding and supporting the 37th Field Artillery Battalion, and was just east of the important communications center of Chipyong-ni.

The area to which Sammy was referring would later become known in official journals and histories as the "Twin Tunnels," and it would be the scene shortly of one of the major engagements until after the winter withdrawal from the Yalu areas.

Ryan suddenly came to life with a start in my rec room. "So this was the start of the well-recorded Twin Tunnels engagement?" he said.

"Yes, Tom, it was indeed the start, but it was off to a rather slow beginning." Radow asked me what platoon I wanted to send on the scouting mission.

"Well, I've got two new crack and eager officers, Dick Kotite and Maurice 'Fendy' Fenderson," I answered. "I suggest we tap Fendy for now. I have something else in mind later for Kotite."

"Sounds like a good choice," Radow replied. "Send him in and I'll brief him."

All this was on January 28, with a relative lull in enemy activity and our contact with the CCF. Fendy was briefed and the following morning the patrol departed.

Did Fendy and his men find enemy troops at the Twin Tunnels? The patrol sighted enemy in the area but they did not engage them. Rather, they made notes and returned with the information.

"And a stronger patrol was then dispatched?"

"That's it, exactly. And the size of the force sent to the Tunnels kept escalating. Over a period of the next day or so the additional patrols engaged the enemy, incurred casualties, and at one point were surrounded. Colonel Freeman personally led the larger force on the

Vehicles of the 23rd Reg. destroyed in an ambush near "the Twin Tunnel" south of Chipyong-ni, about forty miles southwest of Seoul.

Half-track of the 2d "Indianhead" Infantry Division destroyed by a land mine typifies the kind of peril experienced by drivers in the Korean War.

twenty-ninth and was locked in tight contact with as much as a whole Chinese division, or perhaps even more.

By the thirty-first, the confrontation was so intense that someone up high decided to throw in the entire regiment. Our 1st Battalion moved out about daybreak to join the rest of the regiment, which was already engaged, and almost immediately we encountered enemy fire. The Chinese were not lacking in skill. They made good use of the terrain and stayed well hidden. They also seemed to have reasonably good fire discipline, and waited until we were almost upon them before opening up. They fought like little tigers and made us pay dearly for each yard of ground we took.

"So you did take the Tunnels that day?"

"We took the Tunnels, as is recorded, but I think it required at least a couple of days of hard fighting to finally consolidate our gains. Our regimental command report put it this way:

> ...after bitter fighting...the French and 1st battalions, against a fanatical, well concealed enemy, who made every use of every terrain advantage, the "Twin Tunnels" area was taken, at a cost of 1300 counted and 3600 estimated casualties to the enemy.

"Wasn't there some disagreement during the Twin Tunnels fighting between Freeman and the corps commander?" Ryan knew his Korean War history well, and I recognized that he was alluding to one of the most bitter controversies of the war between a regimental commander and his higher-ups. The incident is covered by almost every Korean War writer of any import.

"Yes, there was, but at the time I did not realize just how deep the feelings were running. Some quite acrid interchanges occurred both on the spot and indirectly."

I think it was on the first of February, or the day when most of the fighting was nearly over, when I happened to be near Freeman and his S-3, Maj. John Dumaine, and heard an exchange that would have left one's ears burning.

It seemed that some of the division commanders resented General Almond's tendency to get involved too personally with the operations of his corps components. He wanted a certain village some distance away captured, but the division commander hesitated because of security reasons and the lateness of the day. It seems Almond then directed that the village at least be fired on.

"Was it fired on?" Dumaine was asking Freeman.

"Yes, damn it!" Freeman was fuming.

"Who fired on it?"

"George Stewart," (the assistant division commander), said Freeman.

"Did General Stewart agree that the village be fired on?"

"Hell no," said Freeman, "but he was afraid not to. I think he thought Almond would fire his ass just like he did McClure" (the division commander just replaced by Maj. Gen. Clark Ruffner).

"So what's going to happen now?" pressed Dumaine.

"If the CCF is in Chipyong in any strength, that firing is going to alert them, and they're going to slap the shit out of us here."

Freeman was right. The next morning the whole CCF 125th Division swarmed in with bugles and horns. They were repulsed, however, with an awesome barrage from our artillery that left them stunned. The enemy incurred horrendous casualties and was reeling and decimated. We watched in amazement one of the most effective uses of massed artillery and tank weapons that we had seen to date in the war.

"What did the Chinese then do after the artillery and mortar barrage?" Ryan asked as he diligently tried to catch up on his note-taking.

"They were not only stunned, but were also disoriented and indecisive, to put it mildly. The poor souls fell back in much disarray. Many were trying to remove their casualties from the battlefield, which we noticed they always tried to do, probably as a means of concealing their losses. The barrage ripped into them mercilessly. The dead were everywhere. It was a rather unique phase. Prior to that, most of the fighting had been with small arms, some tank fire, and even hand-to-hand fighting. But in this round, it was mostly an artillery show and our guys laid it on heavily and effectively.

A Most Unhappy Regimental Commander

Most interesting to the lower-ranking officers around the CP early in that Twin Tunnels engagement was the intense displeasure shown by our regimental commander. Freeman was especially displeased with higher-level interference and made no effort to conceal it. I don't think I had ever seen a superior so infuriated. If he could have had the corps commander by the throat I think he would have gladly squeezed him till he popped.

"Who do you think was right? Was Freeman, as a regimental commander, justified in being displeased with his corps commander?"

Ryan had asked a most intriguing question, and it was one I was not sure I was competent to answer, as a junior officer.

"Gee, I don't know about that, Tom. Probably it would be out of line for me as a mere captain then to presume to take sides. I do remember talking with the S-3, Major Dumaine, or the regimental exec, Lt. Col. Frank Meszer, at the time. The fighting had been going on all day, and it was a nip and tuck situation—very delicate. Several of the people from the regimental and battalion staffs were near my company CP. Freeman was stomping around and barking at about anyone within earshot."

"What's the regimental commander so peaked off about?" I asked one of them.

"Why shouldn't he be?" was the answer. "Freeman is no amateur. He has personally led this attack and we've accomplished our mission. We've got the Tunnels, just as ordered. There is no reason for command interference, but we are out on a limb here. We don't need a big enemy counterattack and Freeman feels he knows best how to run the show, since we are on the scene."

I was almost sorry I asked. The officer went on to voice the staff's and Freeman's concern about the village-shooting order. No one seemed to think it was a wise thing to do under the ticklish circumstances.

How a Corps Commander Operates

But that seemed to be the way General Almond operated. At least we lower-ranking officers had the impression that the "Big A," as he was known amongst the ranks, was usually present if there was tactical activity.

Of course, higher-level involvement, within reasonable limits, is not necessarily inadvisable or unproductive. If a higher commander is excessively involved, however, in the minute operations of his lower-echelon units, then one might well ask who is running the store back at the individual's own CP, where he should be in control.

One can always recall the capture of General Dean early in the war, when he was up front firing a bazooka as a corporal, instead of being back controlling his division. Courageous perhaps, but not very prudent. And certainly not very helpful to his men, as he seemed to realize from statements he made at the press conference following his repatriation from the POW camps.

There is, of course, much to be said for the high commander who does not spend all his time sitting around a CP sipping a tall, cool one. He must get out and be personally aware of the situation in his command. We can remember how Lincoln tried with so little success to get McClellan to do so with his army of the Potomac in the early days of the Civil War.

No doubt the line of difference is very thin between actively keeping informed and in touch with subordinate commanders and improperly taking too much operational control away from them. My impression was that Almond was too often guilty of the latter. That seemed also to be the view of my seniors in the 23rd Regiment.

Freeman had been talking to one of his battalion commanders, Jim Edwards, of the 2d, as I recall, and when he heard some of us talking nearby he spun around.

"I don't mind the corps commander being around," he fired out, "and there's no problem either with him telling me what to do. He should as a courtesy go through his division commander, but that's between those two. What I can't accept is his telling me how to do it, especially if I think his way is dangerous to my command and mission."

I had never seen a higher commander more angry than Freeman on that occasion.

"If Almond wants to be a regimental commander, damn it, let him take a reduction to bird colonel and come down and be one," and with that he sped off, leaving us all with mouths agape.

"What do you recall about the rank-and-file feeling for Almond as a corps commander?" Ryan wanted to know.

"I think there was a general awareness that his assignment and operations in the Korean War were surrounded with a considerable amount of military internal political maneuvering. There was an understanding that he was MacArthur's 'fair-haired boy' and favorite subordinate."

We assumed that this influenced MacArthur's decision to keep Almond's X Corps in northeast Korea under direct control, rather than as a part of the Eighth Army under Walker, who had not been selected by MacArthur. I've noted in later years that hardly any tacticians or military historians support that divided arrangement, or "split command." Nor do they believe that it contributed to efficient prosecution of the war in Korea in 1950, when the commands were thus separated.

We also heard rumors of much internal bickering and jealousies involving Almond and his special relationship with the supreme commander in Tokyo. That relationship could hardly be expected to endear him to the Eighth Army commanders, either General Walker earlier, before his death in December, or Generals Ridgway or Van Fleet later on.

But we in the rifle companies, preoccupied with survival and suffering greatly under tactical and climatic adversities, were hardly in a position to objectively assess all those circumstances. We simply were somewhat aware of much talk about the matter.

"But you must have had some impressions of Almond," Ryan persisted.

"Of course. But they were mostly impersonal and, I guess, detached. A rumor made the rounds that Almond had ordered a decoration withdrawn from an officer because he was black."

The rumor has since been confirmed as the incident involving Capt. Forrest Walker of our 9th Regiment, who had courageously led an attack at Wonju.

General Almond's Command Inspections

If I had to name but two of the most widely known and lingering impressions of General Almond amongst the rear ranks in the line companies, I think I would list his almost regular appearances and his "command inspections." For a higher-level general, Almond was seen with unusual regularity around forward units.

Few troops, if any, in my unit in Korea did not know that we had a corps commander and that his name was Almond. I think more troops knew or recognized the corps commander than they did the division commander, and perhaps even the regimental commander. Almond was energetic and ever-present, but perhaps excessively so, judging from the opinions circulated from division and other staff officers.

"And you say General Almond was known for his command inspections? Why or how so?"

"Well, I don't recall ever having such inspections, so often and detailed, as when Almond ordered them and personally carried them out. Apparently he prided himself in being especially supply- and conservation-minded.

American troops have had a reputation for great wastefulness on the battlefield, misusing and discarding equipment wherever they go. The correction of this had been the subject of many directives and much training. Even officers' efficiency reports were modified to include a special section on supply discipline. To his credit, Almond insisted that every soldier and unit have its full supply of equipment, weapons, ammunition and so forth, and that they be in useable or workable condition.

Almond not only directed that units be fully equipped, he ordered them, whenever off the line, to assemble and display their equipment for him, and for their other commanders, he hoped, to see. These assemblies became known as the "Almond command inspections."

A whole battalion would be spread out across a Korean schoolyard or a large rice paddy, with individual and organizational equipment, vehicles, and weapons on display. Almond would then compel unit commanders to accompany him as he walked through the ranks. He knew the canteens, packs, ammo belts, instruments, and countless other items each person or unit was required to have, and if he did not see them, there was hell to pay. He demanded corrective action by supply and command officers.

More on Almond's Inspections

There was no doubt that Almond's inspections were helpful in forcing commanders into administrative action to determine what supplies were needed and to ask for any shortages. But the inspections had one counterproductive, and perhaps humorous, aspect.

To avoid getting caught with their supply "pants down," our battalion and regimental leaders would scurry around and rob Peter to pay Paul. Commanders knew that it would take days or weeks to inventory equipment, ascertain needs, write up requests, submit them through channels, and then pick up and transport them over crowded, congested, and frozen supply routes and distribute the supplies to the units.

Still, small-unit commanders and their staffs did not want the Corps Commander to find that they had fallen down on their supply responsibilities. So when word came that the Big A was due on short notice for one of his famous command inspections, everyone would scamper and scurry around, gathering equipment from one battalion to loan to the one being inspected first.

When a command inspection was completed, and while Almond was having lunch or conferring or engaged in some other interim function, the equipment would be gathered up and rushed to the next battalion in line for inspection. The exercise took on all the elements of a Hollywood comedy.

We often wondered whether Almond knew what was going on with the Mickey Mouse reshuffling of equipment prior to his arrivals. He may have known, but felt, nevertheless, that his action was prodding lower commanders into more thorough supply action after he left. If so, to that extent, I suppose his inspections were a success.

Opinions about the Corps Commander

Overall, in my judgment, and based on limited contact, Almond came across as a vain, arrogant, highly opinionated, self-serving, abrasive, and not very likable person. Still, he was a dedicated, determined, sacrificing, and demanding combat leader. Whether his assets outweighed his shortcomings I must leave to others and to history to sort out.

General Almond has now passed on, and it may be less than kind to criticize one who is not around to defend himself. As with all such noted and controversial wartime leaders, discussions of his effectiveness are not likely to end so long as there are those around who witnessed his performance and leadership and disagreed with it.

Twin Tunnels Aftermath

"What happened with the regiment after the Twin Tunnels operation?" Ryan continued.

"The situation maps and intelligence reports began to show an ever-increasing concentration of CCF strength in the central Korean area around the town of Wonju, just to our northeast, and the road and communications a few miles north of Chipyong-ni. The stage was being set for one of the two or three most critical and decisive engagements of the Korean War."

"Decisive? That's a strong word to use. Why do you think the forthcoming engagement was to be decisive?"

"As you know, I'm sure, a decisive military engagement or action is one of such great importance that it directly impacts on and even determines the outcome of the whole war. There was no shortage of tough, costly, and bitter fighting at various times and places in the Korean War, but I think the truly decisive engagements would be limited to probably only three."

"And those were?"

"I contend that they were the stand by the UN Forces at the Pusan perimeter, our delaying action at Kunu-ri, and the forthcoming stand to the north around Chipyong-ni."

"I think you have to justify your position. There are going to be those who may strongly disagree with you. Why were those actions so decisive, in your judgment?"

"No, thanks, Willie. I'll go look fer some mud wot ain't been used."

As in other wars, including Mauldin's World War II setting in the above cartoon, bathing for troops in Korea was a constant problem. In the winter, streams were generally frozen over and the weather too cold in the open fields and mountains for troops to bathe. Even in warm months the remoteness of troops on mountaintop positions usually made it impossible to maintain a regular bathing schedule. As a result, skin problems and related infections increased drastically in some regions of the forward positions.

Importance of the Pusan Perimeter

"First let's dispose of the Pusan-perimeter phase. I had no part in it, except at its end, so I think no one can legitimately challenge my objectivity.

"It should be noted that had the forces at the Pusan perimeter not withstood the Communist effort to toss them into the sea, there would have been no more Korean War. It would have been over. I don't think there would have been a Chinaman's chance, pun perhaps intended, of our mounting the enormous effort that would have been required to reestablish ourselves on the Korean peninsula. Politically and militarily it would not have been feasible. The public would not have supported it. I think that is beyond dispute."

Importance of the Kunu-ri Defense

I then turned to the Kunu-ri action, as Ryan listened intently. I think also, I told him, that had one division, which happened to be our 2d, not been left behind to delay the CCF and give the remainder of the Eighth Army time to withdraw relatively intact to continue its defense, the UN forces without doubt would have had to evacuate Korea. There are few who disagree with that although, as previously argued, few seem to be around who knew of the key role played in that action by my Baker Company troops.

Even on the eve of the Chipyong-ni battle in February, it was by no means certain that the UN forces could stay. But if they had been significantly smashed on their way down from the north, then for sure a complete evacuation, or even a Dunkirk-type rout, would have been inevitable.

"Yes," agreed Ryan, "I think many experts will agree with you on that. But why was Chipyong-ni to be decisive?"

Importance of Chipyong-ni Action

"Because, in a few words, until that time it was not yet known with any reliable degree of certainty whether the UN forces could stand up to the Chinese oceans of manpower, and whether evacuation might not be required."

After the "new war"* and the entrance of the Chinese in October and November and the withdrawal to our locations mostly south of the parallel, where we now found ourselves, all the engagements of any consequence with the Chinese, and what was left of the North Koreans, had been "rolling-with-the-punches" type of conflicts.

Thus far, by February, we had been only shadowboxing and dancing around to feel each other out. We had not been standing in place to see if we could take all the Chinese could throw at us. As we know, at Chipyong-ni we did just that, and the question was settled. Thereafter, all talk of withdrawing from the peninsula ended. I outlined my views to Ryan.

X Corps in the Northeast

"But what about the X Corps action in the northeast part of the country before its December withdrawal, or the fighting later in the Heartbreak Ridge, Punchbowl, and Iron Triangle areas? Certainly those costly engagements must be considered decisive?"

"Not at all. At least not in any significant or substantive way. They were truly costly. The loss of life in any of those actions was pathetic and gruesome. And I would not detract in any way from the magnificent sacrifices made by those who died in or survived those actions. But none of their outcomes had any deciding impact on the ultimate outcome of the war. The Eighth Army would have had to withdraw, no matter whether the X Corps was in the northeast or not. And its relocation on the main front later was after we had already stopped the Chinese, although, to be sure, their arrival clearly was appreciated and made the burden more equitable all around."

---

* Author Clay Blair in his *The Forgotten War* (New York: Time Books, 1987), on pages 464–65, discusses the November 28, 1950, "posterity paper" sent by MacArthur to the Pentagon upon intervention by the Chinese, in which the General said, in part: "We face an entirely new war."

Heartbreak Ridge Real Estate Exchange

As for the later fighting on Heartbreak Ridge and the other big battles nearby, I continued, they neither added to nor detracted from the outcome of the war. UN forces were by then secure in Korea and would have stayed even if the battles had not been fought.

It's not easy for me to downgrade the decisive importance of the later central Korean actions because I was still in Korea when the 2d Division and 23rd Regiment were on Heartbreak Ridge, and I participated in them and witnessed just how painfully bloody those engagements were. But those battles involved mostly just the exchange of some real estate—and not very much, and not very critical—comprised of almost all high, inaccessible mountains.

The best thing that can be said for the resumed fighting in central Korea in 1952 and 1953 may be that it encouraged the Chinese to get serious at P'anmunjom. Even that may be debatable. Most historians I have read seem to agree that the Chinese were going to accept a cease-fire in due course when it suited their needs, notwithstanding whether fighting was in progress at the time.

Chipyong-ni on the Eve of Battle

"So the curtain was about to rise on your decisive engagement at Chipyong-ni? Do you recall the preparations or events that led up to the battle?"

"Very vividly. It's those kinds of experiences that burn into the memory with an indelible record like hieroglyphics on Egyptian stone," I emphasized to Ryan.

After the Twin Tunnels we returned northward and Colonel Freeman established his CP in the town at some structures that I think were schoolhouses or perhaps municipal buildings of some sort. There was a period of intensive patrolling. Our 1st Battalion CP was close by the regimental CP. Most of the companies of the regiment were placed in position to the northwest, north, and northeast of the town. One battalion, the 2d I think, was designated for regimental reserve.

The village of Chipyong-ni wasn't totally damaged or burned out when we first arrived. There were scattered groups of Korean civilians still in some of the houses. The town was in a small valley almost surrounded by low hills nearby, with higher hills or small mountains several miles beyond and within sight.

A railroad ran through the town of Chipyong-ni in a generally northwest-to-southeasterly direction. The town was also a hub for several key roads. One led south to the Twin Tunnels, from whence we had just returned and to the town of Yoju on the Han River beyond. Others ran to Yangpyong to the west, Wonju to the southeast, and one northeast to Hongch'on and Hoensong.

The road south to the Twin Tunnels passed under the railroad overpass that was to figure prominently in later fighting. On the outskirts of the town there were open farming-spaces consisting mostly of rice paddies. They were frozen, and provided sites for the l05-mm howitzers of the 37th Field Artillery Battalion, and the l55s of the division's 503rd Field Artillery Battalion.

Scattered around the village and in the fields were also tanks from the the regimental tank company, and, I think, from the division's 72d Tank Battalion. Near my CP, the 4.2-mm mortars were in position and across the road the French Battalion and the Ranger Company had gone into bivouac.

"Did your Baker Company occupy defensive positions at Chipyong-ni?"

"Not at first. Later, when the perimeter was formed, my company and the Rangers were designated regimental reserves."

Baker company arrived and occupied the town on February 3, which was my twenty-ninth birthday. Defensive positions were taken by the other regimental companies, but my company was used mostly for patrols. We went out daily in several directions. Sometimes we encountered the enemy, but only sporadically.

While my platoons were out on patrol, I had a bit of time on my hands and I hung around the regimental and battalion CPs. I liked to watch the situation maps. My sister companies in the 1st Battalion had gone into positions on the high ground just a couple hundred yards to the north of the regimental CP. The 3rd Battalion was on the high ground to the east; the 2d generally to the south about a mile away and straddling the road to the Twin Tunnels that we had just come up; and from the southwest to the northwest stretched the French Battalion.

Thus, the 23rd Regiment and its attached units, including the Rangers, had established an all-around perimeter defense. Operations officers Dumaine and Radow had all the units plotted on their situation maps and everything looked well covered.

On the S-2 intelligence maps, Shoemaker and King were busy plotting reported enemy troops arriving in the area opposite our positions, and here the picture looked alarming and ominous.

Defense Preparations at Chipyong-ni

The first several days in the Chipyong-ni positions were relatively quiet; the companies on line were busy preparing and improving their positions. It was known that General Ridgway was tiring of pulling back each time the Chinese attacked his front and that he was now ready to make a stand and test the enemy's will and ability.

All reports indicated substantial enemy buildup in the central Korean sector, and especially around the Wonju area. To the east of Wonju were some of the most rugged mountains in the country, and a major drive through that area appeared unlikely.

If a strong effort were to be made, it seemed it would be toward Wonju itself and the area to its west, which included the Chipyong-ni communications axis, where we were located.

Aware of this, and under instructions from the corps and division commanders Almond and Ruffner, Freeman ordered his battalions to dig in well for a long stay. He wanted all emplacements and foxholes to be extra deep, with several times the normal amount of ammunition, and he directed that fields of fire be plotted and marked.

Freeman also ordered the installation of trip flares, or antipersonnel mines. In some areas rolls of barbed wire were placed across likely avenues of approach, a normal defensive measure when time and facilities permit.

"You people have all been schooled deeply in the textbook methods of laying out an impregnable defense; now let's see you put it to use," I heard him tell his staff and commanders one morning. And days were spent doing just that.

The Fighting French

"And how did you get along with the French Battalion?" Ryan interrupted. "Did you have any personal contact with them?"

"Oh yes, repeatedly. They were just another battalion in the regiment, and we saw them regularly. We relieved each other routinely in various engagements and situations."

Except for the language—and many of the Frenchmen spoke English, especially the officers—one would have thought they were simply another American unit. If there was a tactical difference, it was, I think, that most of the French soldiers were much more motivated to fight the war than we were.

The French had for years been involved in the Southeast Asia colonies, and there was a strong ideological commitment there. While many Americans had strong doubts about why they were fighting a war in Korea, I think the French in our battalion had none, or fewer. The officers, in particular, seemed to welcome the opportunity to fight in Korea, and many had volunteered, unlike the Americans, who were involuntarily recalled to active duty or drafted.

The French battalion commander, Lt. Col. Ralph Monclar, had even taken a reduction in rank from major general to command a battalion so he could go to Korea.

Although French-battalion line-companies were around the perimeter at Chipyong-ni, their battalion CP was just across the road from my Baker Company location, and near our 1st Battalion CP. We intermingled often with the French troops, and sometimes they would share their daily ration of brandy or of Pernod, the licorice-tasting, pale green "bracer" that is almost a French national drink.

Why We Fight in Korea

One afternoon, during a lull in my daily activities, I sauntered across to the French CP either from "nosiness" or to pay my respects. "General" Monclar, as we addressed him out of courtesy, was sipping something to ease the cold and chatting with some Americans. Apparently, the Americans had been griping, as we were wont to do if there was anyone to listen, about the cold, the war, or anything else that came to mind.

Monclar, highly dedicated and ideologically minded about the UN Korean effort, had little truck for their complaints. He looked around the group slowly, fixing a penetrating gaze on several in turn, took a deep breath, and then laced into the bitching Yanks.

"You sunshine soldiers and summer patriots should be ashamed of yourselves," he began, leaning on Tom Paine and his Valley Forge missive, known to any Yank from high-school history. At that point the old French general had everyone's undivided attention.

"There have been wars since the dawn of history," he continued, with an air of a college professor, "but never one like the one you are in now. This war is unique. Most wars have been useless, for greed, power, oppression, or personal whims of some ruler. We in Europe know this more than you Yanks."

"Why is this one any different, General?" someone asked. It was the question the general had been waiting for. He looked sternly at his questioner and continued.

"This war marks the first time in all recorded history that armies have taken to the field to fight for none of these reasons, but simply to preserve the peace and stop wrongful aggression, and do it under the banner of an international organization created for just that purpose.

"No matter what will be the outcome here, historians for all time will record this as a landmark and precedent in man's efforts to eliminate war and preserve the peace by a worldwide organization. These circumstances have never existed before.

"And you men, relatively small in number, are privileged to be a part of this noble and historical effort. Your sacrifices and contributions can long be remembered with pride by your families and future generations. You are making your mark in civilization. You should be grateful. Let me hear no more of your complaints."

Monclar had spoken with deep feeling and sincerity, with words for profound meditation. Whether or not all present agreed, no one dared contradict him. His remarks were undeniably food for thought.

New Mission for Baker Company

About the time of Monclar's lecture justifying our presence in Korea, Freeman called me in to his CP. Several of his staff officers were gathered around, as was George Russell, my battalion commander.

"Pratt," he said, "We have a mission for you." I was suspicious of that editorial "we." If a commander has a real goodie for you, he is usually eager to say "I," but if it is less than yearned for, the human tendency seems to take shelter behind a "we," as though some anonymous source other than the speaker is responsible for the development.

Freeman proceeded to explain to me, the others present having already been briefed, that he was much concerned about the regiment's positions in view of the continuing enemy buildup. He pointed to the situation map and said we were not on the best terrain for defense.

Freeman said, moreover, that he wanted to be farther out on higher ground, but that the size of the RCT* would not allow such a stretch-out. He said that since we must stay where we are, then at least he wanted to deny the enemy the use of an especially critical and dominating terrain feature about two miles away.

Freeman pointed on his map to a hill to the northeast. I noted that it was marked with a "503" for elevation, almost twice as high, or more, than any of the hills on which the regiment was then located. I noted that Hill 503 was about 100 yards northeast of a more prominent hill on the map labeled "491." (Later I learned that Hill 503 had been referred to in the command report as Hill 506.)

"So what do you want me to do, Colonel Freeman, Sir?" I asked, fearing that I knew all too well.

"We want you to take your company out there and occupy that hill."

That was precisely the answer that I feared and did not want, but I knew Freeman and Russell felt I would not protest—or at least not very violently. They waited for my reaction, as I studied the map and made notes on my own.

* Regimental Combat Team.

"Is the hill occupied now by the Chinese?" I asked.

"We don't think so."

"But you're not sure?"

"No. It wasn't, as you know, when your patrol went out yesterday, but who can tell what the Chinks may have done since?"

"How long am I to stay?"

"We're not sure. We'll let you know as things develop. Just be sure you take all precautions on the way out, and if you succeed in closing, set up a good perimeter defense."

"What am I to do while there on Hill 503?"

"Mostly occupy and hold it. As long as you are there, the Chinese won't have it. It's the closest piece of ground to us that is higher than we are; if the Chinese are on it, they can look straight down our throats and see everything that goes on in our perimeter."

I studied the sitmap a bit longer. "There are other hills nearby that are as high as 503, or even higher," I volunteered.

"True, and I wish we could occupy some of them, but we can't. Anyway, most of them are much farther away and are not the direct threat that 503 is."

There was some additional discussion about fire support and other help, and I asked, "When do we leave?"

"As soon as you can get cranked up," Freeman answered. "For sure you should try to be in position before dark, and you have only about four hours."

"Seems to me we could well be cut off out there, so far from the perimeter."

"Don't worry," Freeman said reassuringly. "We're going to play it close—we don't want to lose you—you and the Ranger Company are my only reserves. If the situation gets ticklish, we won't hesitate to call you back in."

I knew I had no time to lose. I also knew the mission could turn out to be an extraordinary challenge, with much uncertainty as to terrain and enemy presence. I did my salutes and buzzed off to the company.

At the company, I hurriedly briefed Mendenhall, Dusseau, Brasswell, Kotite, Fendy, and I think another officer, Lt. Ray Dupree.

Ryan decided it was time for him to join in with a question or two.

"At a time like that, how did your men react to such a mission?" he asked.

"For sure they were not bracing at the bits with uncontrollable enthusiasm," I answered. "While their disenchantment was clearly obvious from the expressions on their faces, still there was no talk of mutiny. I think *resignation* would be an adequately descriptive term."

My men knew their lot inside the Chipyong-ni perimeter was much preferable to being out on some desolate and isolated mountain all alone.

Baker Company Departs for an Outpost

Within the hour Baker Company was on its way, winding along the little levees that separate rice paddies. We passed between the positions of our own battalion's Charlie Company to the north and the troops of the 3rd Battalion on the northeast. Some of the 3rd Battalion troops, upon seeing our column, yelled jibes at my men, and accused them of deserting the perimeter for R and R in Japan. My guys responded with a few not inappropriate expletives and something about a willingness to change places, but no offers from the 3rd Battalion were forthcoming.

Our column passed on out of the perimeter into what would be classified as no-man's-land, and, after clearing a small valley some mile or so in width, the lead platoon entered the brush at the bottom of Hill 503 and began its ascent. I glanced back at the low hills that I knew were the northern and northeastern rim of the 23rd RCT perimeter. We were too far away for me to see the individual foxholes or the men in them, and it became increasingly ticklish as we moved steadily farther and farther from the closeness and comfort of our fellow troopers in the regiment.

With much uncertainty as to the enemy situation around us, I cautiously entered the hill slopes with two platoons abreast in "as skirmishers" formation. As infantry tacticians know, that arrangement gives a unit the most width, with less depth from front to rear, and permits greater dispersion and protection from enemy fire while also permitting maximum fire to be delivered on the enemy from across the entire front. It is the usual formation for an attack, or when enemy defense is anticipated.

As we proceeded ever deeper into the brush and upward onto the hill, I soon realized that if we remained in combat formation, we would never reach our goal before dark.

"Captain, we're never going to get into position before dark at this rate," one of my platoon leaders complained to me.

"You're right for sure," I agreed. "Just what I was thinking. Why don't you think we will make it?"

"The grade is too steep. It's damn near straight up. And the underbrush and trees are thick and tough as steel wool. This growth is almost like a tropical jungle. And there are no paths or trails that we can find."

"Any suggestion?" I asked Fendy, who had just emerged from the woods, also frustrated and seeking directions.

"I'm not sure," Fendy responded, "but for starters we might try changing our formation into columns. We can let the lead men try to clear routes by stomping brush and breaking limbs. And we can rotate the point men to ease that burden. Wish to hell we had a stack of machetes."

"Sounds like as good an approach as any," I told Fendy and the others. "Let's give it a whirl. We simply cannot let the night catch us all strewn out like this on the side of this slope."

Everyone agreed, and off they went to comply. The command started moving again and laboriously made its way up and up, foot by foot.

On top of these difficulties, the snow's depth increased steadily. The going was slow and tedious. I worried that the men were over-heating—a most hazardous condition for men outdoors, through the night, in extreme cold.

Somehow, and after a monumental effort, the company, heavily laden with all the extra ammunition, rations, and other supplies it could possibly tote, struggled to the top of Hill 503, just as the last pink rays of the setting sun faded in the west. We were on our objective, drained, uncertain, shivering in the bitter night air, wondering what lay ahead. I decided it was time to contact Major Russell, the battalion commander.

"Red Six, Red Six, this is Baker Six," I called on the radio, using the standard codes for battalion and company commanders.

"Baker Six, this is Red Three," my radio earphone crackled in the brisk, clear night air. I recognized the voice of Sammy Radow, the S-3. "Are you on your objective?" Sammy was quick to ask.

"Affirmative on that," I informed the S-3. "We are busy securing for the night."

"Congratulations. Well done. Are your FOs laying in defensive concentrations?"

"Affirmative again. They are already busy. I just heard the first round land and they are adjusting."

Sammy cautioned us to be especially watchful, that the area abounded with our adversaries, and to promptly report any and all things unusual.

I "rogered" Sammy's transmission to confirm my understanding, and after some other words, we signed off.

In the last flickers of gray dusk, I set about to emplace the platoons. As I looked around in the thick brush and trees in the rapidly settling darkness, I would have felt like laughing under less unfunny circumstances. A piece of high ground is usually priceless for long-range observation purposes and is a distinct advantage to the army that holds it for keeping tabs on the foe. Any elementary student in military tactics well knows the usual value of the high ground.

On our high ground, however, a body could hardly see a hand in front of a face. The brush and trees were so thick one could not pass or see through them. Even more difficult, we were to find, would be the establishment of gun positions and fields of fire for our weapons.

That night, after roughly indicating areas of responsibility for the platoons, we settled in and shivered through the night, hoping against hope that daylight would come and we would have a chance to study and improve our positions before any enemy emerged. To that extent, we were lucky. The enemy, graciously or otherwise, spared us his presence.

The night was another of the long, cold, nerve-wracking Korean experiences. But daylight did eventually manage to arrive after an eternity and with it a chance to better arrange the platoons and make some attempt to clear scattered limbs away so that we might have some means of detecting the enemy if they showed up. We would not see an attacking enemy until we had almost eyeball-to-eyeball contact, but then neither could they see us either, if that constituted an advantage.

Our first period of daylight passed on Hill 503 without any enemy action. We finally were able to clear some brush and could observe in some directions to some extent. Some of my platoon leaders reported seeing enemy activity off to the north and we reported that to Red Six during one of the several radio contacts during the day.

As the day wore on we made efforts to improve our security. I pressed Red Six for info as to when we might be able to withdraw from this position, which I was rapidly concluding to be an exercise in futility and useless hardship. But I got no encouragement. "We'll let you know" was the standard reply.

Down went the sun the second time on our mission, and again we settled in for another freezing and miserable night on "old baldy," except that our "baldy" was not actually bald at all.

Predawn Fire Fight

About an hour or so before daylight, as I crouched in a shivering semistupor at a scooped-out spot I called my CP, I suddenly heard a burst of fire from one of the platoons. I instantly came to full alert—if there is such a state when one is half-frozen.

At the sound of gunfire, I wasn't sure whether to be annoyed or alarmed. I had cautioned all the platoons that we could not afford to have nervous Nellies firing at nontargets, especially in our precarious and isolated situation; that we neither had the ammunition to waste nor did we need to have the Chinese know we were out here all alone.

As we tried to contact the platoons on the phones to learn what was going on, the firing continued and increased. I had visions of running out of ammunition and then being at the mercy of an enemy who knew where we were from the sound of our firing, and who then launched an attack in earnest and in strength.

Finally, one of the men in the CP made contact with the platoon the firing was coming from.

"Captain, they are being hit over on the right. It's no fake attack.

The platoon leader is away from the phone and in personal charge. They'll let us know as soon as they have more details."

That, of course, was not good enough for me. With daylight now extending its rosy fingers across the eastern horizon, I could see enough to make my way with Rodriguez through the underbrush in the direction of the firing. Before we arrived at the platoon, however, the firing began to drop off. Soon all was quiet again. I heard some stomping and crashing ahead and looked up to see Fendy.

"What's the picture, Fendy? Your men nervous and trigger-happy?"

"Hardly," Fendy shot back with some irritation at my suggestion that the firing had been uncalled for. "We were hit, all right. Chinks were on top of us before anyone could see or hear them. But they fell back smartly when we opened up. I doubt they knew we were here."

"Any casualties?"

"I think so. I was checking on that when I heard you were here. Thought I'd best report in first."

"Glad you did, but let's see if we have any men who need help."

Whereupon Fendy and I scouted his platoon positions. There were half-a-dozen or so dead enemy troops partly buried in the deep snow, and two of Fendy's men lay dead. Three others were wounded, but with less serious bullet wounds in the arm and legs.

By now the sun was rising higher and all platoons were fully alerted in case the attack resumed. No enemy troops were sighted, but most positions reported they could hear the enemy thrashing about in the underbrush over the crest and farther down the hillsides.

Mendenhall wanted to bounce some mortars off their pumpkin heads, but I was reluctant. I knew the sounds of high explosions from mortar rounds would carry far in the cold, especially from high on a hill, and I felt we did not need any more Chinese knowing we were there than already knew. I also had doubts that mortar rounds could be effective and on target in that terrain. But it was tempting and I told Mendenhall so.

Evacuating the Wounded

Our immediate task was to get the wounded men down off the

hill and back to the perimeter and the aid station. We only had two litters. Fortunately, only two men were hit in the legs and would have to be carried. The man with the gunshot in his arm would simply have to try to walk. The first sergeant busied himself in organizing a carrying party, not only for the wounded men, but also for a ration detail.

By late morning the carrying party started down the hill and toward the Chipyong-ni perimeter. I set about to report the situation to Red Six. I hoped, and halfway expected, that we would be ordered back into the perimeter in view of the enemy encounter. Instead, we were given words of encouragement and told to hang in.

During the afternoon, we continued to mill around the hilltop, trying to keep abreast of our predicament and doing what was possible to improve our lot. Around midafternoon we heard commotions down the hill in the direction the carrying party had gone. Looking down, we saw the carrying party returning. I met Sgt. Anton Legault, who was in charge of the party, and commented on the speed of his trip.

"We didn't get very far, Captain," Legault answered. "There are Chinese all over the landscape. They are thick in the valley between us and the perimeter. We decided it was best to return."

"Yes, that was smart, Legault. You couldn't risk a fire fight with so few men, and especially when you are trying to evacuate wounded." I looked down the hillside at his party. I saw the trooper with the arm wound, but not the litters with the other two. I looked back at Legault.

Death from Cold and Shock

"Where are the other two wounded men, Sarg?"

"Captain, they both died, so we left them in place, figuring we could evacuate the bodies later when we passed through the woods on our way out."

"How could they die so quick with only leg wounds?" I asked.

"Shock," Legault answered. "The medic says not from the wound, but from the shock brought on by the wound and the cold. Medic says it happens all the time if you can't keep a wounded man warm."

And Legault was right, as I learned later from the regimental surgeon and as we were to learn repeatedly in later remote mountaintop engagements during that bitter winter. It seemed so sad to me that lives would be lost from relatively minor injuries because of the remoteness of the areas we fought in and our inability to keep a wounded man warm until he could be evacuated to medical channels.

The carrying party had not only been unable to evacuate the wounded men, but also came back empty-handed insofar as rations were concerned. By the end of the second day on Hill 503, we were hard-pressed for food. Either we had to send a reinforced party back on the following morning or Baker Company would have to starve or be returned to the perimeter.

Welcome News to Withdraw from Outpost

On our third day, as we contemplated our worsening predicament, the problem was resolved. Word came over the radio for us to pack up and hustle back to the perimeter. With a sigh of relief that probably could be heard over most of the ridges of central Korea, we did just that. Down off Hill 503 and through the "valley of the shadow of death" we walked, in figurative biblical fashion.

All the way to the friendly positions we spotted Chinese individually or in small groups. Miraculously they did not fire on us on our return trip, and we did not think it necessary or prudent to encourage an ambush by firing on them.

Baker Company Rejoins the Perimeter

Once back in the perimeter, we resumed our former reserve positions and the men caught their breaths and rations were distributed. I hastened over to Russell to report and for any instructions.

Russell took me immediately to the regimental CP. There I learned that the situation overall was growing bleaker by the minute. Corps had wanted to keep us out on Hill 503, but the escalation of enemy activity had increased and there was fear that Baker Company would be cut off and wiped out.

I learned that the enemy had attacked to the northeast in massive numbers and the 38th Regiment, with the Dutch Battalion and other elements of the division and the 7th Division, were withdrawing into Wonju. Freeman was saying he did not like that and his S-3 pointed to the situation map and showed how it left us at Chipyong-ni, out on a bulge and exposed like a sore thumb.

Perimeter Tension Grows

It was February 12, Washington's birthday. Maj. Dumaine, the S-3, collared me with some instructions. He said Freeman was very worried about the situation and was trying to get permission to withdraw to the south before we were surrounded.

"Actually," he confided, "I don't think we could withdraw now if we wanted to. The latest report by Shoemaker is that the south road, our only avenue of escape, is already swarming with Chinese and is closed. Even if we got permission to withdraw, we would have to fight another gauntlet to get out. I think we are going to be told to stay and fight it out."

"Wow!" I remember responding. "That's not been done yet in this war. Can we really hold if the Chinese throw their all at us?" We knew that the army commander wanted a test case to see if his forces could withstand a massive Chinese attack. We wondered though if he had been contemplating anything on the scale coming up, judging by the concentration of enemy divisions and corps shown on the sitmap before us.

"Who knows if we can hold?" Dumaine said. "I sure as hell don't, but it looks as though we are about to find out. At least this regimental combat team has had plenty of time to prepare and Colonel Freeman thinks our units are now well prepared."

The Perimeter Lines are Given the Once-over

"So do you have instructions for Baker Company?"

"Yes, your company is to sit tight. Catch your breath for now, but as you know, you are the reserve and if the crap hits the fan blades, you might be thrown in anywhere there is a breakthrough. So the regimental commander wants you to take your platoon leaders on a survey of the whole perimeter. You are to familiarize yourselves with all company positions so you'll be prepared to reinforce or replace any company on the perimeter."

"That's rather a big order, isn't it? There's lots of terrain to cover, and it's getting dark."

"Right," answered Dumaine. "You can't do it tonight in the dark, but hit it first thing tomorrow morning. Let me know when you have finished. Also, since you may be called upon to occupy them, I would be interested in any comments you might have on the positions you see."

I made some notes on my map and, after a few more questions, I was on my way. Bright and early the next morning, I rounded up all the company officers, and I think one platoon sergeant for the platoon with no officer, briefed them on the mission, and off we went.

"Your inspection of existing RCT positions would have been on the morning of February 13 then?" historian Ryan interjected.

"Yes, the day before the big *'pièce de résistance'*—Saint Valentine's Day, the fourteenth, when the Chinese were to deliver their Valentine gift to us in all its splendor."

"How did you find the positions, in your judgment?"

"Mostly superior, and I think my platoon leaders and I were rather selfishly picky, since it appeared that we might have to occupy some, or any, of the positions ourselves. We did not want to perish in any half-ass foxholes."

The Baker Company officers and I started at the eastern side of the perimeter in the area between the 1st and 3rd battalions. We had just come through there the day before and felt we were more familiar with the lay of the ground at that point. We worked our way southward through the 2d Battalion and then up the west side through the French, to our own 1st Battalion companies on the northern rim of the perimeter.

In each part of the perimeter lines, our inspection team made notes on the best approaches in the event we were committed there, and made efforts to consult and coordinate with the battalion and company officers in position. Some hours later, upon returning to the interior of the perimeter and the regimental CP, I reported that my mission had been completed. One of Colonel Freeman's staff officers asked me what I thought of the positions around the perimeter.

Weaknesses in the Chipyong-ni Defenses

When asked about the sufficiency of the perimeter defenses, I was unsure how to answer. I felt uneasy about criticizing any other unit's efforts. After some hesitation, I replied.

"Well, I think all the positions are relatively well prepared, but I suppose some are better than others," I answered. I thought I was being charitable but also equivocating. The staff officer studied me for a moment suspiciously. He then pressed me for details about why I said some were better than others.

"Which ones are not as good as others?" he persisted.

"Well," said I, "I don't want to step on anyone's toes, but I must say in all frankness that if I were to have to replace George or Fox Company now, I would immediately set about to make some improvements."

"Like what?"

"For one thing, I don't like the depth of their dugouts. Many are barely below the surface. If I were lying in some of those, I would feel most insecure and not very well protected. I think troops in such positions might well be routed if they are hit persistently and repeatedly."

"Anything else?"

"Well, yes," I said, growing a bit bolder but also uncomfortable as a critic of other officers' work. "I think many of the individual positions are too far forward and exposed and down the hill. It gives the occupant a feeling of remoteness and adds to his insecurity. Other positions are isolated so that men cannot render mutually supporting fire."

"You felt that mutually supporting fire was essential?" Ryan asked.

"You better believe it. Ask any infantryman. No trooper wants to feel that he is all alone and without buddies in nearby positions to back him up, and vice versa."

It is comforting and most reassuring to glance to the left and right during a fire fight and see that your comrades are still there. When you can't see them, and don't know if they are there, then you think they are gone, in which case you quickly conclude that this is no place for you, all alone. The inclination is to haul ass yourself. It's human nature. As long as one feels he is part of a surviving team, he is likely to stand and fight, but not hopelessly, all alone. I explained this in the strongest terms to my historian interrogator.

"And you did not feel that the emplacements in the 2d Battalion sector met that requirement as mutually supporting positions?"

"I did not."

"And you passed this along to the regimental S-3?"

"Well, to whatever staff officer who was on duty at the time. It may not have been the S-3, and could have been executive colonel Meszar, or even Colonel Freeman himself. It doesn't matter, really, who received it. I know the message and my criticisms got across, because later that day I was told that when they were passed on to Colonel Edwards, the 2d Battalion commander, he hit the ceiling with indignation and in so many words said to tell that Baker Company commander to get lost and mind his own business—that he, Colonel Edwards, was running the 2d Battalion and not the Baker Company commander."

"What did you then do?"

"Nothing. What could I do? Edwards was quite right. It was his battalion, not mine, and in some ways his resentment at what he considered outside interference was understandable. The problem was that we were to pay the consequences for his battalion's deficiencies in position preparations. As we shall see, the time was coming when we would be called upon to reoccupy his positions, which his companies could not hold, and we would pay a bloody price in doing so."

A 2d Division twin 40mm AA gun at Chipyong-ni. With little or no enemy air activity, the weapon was used extensively against enemy ground troops.

A view to the southwest from the Baker Co. reserve positions inside the Chipyong-ni perimeter defenses in central Korea near Seoul in February 1951.

CHAPTER TEN

The Decisive Battle of Chipyong-ni

The battle of Chipyong-ni, a name and location known to very few Americans or the rest of the world, began on the eve of Saint Valentine's Day, on February 13, 1951.

The battle was to be one of the most critical of the entire Korean War and clearly marked the turning point in that conflict.

Chipyong-ni would be the "Battle of Gettysburg" and high-water mark for the Chinese Communist cause. Afterwards, the battle lines would surge to and fro for almost three years, but the enemy would never again have the clear initiative.

Like Pickett and his Virginians with their valorous and costly but futile charge through the cornfields of southern Pennsylvania in early July of 1863, the Chinese would flood through the Korean rice paddies at Chipyong and up the slopes to our positions and be repulsed. Also like Pickett and his men, the Chinese would never again penetrate so

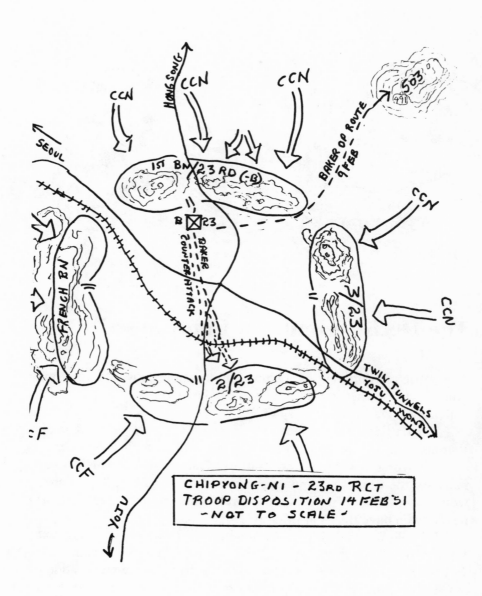

CCN

CCN

CCN

HONG SONG

503
491

BAKER OP ROUTE
9 FEB

SEOUL

CCN

1ST BN 23RD (-B)

CCN

B ☒ 23

CCN

BAKER
COUNTER ATTACK

3/23

FRENCH BN

TWIN TUNNELS

2/23

YOJU
YONJU

:F

CCF

YOJU

CHIPYONG-NI - 23RD RCT
TROOP DISPOSITION 14 FEB '51
- NOT TO SCALE -

deeply into the enemy's lines. Thereafter, the overall initiative would remain with the UN, as it did with the Union in the American Civil War, until the fighting ended. The ultimate outcome would never again be in much doubt—only the question of when and where it would occur.

My regimental commander had not wanted to stay at Chipyong-ni. One day, just before the big battle commenced, I saw him at the battalion CP conferring with Major Russell. Freeman was fuming and ranting.

"Colonel, you don't look especially happy," I told him.

"Pratt, you are always stating the understatements of the year. You bet your arse I am not happy."

"Is the situation really that gloomy?" I asked.

"Well, we've seen brighter days," as he tried for an understatement himself. "We are sitting here constantly being surrounded by ever-increasing hordes of enemy. Look at that damned map."

Freeman pointed to the S-2 sitmap, which shows enemy dispositions. The little boxes showing corps and divisions were almost solid around the whole perimeter. It was indeed a most ominous and alarming picture.

"I don't mind making a stand when the odds are at least somewhat in our favor, but with this overwhelming tide of enemy forces, I fear it's little less than suicide to stay here."

"But we are in unusually strong and well-prepared positions, aren't we?" I asked timidly and with a tone that did not sound very convincing.

"Yes, I'm sure of that. But look at our position here in relation to the rest of the Eighth Army. We are stuck out way ahead like the sore thumb. I'd like to think we could be reinforced if the going got too rough. But how?"

I studied the map for a bit. It was not difficult to see the gravity of our situation and the vulnerability of our location.

"Perhaps you should order a pullback," I suggested, naively, it turned out.

"Pullback? I've been on the box most of the day trying to get permission to do just that. But the corps commander so far will have none of it. He wants to stand pat and test the enemy's power."

"And that's bad?"

"No, of course not. But not, I think, here. I don't think the terrain is ideal. There must be a better place and time."

Speaking of the time, I decided the time was ripe to leave before I got into some sort of trouble from a frustrated and overwrought senior commander. Under those stressful times he could think up another undesirable mission for Baker Company, which I considered was just then not needed in the least.

The fighting at Chipyong began shortly after dark on the night of the thirteenth. At first there were mainly only trip flares, widespread tooting of horns and blowing of bugles, and rattling of various noisemaking instruments. Then, shortly before midnight, enemy troops launched assaults on the positions of my 1st Battalion on the north rim of the perimeter.

Between midnight and daylight the attacks had spread to the positions of all battalions around the perimeter; the 3rd Battalion to the east, the 2d in the south, and the French on the western sector. These attacks were all repulsed with heavy casualties on the enemy by intense and almost uninterrupted fighting. I was awake most of the night. After all, who could sleep? On the brighter side, all reports indicated that casualties in the battalions were almost nonexistent.

For most of the rest of the fourteenth of February, the second day of the siege, the Chinese continued their attack. They came in waves and were mowed down by the Chipyong defenders until they lay in rows and stacks up and down almost every draw and gully around the perimeter.

The slaughter was ghastly. Our troops, however, mostly in well-prepared and deeply dug emplacements, were to incur incredibly light losses that in some companies would be as little as five or six men.

During this time, enemy artillery and mortars pounded the frontline positions and fell at random throughout the center of the perimeter. One barrage blanketed my company position and extended to the regimental CP and some other nearby units.

After a particularly heavy barrage on my company slackened up, I made my way to one of the platoons near the French Battalion. I found Lieutenants Kotite and Dupree lying in a ditch for cover.

"How are you making out?" I asked Dupree. "Have any of those shells landing in your area?"

"Yes, Captain. Sure have. Two of my men are dead, and two or three others wounded."

"Have you evacuated the wounded?"

"Evacuated to where, for God's sake?" Dupree responded impatiently. "The whole damn area is under fire. I just saw rounds hitting alongside the aid station. No point in taking them over there."

"OK, OK. I see your point. But are they being patched up? Is your medic available?"

"Affirmative, Captain. He's done all he can. No bleeding. But they need a doc badly. First chance we get we are going to carry them over to the aid station."

With that I had to be content and after a bit I crouched and ran for the battalion CP. Sammy Radow was in his dugout.

"Pratt, you're going to get your fat ass shot off, running around the perimeter like this," Sammy scolded.

"Major, my ass is not fat at this moment. In fact, it's doing its share of twitching. Thought I would give you few words on our casualties," which I then proceeded to do.

"What's the situation otherwise?" I asked.

"Well," started Radow, "we seem to be doing worse within the perimeter than on the frontline positions up the hills. These artillery barrages are playing hell all around. The regimental CP caught several. Colonel Freeman has been hit."

"My God!" I sputtered. "How badly?"

"Not sure, but we understand it's not very serious. Piece of shrapnel in the knee. He's still carrying on. Worse news is Shoemaker, the S-2. He's dead."

The news hit me hard. I had formed a special liking for the regimental intelligence officer. He was a dedicated and efficient staff officer. He knew his job well. I enjoyed his company, brief and spotty as it usually was. It was hard to picture him no longer around and my thoughts turned to his family, whom I had seen in his billfold snaps. But only for a moment. Radow continued.

"Two of the sergeants were also killed. Colonel Meszar escaped serious injury, although he was thrown all the way across the dugout."

I didn't need more of that kind of news and so made my way back to my own CP to be with my troops and await further developments. Later I was to learn that our popular and respected regimental com-

mander would be forced to evacuate in deference to a new commander, General Almond's Corps' G-3.

Twice during the siege, we were resupplied by spectacular
airdrops, since we were completely cut off and all roads were closed,
including the MSR from Yoju, to the south. The big clumsy C-119
Flying Boxcars came in low, opened their tails, lifted their noses
slightly, and their cargoes on parachutes would roll out the rear, filling
the air with multicolored billowing nylon balloons.

Most of the supply planes, as they approached or left the drop
zone, would be fired on by the enemy in the higher hills around us.
Some of the planes barely cleared and were low over the hills and easy
targets for even small-arms fire.

To avoid enemy fire, the later waves of supply planes were forced
to drop from a higher altitude and found it more difficult to land their
cargoes within our perimeter. Unfortunately, some of the supplies
dropped from higher up drifted away from us and landed in enemy
positions, no doubt to the delight of the Chinese.

Later on the fourteenth, the first full day of the siege, while our
companies were fighting desperately and almost continuously, I
wandered again over to the battalion CP to see what I could learn.
Major Russell and some others greeted me.

"Any word on what's happening elsewhere in Korea, Major? Or
are we the only ones catching hell?"

"No, Pratt, we're not the only ones, although for sure we have
our share. The guys over at Wonju," he pointed on his map to a
location about twenty miles to the east, "are also being kept awake
and busy. The 38th and 9th are fighting hard. They are also the target
of a major Chinese attack. But they are not as stuck out as we are."

I could keep some tabs on the progress of some of the other
engagements across the landscape since my company was still in
reserve and I was not preoccupied. I liked hanging around the
regimental and battalion CPs to eye the sitmaps.

I noted that the division forces at Wonju were not in a perimeter
situation like us at Chipyong but, rather, were being struck by an
essentially conventional frontal assault.

"Who's in charge over there at Wonju, Major?" I asked Russell.

"The assistant division commander, Gen. George Stewart. He's
directing the whole show and has plotted that defense."

"Are they holding out OK?"

"Word is they are."

"Casualties heavy?"

"Not among the infantry troops. They're using a different approach to stave off the Chinks."

"What different approach?" I asked with considerable curiosity.

"Artillery. Word is that they are laying down one of the damndest barrages of the war—almost melting their gun barrels, enemy piling up by the thousands. Ferocious and awesome," Russell continued, with obvious satisfaction.

"Not exactly breaking your heart, eh, Major?" I commented.

"You can believe that," Russell replied. "Not that I take any satisfaction from all those poor souls spilling their blood, but let's face it. The fewer that survive there, the fewer they can throw against us here—or later."

"Why don't we do the same?" I asked, but realized the probable answer almost before the words cleared my mouth.

"Because we don't have an endless supply of ammo for the arty. We're cut off. If we fire it all up, there might not be any more. You know that, for Christ sake."

I admitted that I did. I couldn't argue with that. After asking less than a very intelligent question, I felt the time might be ripe to steal away and wind my way back to my own CP again, which I did.

Back at the company, one of the automatic riflemen, Corporal Perkins, saw me and tried to be friendly.

"Hey, Captain, Sir, I'm due a three-day pass. If you don't grant it, I'm going to file a complaint with the IG." I smiled and passed on. He knew his question didn't need an answer.

New Regimental Commander Arrives

Sometime on the afternoon of the fourteenth, the first full day of the defense of Chipyong, and after word of Colonel Freeman's wound reached higher headquarters, the new CO, Lt. Col. Jack Child, was flown in by helicopter.

Freeman was most displeased. He did not want to be evacuated. I was not far away and watched a most unusual drama unfold.

81mm mortar emplacement of the 1st Bn./23rd Reg. in the Chipyong-ni perimeter defenses in February 1951.

Korean civilians and pathetic victims of war inside the 23rd Reg. defense perimeter at Chipyong-ni in February 1951.

"There is no damned need for me to be evacuated. My wound is not that serious. I can have it patched up," Freeman was saying.

The new CO stood by as Freeman continued to command and direct his CP. Outside and nearby the helicopter sat, with blade idling. Shells dropped, exploded, and sent fragments screaming and whistling into vehicles and other equipment. Men stayed low. The pilot grew increasingly impatient and rattled. Finally, he took off without his wounded passenger. Clearly Freeman had stalled so that the chopper would take off without him.

"He's pissed off to a fare-thee-well," one of the staff officers told me. "He knows he's being forced out to make room for another of the Big A's fair-haired boys."

Later, under direct orders as I understood it, Freeman was evacuated when the chopper returned. Upon his departure Colonel Child assumed his office and we had a new commander in the thick of battle.

All through that day and into the night the enemy continued to pound and batter the defenders at Chipyong. There was hardly a moment at any time when some company in the circle was not under assault. Mortar and artillery and shells from enemy self-propelled guns rained down on the relatively small and tight enclave.

By early morning on the third day the unrelenting pressure by the enemy began to tell. Troops were growing very weary. The strain and tension were terrific. Finally, around 3:00 A.M. on the fifteenth, the third day of the battle, our defenses began to crack, and most perilously.

On the south, George Company and part of Easy Company of the 2d Battalion were overwhelmed and forced to withdraw. The ring had cracked. Everyone around the CPs immediately recognized the criticality of that development.

The whole regimental combat team was in the gravest of danger. If the enemy exploited its gains and poured troops through the gap— and it seemed the enemy had endless supplies of troops—the inside of the perimeter would be swamped by masses of the enemy; the CPs and supporting forces would be overrun, and combat troops on line would be easy prey for attack from their rears. The situation was nothing short of terrifying to the extreme.

The hope was that the enemy might not realize the magnitude of its breakthrough and be slow in following up. There was nothing in, or behind, the 2d Battalion sector to prevent the enemy from pouring through the gap like water through a break in a dam. The regimental commander and his staff knew this and urgently ordered a counterattack by the 2d Battalion.

The 2d Battalion counterattack got underway using a platoon from Fox Company and what men could be rounded up from George Company. The Ranger Company from regimental reserve was also sent along to help. The action was launched just as dawn was breaking, but the effort was stopped dead in its tracks by a determined enemy that now held the high and commanding ground.

Baker Company to the Rescue

It was at this critical point at the failure of the counterattack when the regimental commander ordered me to rush Baker Company to the south edge of the perimeter and report to Colonel Edwards, the 2d Battalion CO. After coordinating with him, I was to counterattack and close the gap in the perimeter defenses in that sector.

Tom Ryan again looked up from his notes. "Isn't all this pretty much a matter of record?"

"Yes, more or less, in general outline, and in varying degrees, depending upon the writer and source. What I am about now to relate, however, has never been recorded in pertinent detail, anywhere, that I have been able to determine, and yet it is of the utmost decisiveness and important in determining the outcome of that critical engagement at Chipyong."

"But don't the accounts credit Baker Company with being committed and counterattacking?"

"Yes, in substance and to that extent. But beyond that, most accounts seem to suggest, without expressly saying so, that we did not succeed or contribute meaningfully to the outcome of the engagement. The facts are otherwise and the record needs to so reflect for historical accuracy and completeness."

By the time I had been briefed on my mission and returned to the company, it was past midmorning. As we started moving out across the middle of the perimeter, I learned that the rest of my lst Battalion

1989 photo by official 8th Army historian showing northern edge of Chipyong-ni perimeter (near hills). Distant hills and valley between Chinese-occupied territory. Rice paddy was interior of perimeter. Circle shows location of Regimental Reserve Company (Company B) at time order given to counterattack to close gap in defense. Official U.S. 8th Army photo.

was again under very heavy assault on the northern edge of the circle. Reports also were that a relief column from the 5th Cavalry Regiment was driving up from the south but was still almost ten miles away and meeting stiff resistance. The question, then, was: Could we close the gap and do it in time so we, rather than the enemy, would be on the high ground, when and if the column approached our southern rim?

Behind the 2d Battalion the 155-mm howitzers of the 503rd Field Artillery Battalion were in position. As we passed through their area I noted the guns were silent and unmanned. With the hills just above them now occupied by enemy troops, the artillery men had fled. The 503rd was a black battalion, one of the few remaining segregated army combat-units. Groups of the gun crews were huddled here and there seeking cover and concealment for protection. I spotted a couple of officers and shouted to them.

"Hey, Lieutenant, we are moving up to counterattack. Get your men rounded up and join us. We need all the help we can get."

"No way, Man. We're not infantrymen," came back the quick answer. "We don't know how to attack."

"You can damn well learn fast," I shot back, getting more annoyed by the minute.

"No, Sir," he insisted, "we're not trained for that kind of fighting. We'd better stay with our guns."

"Then why don't you get on them?" I said, with no attempt to hide my irritation. "If we need a fire mission and don't get it, you may be learning next in a POW camp." With that I gave up.

Baker Arrived at the Line of Departure

Within moments we had cleared the artillery positions of the 503rd and began passing under the railroad overpass. We were on the road that ran south and southwest to the Twin Tunnels about twelve miles away, and to the town of Yoju beyond.

Looking up from the road and about 200 yards farther away, I could see the near slopes of the hills to the left of the road that I knew from prior reconnaissance to be the former locations of George Company and part of Fox Company. The hills were mostly barren,

Modern-day view of the Chipyong-ni Valley southeast of Seoul in Korea. Arrows ("C") show counterattack routes of 23rd Regiment's Company B to close gap in perimeter line caused by Chinese occupation of southern rim of perimeter ("A"). "D" indicates road from the south used by relief column from the 1st Cavalry Division's 5th Regiment and the British Commonwealth Brigade.

with ridges and irregular slopes. Near the top I thought I could see human forms and some movement.

About then, a trooper motioned to me and pointed over to several people in a low spot, one of whom I recognized as Colonel Edwards. Another I knew to be Capt. Tom Heath, the CO of George Company.

"What's the picture, Colonel Edwards?" I asked. "I'm Pratt with Baker Company. We've been ordered to counterattack and retake your positions."

"Yes, I know," he said, and prepared to further brief me.

Gathered around me with Edwards were some of my own officers. Specifically, I had Kotite and Fenderson at my elbow. I had told them the good news that I was going to use them initially in the attack. They were not exactly overcome with joy. But neither did they throw a temper tantrum. Both were exceptional officers. I felt, and they knew I felt, that if our mission could be accomplished by any of the platoons, it would be under their leadership. These two were courageous, bold, and aggressive combat leaders. As I recall, my other platoon at the time was without an officer in command and was led by the platoon sergeant. I thought it best to start out with my officerless platoon in reserve.

"George Company's positions are just up there to the left and right of those points," Edwards was explaining to us.

Just then several mortar rounds slammed into the ground just to our rear and we all ducked instinctively. I heard a man scream out in pain, and saw another fall to the ground and not move. Edwards continued to brief us on suggested routes of advance. To me he seemed irritatingly complacent and self-assured.

"Are there any of your men still in position atop the hill?" I asked.

"No, there are only enemy troops up there."

"I saw some bodies moving, I thought, a few moments ago."

"If you did, it has to be Chinks."

"And if we reach the top, there are emplacements in existence that we can drop into?"

"Oh yes," Edwards said reassuringly. "The companies' dugouts are just over the crest and all prepared. All your men have to do is go up cautiously, then rush over the top and drop into the existing positions. Shouldn't be a big order."

I studied Edwards for a moment or so, and glanced at my officers. We were reading each other's minds. We had been in these positions only a couple of days earlier, before the big attack, and had found the positions wanting in many respects, as we had pointed out to the regimental S-3. I looked at Edwards again and tried to imagine what he was thinking.

I realized that the 2d Battalion's positions might have been improved since we last saw them, but I had the feeling that Edwards was being far from candid. I was tempted to ask him if the mission was such a piece of cake then why in hell didn't his own battalion reoccupy their own positions. But better judgment prevailed and I did not embark on an exercise of insubordination.

Command Frictions

Perhaps Edwards was right, I tried to reason to myself as the anger built within me. After all, he was on the scene and must have known better than I the condition of his defenses and the strength of the enemy? Perhaps he did, and perhaps not.

My mind reeled. Thoughts flashed through my head as I looked around the confusion, tension, and slaughter. Was I really in Ch'pyong? Or was it Salerno, Anzio, the Siegfried Kine, Kunu-ri, or Casablanca? Better yet, I would awake at any moment from simply a bad dream.

Two recently assigned officers, Lt. Herschel Chapman from the last West Point class and Lt. Raymond Dupree, were at my elbow. I thought that Chapman, whom we called "Hawk," a name from his academy days, made a most salient point just then.

"If the retaking of his positions was such a snap, Captain, why had the earlier counterattack under his command not succeeded? Or why did he not make another effort?" I looked at Chapman in agreement.

"Hawk, my boy, you couldn't have said my thoughts more clearly." Several more shells landed. I was about to say something more to Chapman when suddenly a burst of machine-gun fire raked our area and I heard him let out a moan. One round hit my carbine stock and splintered it and almost twisted it out of my grip. We all crouched down closer to the ground, if that was possible.

My thoughts turned to my Third Platoon, now without a platoon leader since Lt. Ray Kampe had been evacuated after the fire fight on Hill 503 a few days earlier. Kampe had lost an ear, shot away by an enemy burp gun, leaving the platoon in charge of the platoon sergeant.

"Are you hit, Chapman?" I asked anxiously.

"I think so, Captain."

"Where?"

"My arm stings."

I saw blood running down his sleeve and hand.

"Are you dizzy, lad? Are you about to pass out?"

"Not really," he answered rather calmly, but with a slightly quivering voice.

"Here, let me take a look at you," I told him, as I reached for my first-aid packet, which each soldier carried on his belt. The only medic near us had already been busy on several other downed troopers nearby.

As I quickly examined Chapman, I could see that he had only a slight flesh wound on the lower arm and I so told him. He was obviously relieved that the bullet had missed his head and body. The bleeding seemed to have stopped.

"Make your way back and out of here when you can, Hawk. Looks like you have the million-dollar wound—not serious but good enough to get you off the front lines."

"No way, Captain. I'm staying. If I withdraw with this slight wound I will be the laughing stock of my graduation class at the Academy. I would never live it down. Just give me an assignment and let's get on with it."

I looked at Hawk with surprise, but also with admiration.

"OK, fellow. If you feel that way, are you up to taking over the third platoon at this time? As you know, we have the platoon sergeant in charge and I'm sure he could use some help. I was going to wait a few days for you to get your feet better planted, but we have a bit of an urgency just now, I think."

I felt no small degree of guilt. What a hell of a time to ask a new officer to take over a command. Hardly fair to him at all. I had not planned it this way, but events were overtaking me.

"Damned right, Captain. Thought you would never ask."

"Then up and away. The platoon is just behind us. Find the

platoon sergeant and let him know you're now in charge. I think he will welcome your arrival. Get ready to be committed. I'm sure we are going to have to commit the reserve platoon but don't yet know just where. I'm going to send Ray Dupree along to help you, or take over in case you are hit." In short order, Chapman was up and running and away.

Still I had what I considered to be the problem of Edwards, the 2d Battalion commander. It was clear that he and I had no love for each other. To him, I must have been the pip-squeak company grade officer from another battalion who, a couple of days earlier, had had the audacity and the impertinence to question the adequacy of his battalion defense-preparations. He had already shown that he highly resented my comments to the regimental staff or commander.

Edwards' reactions were, of course, quite understandable. No commander is likely to be graciously receptive to criticisms from outsiders, and especially anyone junior in position or rank.

From my point of view, on the other hand, I saw the situation as one where we had to bail out Edwards and his outfit, probably because of their ineptness, and at possibly heavy losses to us in men and lives. I felt that I, not he, was the one entitled to satisfactory reassurances and answers, and not misleading overstatements and gloss-overs.

"Do you know just how many of your company's positions that were vacated have actually now been occupied by the enemy?" I inquired in not a little nervousness.

Before Edwards or his staff officers could answer me, several more bursts of machine-gun fire sprayed the area and I saw several of my men in one of the platoons a few yards ahead hit the ground. I felt my own field jacket pulled back and out as a bullet went through the right-shoulder sleeve. We all hugged the ground more closely. I felt sure there was no room for cigarette paper between my belly button and the ground beneath.

One of Edwards' officers mumbled something in answer to my question and pointed to the left front, up the closest slopes to where he thought the machine-gun fire had come from. I felt my right shoulder to see if I had been hit. I saw no blood and felt no pain, so I assumed the bullet had missed my body. Twice in a short span I had missed being hit by a hair's width. I wondered how long my luck would hold out.

"Did Colonel Edwards make any commitment to help you in your counterattack at that time?" Ryan asked when I paused for breath.

"No. None. He seemed quite content to pass the ball to me and my Baker Company. His whole attitude seemed to be one of complacency and almost unconcern, as though the reoccupation of his positions was a mere formality—as we say nowadays, 'a piece of cake.'"

"But you had your doubts?"

"That is putting it mildly. I didn't trust Edwards as far as I could throw one of our medium General Sherman tanks. I had seen his positions earlier and formed my own conclusions as to their unsuitability, which had now been confirmed, in my judgment, by his forced withdrawal from them."

Also, as I studied Edwards at that critical moment, I simply was not persuaded, even then, that he knew precisely what he was talking about. In particular, I felt he was understating the situation to our detriment, hoping we would go charging into the buzz saw of his creation that he had left behind.

The situation was growing more tense and desperate with each tick of the clock and we had no more time to jaw. We could see the enemy up the hill, they could see us, and they were firing on us with small arms, automatic weapons, and mortars. We had to move out, and fast. Lingering in that place could only mean more casualties.

"Fendy, you and Kotite charge out. The time has come to bite the bullet."

I pointed up to their objectives. As they began to move, enemy fire increased. I could see men go down all across the line as they rushed in leaps and bounds from defilade to defilade. Some I could tell were hit by fire, some merely seeking cover.

Kotite and Fendy were almost constantly exposed and urging their men forward. Their outstanding leadership and forcefulness under fire was an inspiring sight. I had visions of Teddy Roosevelt and his Rough Riders at San Juan Hill, Lord Kitchener at Khartoum, General Santa Ana at the Alamo, the Charge of the Light Brigade in the Crimea War, and other great assaults in history.

As in other great and notable historical charges, neither of my officers flinched or hesitated to command, but continuously urged their men forward and directed fire and movement. Especially effective and admirable were our squad leaders, who, it seemed, tried to perform with no less valor than their commissioned leaders.

I have long maintained that the most challenging assignment given to mankind is that of an infantry squad-leader in combat. Under the harshest and most dangerous conditions of life and death, closer to the enemy than anyone else in the war, he has more men to control than any other leader. Squads normally number about ten to twelve men, or a bit higher, with occasional overstrength. Controlling and directing that number of people when an enemy is shooting deadly weapons at you and trying to kill you is an assignment of staggering immensity.

In theory, platoon leaders have a less challenging role than do the squad leaders. Through, and with the help of, their platoon sergeants, officers have only three squad leaders to command. In practice, however, they may have as many men to control directly as the squad leader because in an actual situation, the NCOs may be less experienced and less aggressive and require more help from their commanders.

No one who has never been in combat can properly appreciate the difficulty of the task assigned to the humble sergeant leading a squad in an infantry company in a fierce tactical situation.

On the morning of our attack at Chipyong, Baker Company's squad leaders were performing magnificently. In about a half-hour, leading elements of the company's attack platoons were near the top of the hills on the southern rim of the perimeter, with their objective almost within grasp. But the enemy fire had reached a peak of intensity. Some of the squads, with only a few men left, were starting to fall apart. Here and there men were pulling back. I could see Chinese coming up out of their holes and charging toward the men in the forward squads. Something had to be done and fast.

I decided it was time to commit the reserve platoon. Earlier it was without a platoon leader, but now it had energetic and daring Hawk Chapman as its new leader, even if only very recently.

Just as I was about to rise and go to the waiting reserve platoon, another shower of mortar rounds landed all around us. Several men were knocked down, and I felt shell fragments tearing through my right pant leg and my waist area. I swore in annoyance. When I felt liquid running down my leg, I concluded I had been hit. Finally my luck had ended.

But the liquid running down my leg was cold. I remember wondering why my blood would be so cold. On the other hand I feared that I knew all too well why it was cold. After all, I felt quite cold myself. I glanced anxiously down at my leg. To my chagrin and relief, I saw that the fragment had only torn the bottom out of my canteen and its cover. The water inside had doused my leg and clothing. But two of the men in company headquarters were not so lucky. They lay bleeding to death from those rounds.

Mendenhall, or Dusseau, nearby, helped me get word to the reserve platoon to join in the attack in the area where our offense was crumbling. By now, we were in very serious difficulty. Our casualties had been heavy and many of the squads were left with only a fraction of the men with which they had started out.

The Price of Victory

I made my way partly up the slope behind our advancing reserve platoon. Bodies of my dead and wounded men were on all sides. Some were pleading for medical help. Others were ominously silent and I knew they were probably dead. I learned that Kotite had lost his platoon sergeant, Gene Nabozny, who had been killed near the top of the hill.

It was about an hour or so after high noon. I crouched in a ravine with some of the company-headquarters personnel and worked on the radio with regiment to see what help we could get. Up ahead the reserve platoon was almost on top of the twin rises that constituted the main objective for us. I could see that they were intermingled with what was left of Kotite's platoon. The high ground was barren in spots, but in some places there was a cover of thin, scrawny, and low trees. The growth provided some cover for the men as they tried to move forward.

"Captain, it looks like we got a real stalemate on our hands!" It was Dusseau. He came running up and slid into my ravine. He had been up with Kotite and Chapman.

"It sure seems so, Dussy," I agreed. "What news from the platoons?"

"Our men are just short of the crest of the hill, and the enemy forces are just a few feet away, over the crest and near the top of the slope on the other, or south, side."

"What are they doing?"

"It's hairy, Captain. They mostly can't see each other, but they know each other are there. They're within a hand grenade's throwing distance and have been doing just that for over an hour."

Just then we reestablished radio contact with the center attacking platoon. The picture could hardly have been more grim. The platoons reported that each time they rose up to charge over the crest, enemy gunfire could cut them down in their tracks. The platoon leaders insisted that further efforts were simply suicidal, and wanted to know what to do.

"Hang on in place," I instructed the platoons. "At least we are denying the enemy any observation of the center of the perimeter and regimental and battalion CPs. Let me see what I can do by way of getting armored or air support."

The platoons answered with their approval, but cautioned against asking for any artillery.

"You don't want artillery?" I asked in disbelief.

"We don't think so," Fendy came back on his radio. "The enemy is so close to us that I fear any rounds aimed at them are sure to fall on us also." Fendy was right and I quickly agreed with him. But perhaps tanks were the answer.

The road south through the perimeter and toward Yoju and the Twin Tunnels was just to our right. It passed through the hills that were our objective and out of the perimeter and through the enemy positions. I figured that if we could get some armor down that road, even a short distance, the tank guns could then swing around and fire on the rear of the enemy troops on the reverse slopes of the hills we were attacking.

Failed Attempt at Tank Support

I radioed regiment and asked if there was any tank support

available. To my delight, regiment said there were plenty of tanks around just looking for missions. I outlines my plan and request. Very soon afterward I saw three tanks in the perimeter valley behind churn out of their positions in a farm field, grind up on the road, and head our way. I sent Dusseau, as I recall, down to the road edge as they approached to outline our plan and their mission and explain what we wanted the tankers to do.

About that time I heard the low rumble of aircraft engines and looked up to see a group of Flying Boxcars approaching from the east. As they arrived over the perimeter, their doors were open. With a slight gunning of engines, one by one their noses tilted upward and the familiar cargo racks rolled out the rear of the fuselages and into the cold February air. Parachutes opened and they drifted into the perimeter—or at least most of them.

Again, as on previous airdrops, some of the chutes went wild and I could see them drift down into enemy-held territory. If this was the vitally needed small-arms and artillery ammunition, I could only hope it did not fit the enemy's guns, or that they too could not reach where it landed.

As the last Boxcar dropped its cargo and cleared the area, my attention turned again to the predicament of my company, and specifically to the progress of the tanks. I watched as they approached the cut in the hills where the road passes through. Just a little further I thought, and they will be in a position to open fire with their turret cannon and machine guns and the enemy resistance on our front will crumble. The lead tank had passed into the cut and out of my sight when I suddenly heard an ear-jolting explosion. I saw a column of gray and dusty smoke rise above the hill behind which I knew the lead tank to be.

Instantly I knew with a sinking heart what had happened. The other two tanks had ground to a halt and were backing up. The lead tank had hit a land mine in the road. Apparently the Chinese, during the earlier hours of the siege, had slipped in and planted antitank mines under the cover of darkness. Thus ended our best-laid plans for armored support to help reduce the enemy to our front. Other than the road, there was no means of getting the tanks into a firing position. The hills on each side, up which we were trying to advance, were simply too steep for armored vehicles to negotiate.

But there was a ray of hope. I was advised that an air strike had been requested and was expected at any minute. I expressed joy, but also apprehension. I asked regiment if it was advisable to have an air strike on enemy forward-troops when they were almost in eyeball-to-eyeball contact with our own friendly forces.

"Not to worry," the regimental staff officer said. "The pilots have been well briefed on your location, and the air force ground-control officers are right here and will be in continuous radio contact with the planes." With that I had to be content, but I remained wary.

Air Strike at Baker Company's Fingertips

I had barely gotten off the radio when I heard the whine of fighter jets. They circled the area a couple of times, then dropped down to come in low from the west with the sun to their rear and in the enemy's eyes. The chatter of their machine guns was a deafening and frightening sound. I was so grateful they were aiming at the enemy and not us. That was one great advantage and relief in the Korean War. I don't recall that we ever had enemy air to contend with. We could hear the planes' bullets tearing into the earth just over the hill in front.

We stayed low and hugged the ground, fearful that stray rounds might not stay on the other side of the crest, where the enemy was. But they did, and the planes, close as their impact area was, did not endanger my men, except for one napalm drop.

Napalm is an oily mass that explodes and burns as it spreads itself over a wide area of the ground upon impact. Globs of the burning mess can splatter over a wide area. It burns hot, reaching searing temperatures.

Napalm is a particularly nasty and controversial weapon. Some people have wanted it banned, but it is more effective in reducing enemy resistance in bunkers and caves than most any other weapon. At one point, some of the burning napalm bounced over the crest and was blazing throughout a Baker squad position. Some small amounts landed on the clothing of a couple of my men. Because of the heavy winter clothing, they were not burned on the skin, and the flames were doused. But they had a frightening experience from it and for some weeks afterward would not surrender their burnt clothing as they proudly showed off their "battle scars."

The air strike ended at about 1500 hours and I ordered the platoons to resume their attack. They did, and this time were able to pass over the crest and occupy the high positions where the enemy troops had been. The enemy dead littered the area. Some were charred from the napalm, although most napalm had landed further down the slopes and as far as the valley at the bottom.

By 1600 hours the combat situation was considerably more rosy. We had consolidated our positions and were in firm control of the high ground. There was no longer any enemy there who could observe the interior of the perimeter or who constituted a threat to its security. Down the slopes toward the enemy main territory, scattered groups of enemy troops could be seen or heard, but they were clearly disorganized and were trying to withdraw as best and fast as they could.

5th Cavalry Relief Column Breaks Through

Just as the sun was setting, we looked out and could see the leading elements of the 5th Cavalry Task Force about a thousand yards away. Lucky for them, I reflected, that we were where we were on the high ground overlooking their approach to the perimeter. If we were not on that ground, the task force could hardly have approached and entered the perimeter without devastating casualties, if at all.

Within minutes the lead vehicles of the 5th Cavalry passed through the gap to our right and into the perimeter.

A little before midnight, my radio crackled with a message from regiment. I was told to withdraw from my positions, that 2d Battalion would take over, and that I was to rejoin my battalion. The battle of Chipyong-ni, the high-water mark for the Chinese Communist Forces and the turning point of the Korean War, was over.

Aftermath of a Decisive Battle

It had been a tough day for Baker Company of the 23rd Regiment. We retook the key ground breached by the enemy. We closed again the perimeter ring on the south edge. But the cost to Baker Company was ghastly. We had suffered over 50 percent casualties. Two of my officers had been wounded; all four of my platoon sergeants had been either wounded or killed. But still, we had accomplished our mission and had played a most decisive role in one of the two or three most critical battles of the entire war. Had we not reoccupied the positions lost by the 2d Battalion, I believe the outcome of the battle, if not of the entire war, would have been profoundly different.

"So you are saying that Baker Company did reoccupy all of the 2d Battalion positions?" Ryan challenged.

"No, actually, not quite. We did not go down the forward slope of the hill and completely reoccupy every position formerly occupied by the ousted troops of the 2d Battalion. Some were far down the hill, and in fact too far to be of any significant value or defensive need. Some should have never been occupied at all, unless only for outpost and early-warning purposes, with the intent of vacating them in event of a major enemy thrust. We were able to work our way to few of those, nor did we particularly try.

Baker Company did occupy all the ground along the high ridgeline, contrary to any assertions otherwise by anyone.

"And you think that of critical importance?" Ryan persisted.

"Absolutely. We can't say that the occupation of those positions, unless improved, would have withstood additional enemy attacks, since none were made. But our presence there denied their use to the enemy and eliminated a major and crucial threat to the defense of the perimeter. With the enemy in our positions, complete surveillance of the perimeter's interior would have been in their grasp. The enemy could bring precision fire to bear on our command and support facilities, and they could have infiltrated at their pleasure and attack our frontline units from the rear. Under those conditions, continued defense would have been all but impossible. To this day, no one seems to have known that fact."

"Why do you think no one realizes the role Baker Company played in the Chipyong-ni engagement?" my historian guest and quizzer wanted to know.

"Because it is hardly dealt with in any detail, or correctly, if at all, in any historical or other document that I have been able to locate in some rather persistent research."

Even our own regimental command report barely mentions Baker Company's participation. There are only a couple of short entries: "Heavy small-arms and automatic weapons fire from the reverse slopes of 'B' Company's objective prevented them from taking and holding the position," and after describing the air attack it states the raid "routed the enemy and enabled 'B' Company to proceed to their objective."

In other writings, Baker Company was either omitted entirely from mention or its activities were completely understated. No less an accomplished and scholarly author than Clay Blair, in his *The Forgotten War*, incorrectly wrote: ". . . Freeman committed his last infantry reserve, B Company, to the 2/23 sector. Going into battle hurriedly and piecemeal, it was unable to restore the 2/23 positions."*

"And you maintain this is an incorrect assessment?" Ryan asked.

"Well, not entirely, I suppose. Literally, we did not restore all the 2d Battalion's positions. As I say, we did not occupy those remotely down the forward slopes that I considered not important or critical at the moment to a successful defense of the ridge. But in substance, Blair's statement is without merit and incorrect."

"To what do you attribute these oversights? Are you suggesting commanders and historians have had ulterior motives with respect to recognizing Baker Company's true battle contribution?"

"By no means. I am not saying that the world is out to get Baker Company, except perhaps for Colonel Edwards, the 2d Battalion commander. I would suggest that anything he may have said or written about the incident that downplayed, incorrectly represented, or omitted our contribution, could have been motivated by a guilt complex or self-justification over the failure of his unit to hold, or retake, his defensive positions.

"Otherwise, I imagine, that in the haste of developments of major scope, and preoccupation of higher leaders some distance away and mostly out of sight and sound, there was just simply a lack of realization of what was happening in our relatively small combat area, or its critical importance to the survival of the perimeter combat-team."

In fairness, other points concerning the general ignorance of Baker Company's role at Chipyong should be documented. As we

* Blair, *The Forgotten War*, p. 701.

were at our most delicate point of the attack, around noon and shortly thereafter, bristling activity was occurring all around. I doubt it was possible for higher headquarters staff to keep an eye only on us, even if they had been disposed to do so. I stressed this to Ryan. Higher commanders and their staffs were reeling, for sure, over the disappointing failure of one of the battalions to hold its positions on the line.

Also, concurrently with the Baker counterattack, there was a major airdrop, and an air strike, in the process of arrangement and implementation. Efforts were required to establish and maintain meaningful communications with a relief column attempting to fight its way northward to the Chipyong perimeter.

On top of these developments, a major sister engagement was underway off the right around Wonju. All these circumstances combined were enough, apparently, to overshadow and eclipse our frenzied and costly activities, no matter how important and essential they were to the survival of the perimeter force. In the confusion and aftermath, our efforts have escaped the attention of about everyone except those of us who were there and personally involved in the southern slopes that cold and sunny and desperate day in mid-February 1951.

The record needs now, better late than never, to be set straight, in the event that anyone ever hereafter cares. Hopefully, this narrative might accomplish that purpose.

"But isn't it really the 5th Cavalry Task Force that is entitled to the credit for saving the 23rd RCT at Chipyong? Or the air strike by the tactical command?" my interrogator persisted.

"Certainly those two events deserve great credit, and I would not detract from their contribution in any way. We were all grateful to the people involved, and enthusiastically welcomed them over and into the perimeter. But I must stress most strongly the critical timing involved in the arrival of both, and especially the armored task force.

"It is well recorded in numerous places that the 5th Cavalry had been meeting continuous and stiff enemy resistance all along its way north to us. By early afternoon it was still several miles away and moving at a snail's pace. Casualties were heavy. It seemed highly unlikely that the column could reach the perimeter before dark, and particularly if the enemy along its path continued in strength and maintained its ferocious defense."

When Baker troops pushed over the crest in midafternoon, however, the enemy forces fell rapidly back and began to dissolve throughout the area. I think it is indisputable that this melting of the enemy to our south, and directly in the path of the approaching armored force, is the only reason that the force reached us by dark. But let's carry the scenario one step further, and consider what would have most surely have happened had we not hammered our way up to the southern ridge and routed the enemy forces there.

With the arrival of darkness at the end of that third day of the Chipyong siege, and with the enemy still on the high ground of the southern rim of the circle, the approaching armored column most certainly would not have been able to enter the perimeter. No sensible tank commander is going to take a column of tanks through a narrow pass with the ground on both sides held by hostile forces, unless he in desperation and with no other recourse is trying to escape, as in the gauntlet at Kunu-ri earlier. It would be folly and suicidal, especially in the dark.

But consider now the probable course of action the enemy, under cover of darkness, would have taken had their troops still held the high ground on the southern side of the perimeter. There would have been nothing to stop them from pouring through like water from a broken dam. I think it clear, again beyond any doubt whatever, that had they poured into the perimeter, the defenders would not have been able to cope with an enemy to their rear who was vastly superior in numbers. The outcome of Chipyong would not have been successful for us. I've made this point before, but it merits repeating.

There may be those who would disagree with that conclusion but if so, let them come forward. I would be keenly interested in hearing their rationale.

"So Baker Company won the battle of Chipyong mostly by itself?"

"Hah, but no. Of course you are needling me now, Mr. Ryan. I've said no such thing and have not meant even to imply it. I'm simply trying to include in the record that which is missing, but should not be, for the sake of historical accuracy. I'm well aware that within the depths of perhaps every combat veteran lurks the subconscious dream that he won the war, or a major engagement, or nearly so, all alone, or substantially alone. At least he likes to think he made a worthwhile contribution and did not fight or sacrifice in vain."

I don't suggest that Baker Company of the 23rd fought any better than any other unit in that painful and mostly thankless struggle.

I do contend, however, and most strongly, that Baker contributed in a most essential and commendable way in two of the most decisive engagements of the war, at Kunu-ri and Chipyong, by being in those critical spots at those critical times. I also maintain that had Baker Company not performed reliably on both, or either, of those occasions, the whole course of the war would have taken an entirely and disastrously different turn.

Sadly though, in my judgment, these facts have not been known or recorded to date, which I think is a travesty on the actions of my brave men who took part. Nor do I claim personal credit to any important degree. I was there in command, but on neither occasion was it necessary for me to individually engage in enemy contact, except for in self-defense from time to time.

Stinginess in Combat Awards

The room fell silent. Ryan and I took a break. Outside my Arlington, Virginia, home, we could hear the whine of traffic on nearby I-395, the major road into the nation's capital from Richmond and the South. Across the highway were the rolling links on the golf course of the privately owned Army-Navy Country Club. Just outside the entrance were the lower-income Nauke and Shirlington neighborhoods and the locations of Arlington's main drug-dealing activities. A string of sirens and honking fire engines went by, indicating another accident on the interstate, a regular occurrence. As the sirens faded into the distance, Ryan returned us to Korea, so far away, and to the war there in the remote past.

"To what extent were your men decorated for their action at Chipyong-ni?" Ryan next asked me.

"Glad you asked," I said with not a little satisfaction. "This brings me to another bone of contention that I have harbored and complained about through two wars. It involves the difficulty, in too many instances, of a commander in his efforts to adequately reward his men for acts of merit and heroism. In my experience it has always been an uphill climb and a frustrating experience."

I then proceeded to give vent to this matter, which has long annoyed me. My feeling was that our day of attack at Chipyong was a walk through the corridors of hell. Anyone there who survived, or didn't, was due special thanks and praise, even if their individual acts could not be characterized as extraordinary or unusually remarkable. Just being there was enough to merit special attention. Many who did perform exceptionally well deserved special treatment and higher recognition.

Although it was extremely difficult to find the time and wherewithal to honor our troops in the height of a war, I and many another commander spent long hours, by candlelight and otherwise, writing up officers and senior NCOs for awards. I did so after Chipyong. I pressed my subordinates to do likewise for all their men of whose activities I was not always personally or directly aware.

I recommended all the officers, senior NCOs, and many others for Silver Stars, for "gallantry in action," some posthumously. Three officers and some NCOs I also recommended for the higher Distinguished Service Crosses (DSCs) for "extraordinary heroism in action." The DSC recommendations were all knocked down to Silver Stars by the division awards-committee, except the one for Lieutenant Kotite. He received his and was written up, deservedly, in *Newsweek* magazine. For all the remainder of the company, at considerable personal effort, I recommended Bronze Star medals.

The Bronze Star is awarded for simple "meritorious service" and in combat it can be awarded with a "V" for valor. Its about the least a commander can do for a man who has experienced a frightful period in combat. The Bronze Star is relatively new among military awards and dates from World War II. It was then established as a sort of army counterpart to the air force medal, which was routinely awarded to flight crews or pilots for five combat missions, whether or not engagements with the enemy took place. It was never intended that a candidate for a Bronze Star must have moved heaven and earth to earn the award; simply that he serve "with merit."

Herein lies my complaint. To me there could be no doubt that my men served at Chipyong, and that they did so with merit by merely being there under those horrendous conditions of death and destruction. It doesn't matter if they did not do anything particularly unusual or out of the ordinary. If they were not more highly decorated, I felt they should receive Bronze Stars as an absolute minimum and I recommended it for all members of the company who were not otherwise recommended for a higher award.

"But the awards were not granted?"

"That's right, and to my great irritation and disappointment. I even made a trip back to the division's rear echelon later to argue most vehemently for the awards, but to no avail. When my commanders heard about my effort, which involved going over their heads without their knowledge or approval, they hit the ceiling and let me know how angry they were in no uncertain terms. I didn't really care. I was furious. I raged at the panel members I could locate and accused them of living in a world of fantasy and of being callous and ignorant of the world of the combat soldier."

"But it didn't get you anywhere with them?"

"Not at all. They were firm and would not yield. They insisted that my recommendations were insufficient when they did not spell out in precise detail exactly what the candidate for the award had done on the field of battle."

"And you think they were too rigid in their application of the regulations?"

"Clearly. Beyond dispute!"

"Why were they that way, in your opinion?"

"Good question, and a hard one to answer with certainty. We can't go into the heads or minds of the men on the award panels to see what they were thinking. I'm sure other divisions, or award panels, had the same problems. Part of the answer must lie in the fact that the rear-echelon award-committees were, and are, usually comprised of officers from units nearby, which usually means service outfits such as ordnance, quartermaster, signal, and so forth. They are the men who are available and at hand."

Combat officers are up front with their units and not around the rear to sit on award panels. So recommendations are acted upon by people, through no fault of their own, mind you, who have not lived through the conditions experienced by the men whose services they are evaluating. They do not recognize, I suppose, that any doubts as to the eligibility of a trooper for an award should be resolved in favor of the candidate.

Award-panel members, not being people, ordinarily, with frontline combat experience, also cannot well understand that for every incident where a commander can learn of and write up a trooper for an award, there are probably many other incidents that go un-recorded and unrecognized. Many acts of heroism and good perfor-mance are simply not witnessed. Even if they are, commanders seldom have enough time and opportunity in rapidly moving and cramped combat conditions to stop and write up all deserving men for awards for each and every act deserving attention. Moreover, witnesses, as the days pass, and casualties occur, may simply evaporate from the scene.

All of this means, in my judgment as a combat commander with not a little experience, that when a trooper is considered for an award, every effort should be made to insure that it gets favorable action by rear-echelon panel-members. Their time should not be consumed trying to find reasons for not granting the award, as I feel has too often been the case, specifically for my Baker Company in Korea. I think the public is, for the most part, totally unaware of this aspect of military operations in wartime.

Too often one may see a military man walking around with a chest full of ribbons and the folks on the homefront have doubts as to whether he has properly earned them all. My feeling is that if he is a high-ranking member, some skepticism may well be in order.

If, however, the decorated serviceman seen walking down a street back home is an enlisted man, or a lower-grade officer from the combat branches, it is far more likely that the ribbons for awards on his uniform are but a small fraction of the ones he should be wearing if he were to receive full recognition for everything he did during his combat service.

I would like to think that more people on the homefront realize and appreciate this fact and how underdecorated, and not over-decorated are the combat-branch junior officers and enlisted men who have fought this nation's wars.

CHAPTER ELEVEN

The UN Takes the Offensive— Operation "Killer"

"Pratt, we've got some good news and some bad news for you. Which would you like first?"

I looked up from my can of C rations at the company CP in some shells of burned-out Korean huts. Standing above me was none other than my glorious leader and battalion commander, Maj. George Russell.

We were bivouacked on the outskirts of Chipyong, nursing our wounds and trying to get reorganized with equipment and personnel replacements.

"Gee, I don't know, Sir," answered I. "Let's try for the good news first. Seems to me we could use some large doses of that."

"OK. Here 'tis. We're going to continue the advance northward and pursue the enemy."

I gazed at Russell for a prolonged moment. Was he serious, or was he engaging in a bit of levity?

"That's the good news?" I asked incredulously.

"Sure is," Russell answered quickly and with obvious conviction.

"Perhaps you could explain to this poor misguided soul why, after the torture we have just been through, it is good news that we are going to continue the same? Is this a case of welcoming pain because it feels so good when it stops?"

Russell ignored my last observation.

"Well, we must get this war over so we can all go home. Isn't that great news in the long run?"

"Perhaps," I conceded, "but that's the long run. Not now. And why us? We aren't the only ones in this damned war."

"No, but it's not just us. The whole UN command is going to launch a general offensive northward, now that we have shown the Chinese are little more than a paper tiger."

I studied Russell for additional moments. I was far from agreeing with his paper-tiger observation. Nor was I able to determine the depth of his sincerity. He had a most engaging sense of humor and appearance with his handlebar moustache and usual cigar.

Russell also had only recently assumed command of the battalion with the departure of Hutchin and probably would not look with disdain upon additional experience as a combat-battalion commander and—who knows?—probably a promotion to light colonel. Still, it was hard for me to imagine that even he would be bubbling over with enthusiasm at the prospect of more painful days or weeks of close and bloody combat with a determined enemy in midwinter.

"So the high command isn't prone to letting well enough alone and sitting tight where we are?"

"By no means," said Russell. "General Ridgway is delighted with our stand at Chipyong and Wonju and now wants to push northward to prove the UN capability to eject the Communists from South Korea."

"Then what is the bad news?"

"The bad news is that when we jump off tonight and move out to find the enemy, the 2d Battalion will lead off the attack."

"That's the bad news? Why is that such bad news?"

"Because it means that our battalion will not be center stage—we will have to forfeit that honor to another battalion."

"And that's bad news?"

"Of course. We should be permitted to continue and defend our outstanding battle record."

At this point I simply decided to give up trying to figure out whether my commander was serious or had tongue in cheek. I wasn't sure I could handle whatever conclusion I would reach. As Russell turned away, he told me to make ready and stand by for march orders that would be forthcoming shortly after dark. I could hardly wait with breathless anticipation.

Turning Point of the War

There can be but little doubt, if any, that the battles of Chipyong-ni and Wonju in middle February 1951 marked the high-water mark of the Korean War on the ground following the Chinese intervention. The period just after also marked a turning point in the direction and future of the overall struggle. We were to see big things take place.

The Truman–MacArthur Confrontation

A casual stroll through the pages of any world or Korean history book will reveal that it was then in the late winter of 1950–51 that the confrontation between President Truman and General MacArthur took place. It reached its bursting point with the firing, or relief, of the general in mid-April and his return to the States with all the ticker-tape parades in San Francisco and New York, and his famous "ole soldiers never die" farewell speeches to the Congress and elsewhere.

The arguments for and against the relief of MacArthur are many and complex, and are well spelled out in many places. I think repetition or detailed elaboration here is beyond the scope of my interview with the Eighth Army historian or this narrative, even if I had the knowledgeability and background to do so, which I do not claim to have.

We can simply say briefly and in passing that General MacArthur and his president and commander in chief did not see eye-to-eye in the conduct of the fighting in Korea. MacArthur wanted to widen the war and complained constantly of the restrictions placed upon him by the president and the GHQ in the Pentagon and Washington.

MacArthur wanted far more troops, to bomb Manchurian bases of the Communist Chinese, to blockade the China coast, to bring up a hundred thousand or so troops of the Chinese Nationalists on Formosa, and to undertake certain other measures to intensify the effort to achieve total victory. MacArthur had spent much of his life in the Far East, had led us to victory in World War II in the Pacific, and believed the center of the planet was, and is, there, insofar as American defense and other interests were concerned. Many Americans agreed with him then, and do to this date.

Truman and many of his advisors did not agree with MacArthur. They wanted to end the fighting, through diplomatic or political means, if possible. They feared Russian intervention and World War III. They were concerned about our allies and their fears of an escalation in the fighting in Korea and the curtailment of even the previous little support we were then receiving from them in Korea.

NATO in Europe was just getting underway, the Berlin airlift had barely ended, and the cold war was in full swing. Europe was held in higher priority, Germany had not raised its twelve divisions for NATO, and any increase of effort in Korea could only be at the expense of our effort in Europe, so the antiexpansion argument went.

As is recorded, General MacArthur continued to complain publicly to House Speaker Martin and others and finally Truman made the decision to remove MacArthur. Secretary of the Army Frank Pace, who happened to be in the Far East at the time on an inspection trip, was assigned the job of informing the general, but through a leak it hit the press shortly before he did, and another controversy was created. Truman was accused of insensitivity by relieving the general without first informing him.

General Ridgway was sent from the Eighth Army to replace MacArthur, and General James Van Fleet came out to replace Ridgway as army commander. Just after Chipyong we were to see Ridgway's Operations "Ripper" and "Killer" (later renamed "Courageous" for more public palatability) get underway.

The Front Lines in Spring 1951

By the end of February, our forces would occupy a line running roughly along the south bank of the Han River at Seoul and eastward across Korea, well below the 38th parallel, through Yangpyeong, Hoengsong, and then upward to the east coast just north of Kangnung. Objective lines of "Idaho" running northeast of Seoul toward the parallel, and "Topeka" and "Kansas" just below and above the parallel across most of Korea, and "Wyoming" well into North Korea, were to show up on our tactical maps.

At that time, the Eighth Army was spread out across Korea with the I Corps on the west around Inch'on and Seoul with its 3rd and 25th infantry divisions and the Brits, Turks, and Canucks. To their east was the IX Corps with its 1st Cavalry and 24th Infantry divisions and ROK divisions. We in the X Corps, with our own 2d Infantry Division, and some ROK divisions, and the marine division down south in reserve around some bypassed North Koreans, occupied the front up to the stretch along the most mountainous east coast. That area, about fifteen miles or so in width, was assigned to several ROK corps.

2d Division Springtime Activities

"And how did your own 23rd Regiment and 2d Division fit into this big picture in the period?" Ryan asked.

"In the days immediately after Chipyong, the Chinese pulled back slightly and, we assumed, licked their wounds. In many ways, so did we."

Two days after Chipyong, as Russell had indicated to me at our "good news, bad news" conference, our battalion patrolled just north and ran into a fire fight on some hills overlooking the small village of Wolpa. We had several casualties in Baker Company there. We also spent some more cold and miserable nights on windswept knobs. On February 20, the regiment was reassigned far to the east and south and we closed into an assembly area on the outskirts of the town of Nodong-ni, north of Chech'on and about fifteen miles southeast of Wonju.

Except for a couple of weeks in late March in a rest area near the

Airdrop of supplies to the 23rd Reg. combat team at Chipyong-ni that was surrounded and cut off from the main Eighth Army forces for five days.

Hordes of fleeing Korean civilians pouring through the author's company positions in central Korea. Such refugees usually signaled the enemy attack.

small town of Singyang Dong about five miles northeast of Wonju, we were to spend the next couple of months slowly struggling northward up to and across the parallel in the Hwach'on Reservoir area.

The 2d Division, as well as other combat units, was to find in that fighting phase that the terrain was an even more challenging opponent than the enemy forces. There were to be stiff fights at times, and more casualties, but I think most veterans would remember more the punishing terrain and environmental conditions under which we had to fight and move.

In March and April in Korea, spring was arriving and the rains came in torrents. Roads, or trails, turned to mud and swamps, and vehicle passage became nearly impossible. Streams flooded and bridges washed out, slowing supplies and fire support. Up high in the mountains, where we mostly were sent, we were far removed, and had little hope of rapid or adequate resupply in the event that we became heavily engaged.

Security and survival of forward units isolated by flooded streams depended not only on the enemy's activity and perseverance, but even more on the ability of our own native pack columns to locate us on some remote hilltop. Often, in the hours required to backpack supplies, we would have moved on ahead and the supplies would arrive, not where we were, but where we had last been.

Ridges and Mountaintops

For us the fighting deep in eastern Korea in those spring weeks of 1951 was a war of ridges and hilltops, and canyons and crests, and hours from bases and supply routes, and in rainy, muddy, restrictive, and miserable weather.

On February 20 Generals Mark Clark and Ned Almond visited our regimental CP as our lst Battalion was moving out in the attack. Two days later, on Washington's birthday, we were starting the long, tedious ascent to the high, rough, and rugged terrain north of the town of Chuchon-ni, almost fifteen miles due east of Wonju. By night we had limped onto and closed on our objective, Hill 642, with no enemy contact. The troops were exhausted, weary, and hungry. The night and following day passed without food or resupply. We were outrunning the backpack columns.

Two days later the picture brightened somewhat as we began to descend into the valley through which the Korean Highway 42 runs east and west. We took up defensive positions on the lower hills overlooking the village of Ungyo-ri. There we were within sight of the road and were able to be resupplied. During the pause, I hotfooted over to the nearby battalion CP. I was eager to learn as much as I could about the tactical situation.

"Did you?" Ryan asked.

"Somewhat, but not much to my satisfaction."

As always in combat, keeping up with developments was a challenge. I did spot Sammy Radow and the battalion commander at the CP around the map boards. I was worn out, frustrated, and impatient, and probably a bit on the insubordinate side. I had been catching flak from my troops who were at a loss as to the need or purpose of our tiring ordeal and I needed to vent my feelings somewhere, or on someone.

Always Take and Hold the High Ground

"Major," I said with obvious indignation, "just what the hell are we suppose to be accomplishing, traipsing over these mountains like a bunch of boy-scout campers?"

George Russell needed a shave like all the rest of us. He too looked weary and much the worse for wear. His scraggly whiskers almost blended out his neatly trimmed and usually dominant moustache. He slowly removed his cigar and gazed calmly at me for a moment. Then, in an almost fatherly manner and with the air of a patient commander burdened with weak and faithless helpers, he answered me.

"Not sure what you mean, Pratt. I didn't assign the objectives. I just work here too, and do what I'm told." I didn't miss his implication that perhaps I should do the same.

"Of course we will also do as we are told, Sir," I responded, backtracking a bit and readjusting the chip on my shoulder. "But can you shed any light on why we are scouting ridgetops where there are no enemy and exhausting our troops so unnecessarily? Is this simply an exercise in mountain climbing, testing just how much our troops can take?"

"Higher-ups didn't know those mountains were unoccupied by the enemy, Pratt," Radow joined in. "And don't gripe too soon—the next ones may be so loaded you will wish you were back on the last ones."

"But wouldn't we be better utilized if we controlled the valleys, towns, and roadnets and left the mountaintops to the enemy? In those remote and isolated hell spots we're at a big disadvantage. Even if we run into the enemy and get in a fire fight, we will run out of ammo with little hope of resupply. We are fighting where we are weakest and the enemy is strongest. Doesn't make sense to me."

"You may have a point, Pratt," Russell said, "but how would we be secure if the enemy held all the high ground? That's against every basic principle of ground warfare we've ever been taught. Have you thought that one out?"

"I know the high ground is a must, as a general rule. But does that mean we have to occupy Mount Everest? Every principle has its limits. Some high ground can be more of a burden than a benefit. That's all I am saying."

"And you think the high ground we have been on is not a benefit?"

"If it is, I sure as hell don't see how."

"But high ground is necessary for observation and surveillance."

"It is if it's not so remote that it can't be used for observation. Even if we were on it, miles up there in the clouds, we couldn't keep the enemy from using this road and valley. The lower hills we are on now make sense to me. But not those pinnacles in the sky. Our tanks can't accompany us. The forward areas most often are beyond the range of our own supporting artillery. And, worst of all, our troops are so restricted by fatigue and demoralization that they cannot put up their best effort."

"Well," said Russell, "I'll remember how you feel and pass it along to the regimental commander, but Colonel Chiles just took over a few days ago, as you know. I'm not sure he will want to go complaining to Ruffner that his company commanders are dissatisfied with the division or corps commanders' tactical decisions."

Some days later when I ran into Sammy Radow in the battalion sector, I asked him if Major Russell had passed along my criticisms about our tactical methods.

"I don't think so, Pratt," answered Sammy. "At least not just yet. Surely you can see that it is not very easy for him to do so, for the reason he told you the other day. But he will if the right opportunity comes along. We both think you have some good points."

With that I had to be content, I concluded. No doubt Russell also had other things on his mind. No commander is ever enthusiastic about complaining juniors who gripe about their missions. So my complaints were sure to be off for a poor beginning, even had the battalion commander agreed with me, which I suspected he did more than he wanted to say. Russell was no dummy. He knew his battalion could not fight its best on a remote mountaintop. But he too had a limit on what he could do about it.

In the following weeks, the tactics used and loyalty to the classic military-school solution of occupying the high ground did not change as we advanced on and on. All the way to Heartbreak Ridge, the Punch Bowl, the Iron Triangle, and other engagements, at least in central Korea, it seemed to me the war was prosecuted under conditions where we were weakest and the enemy the strongest.

I was not of the opinion that the war was best fought as we were then fighting it. I thought it was unnecessarily punishing and costly to our forces. We had the modern firepower and fire support and armored strength, and could have fought a modern, highly mobile kind of warfare, but did not. Our leaders chose to engage the enemy on his ground, where his more primitive army was strongest and we were weakest.

"But you don't argue with the basic concept that control of high and dominating terrain usually determines the outcome of a battle, do you?" again asked Ryan the historian.

"No, up to a point. The importance of controlling the high ground is fundamental, but provided it is high ground that can be used to your advantage.

High Ground at Gettysburg

"Didn't possession of the high ground at Gettysburg play an important part in the Union victory in July 1863?" Ryan asked me.

"Absolutely, it did. The Union forces of General Meade were spread all along the high ridge and up to and including Little Round Top. But it should be remembered that Meade's generals did not place much importance on the highest ground at Gettysburg, the Big Round Top, but occupied Little Round Top instead. They concluded, and rightly, that the highest ground is not necessarily essential to dominate the battleground especially if it is so massive and remote as to be beyond practical use or value."

"And you think the generals and their tacticians in Korea did not realize that?"

"That's right, I think they did not, and their error caused great suffering and misery on the part of the troops who paid the price for those decisions."

"Why do you think those mistakes were made?"

"Another interesting question. I've never presumed to know the answer. We argued it from time to time in various forums at the infantry school and elsewhere in bull sessions. I don't fault the sincerity, of course, of anyone who holds the view contrary to mine. In fact, I'm probably in a tiny and unpopular minority among small-unit military tacticians. Nevertheless, I hold to my convictions that those tactics in Korea were a mistake. The recent *Blitzkrieg* generals of Germany would never have used them, and I think we must admit that 'ole' Hitler's generals did win some key battles, at least earlier in the war, before he began to substitute his will for that of his professional army leaders."

Fortunately, the misguided, burdensome, and painful mountain tactics of which I complained were not used throughout Korea. And there are other vets of the war who can also, and perhaps better, respond to these points. In the western areas of the I and IX corps, for example, the terrain was less mountainous, and there was probably not much occasion to position troops or units in high, isolated mountains. I'm under the impression that there they made much better use of the armor and support fire and did not position infantry units very much in places where they were beyond reach.

Generals Up Front in Korea

Ryan again was in deep thought and scribbling madly. "Were these practices of assigning infantry positions in too-remote places, which you think was a tactical mistake, made at all levels of command?"

"Here again, I doubt I am in a position to comment responsibly on that question. Ordinarily, an infantry battalion or company objective would be determined at the regimental level, and certainly not higher than the division level. But as we know, in Korea, at that period in 1951, we had army and corps commanders who distinguished themselves for personal involvement in the fighting at the very lowest levels, so it is hard to say just at what level the decisions were made."

Stories are told of how often and closely General Ridgway monitored the frontline activities of combat troops. He flew directly over the positions, sometimes landing right in a battalion or company area. The "Big A" did the same, and, as I said earlier, it was not surprising to see either materialize out of the mists or around bushes within small-arms fire of enemy positions.

With that kind of close supervision, I would not be surprised to hear from regimental or divisional leaders that very often their company and battalion objectives and routes of advance were determined by the army or corps commanders. To the extent that this is true, then, in my judgment, the errors of forcing troops to needlessly occupy remote and unimportant real estate, with negligible, or no, benefits, at enormous human physical drain, must rest also with the higher-ups.

"And again, why did you think the tacticians, at any level, or all levels, ordered the highest ground to be taken?"

"I guess it stemmed from their training throughout their military careers. An army officer is taught from his earliest days in the academy at West Point, in the ROTCs, and in the branch schools such as the Infantry School, or the Command and Staff College at Fort Leavenworth, that the key to success on the battlefield is taking and holding the high ground."

This writer and combat veteran has not been to all these institutions, but I suppose that in the process, there is no, or too little, emphasis on the question of distinguishing high ground that is critical from ground that is merely high. At the "Advanced Infantry" course at Fort Benning that I did attend, I recall no emphasis on distinguishing between just any high ground and high ground that is critical to success on the battlefield.

The finished product from army tactical schools is too often unable to differentiate between just any high ground and that which is also critical and must be taken and held at all costs.

It is a question of relativity or degree, and our tactical training has not enabled our senior officers to determine just where the proper balance lies. As a consequence, much effort and many resources can be wasted wearing troops down to a pulp on needless pieces of land, the possession of which does not really contribute to victory in battle.

"So your company just went ever forward, occupying the high and noncritical ground?"

"Well, not always, perhaps, but too often so."

Predawn Fire Fight on Hill 1126

An exception to my complaints about the futility of occupying the highest ground, or perhaps proof of my position, since we were on lower ground, occurred in early March.

After a couple of days in defensive positions along the valley overlooking Route 42, which runs from Wonju across the battlefront to the east coast, we crossed the valley and again took to the high mountains. Objectives such as Hills 1126, 801, 884 and others came and went as we pushed ever onward at great effort.

On March 2, my Baker Company was in position about a mile north of Hill 1126 when mortar fire began to fall, at around 0200 hours. I alerted all the platoons and urged maximum care in case of a predawn counterattack. At about 0400 I learned that Able Company on the next rise, some 300 to 400 yards to our left, was under attack. Barely an hour later, small-arms fire broke out also across the Baker Company front.

Within moments, all platoons were heavily engaged, and enemy troops, in the faint early glow of daylight, were prancing all about. Several were in the company CP area and most of us in the CP were firing and being fired upon. After more than two weeks of little or no enemy contact, we were suddenly heavily engaged and fighting for our

The scene at a Baker Co./23rd Reg. central Korea position in early morning following a fierce predawn fire fight.

Warrant Officer Ralph Dusseau and 1st Lt. Jessie Mendenhall (Baker Co./23rd Reg.) at mountaintop blocking position in central Korea, early January 1951.

The "after-battle" scene on Hill 1126 overlooking Korean Route 42 northeast of Wonju. Dark spots in the snow show where artillery shells impacted.

228 DECISIVE BATTLES OF THE KOREAN WAR

lives. I wondered if the platoons had all been overrun and if we were all alone in a classical "Pratt's Last Stand," reminiscent of good "ole" George at the Little Big Horn in 1876.

As daylight increased and our ability to spot and aim at the enemy improved, I was able to determine that my platoons had not been overrun at all. On the contrary, they had held like steel and were very much in place. The enemy troops we saw and killed around the company CP were only a handful who had infiltrated our platoons during the darkness. As the sun rose, the enemy pulled back, as had been their custom more often than not, and calm returned.

During the morning I made an assessment of the engagement. We had only seven or so casualties. Based on conservative counts from the platoons, we estimated that around 400 enemy troops had hit us in that dawn attack, and we counted just under a hundred dead. We estimated that at least twice that number of enemy had been wounded but removed from the battlefield. Also, we knew that many dead would have also been removed, as was the practice of the Chinese. The Chinese always went to great lengths to evacuate their dead. We believed it was more for intelligence purposes to conceal their losses, and thus their weaknesses, than for any compassionate reasons.

The battalion estimate of enemy strength and losses from our Hill 1126 engagement was more conservative. They reported to regiment, and it was included in the command report, that we were hit by 250 troops, and that only ninety-one dead were left behind. This reflected the tendency of higher-level military commands in all wars to tone down claimed combat figures to compensate for exaggeration by lower-echelon units. Still, we felt our count was more accurate.

Novel Resupply Situations

The Korean War not only often presented unique and challenging situations to tacticians, but also to those responsible for resupplying combat troops—activities known as "logistics." One such situation occurred just after Baker Company's predawn fire fight on and around Hill 1126.

As I was shivering in my "accommodations" at the company CP, I heard some thrashing about in the nearby underbrush. Looking up,

I beheld Warrant Officer Dusseau charging toward me. I could see he had something on his mind underneath his grim and disheveled appearance. If ever there was truly a Korean War "GI Willy" à la Bill Mauldin, it was Mr. Dusseau at that moment. He was unshaven, muddy, unwashed, and smelly, to list but a few of his less than socially acceptable features. His eyes were sunken and bloodshot from fatigue and lack of sleep and his uniform was unpressed. I probably would have considered his appearance to be humorous and amusing but for the realization that he could hardly have looked worse than any of the rest of us.

"Captain, we got problems," Dusseau announced with an earth-shattering ring of importance as though he had just invented the wheel.

"Really?" said I drolly, "I would never have known. What would I ever do without the likes of perceptive company officers like you, Mr. Dusseau?"

"No, really, Captain. I mean we have serious problems. I don't see how we are going to get supplied."

"Well, that is your job, isn't it?"

"Oh, yes. I'm not denying that. But I am worried that I am not going to be able to do it. We keep advancing through these mountains and we are outrunning the carrying parties. Every mile we advance adds to the distance the parties must travel to reach us. Each day, they barely reach us before darkness sets in. I don't see how we can continue on this way."

"Have the parties encountered the enemy en route? Any ambushes so far?"

"No. They have been lucky, I guess. But not sure how long the luck will hold out. Awful lot of real estate back behind us between our positions and the supply dumps they leave from. Cruel terrain—and there must be pockets of bypassed enemy—they could be at any bend in the trails."

"So what's to be done, Mr. Dusseau? Call off the war for a while?"

"We wish, don't we? No, I realize that's not in cards, but I think we should explore possible alternative routes to our positions."

"Such as?"

"Well, let's do some skull practice with your maps, *mein Kapitän*. I think I may have an idea. Hand me a beer and show me where we are now."

I ignored his suds remark and reached for my map board. With a couple others around the CP, Dusseau and I went into a huddle. I pointed to our position on the crest of some lower mountains sloping into a valley running across our front.

"What's the road in front of us, Captain?" I was asked.

"That's Road 42."

"And that village out there?"

"I believe that's Ungyo-ri," I answered.

"Notice how Road 42 runs across our front and, a short distance to the west, turns southward and passes through friendly lines." Everyone nodded their understanding.

"Now notice," Dusseau continued, "how it finally connects with the main north–south Wonju-to-Hoengsong road."

"So what's your point?" someone asked Dusseau.

"Well, don't you see?" continued Dusseau. "Since the southern part of the Wonju-Hoengsong road and Road 42, almost to Able Company's positions on our left, are in friendly hands, we could motor our supplies to a location just behind Able Company."

"And then what? Teletype them on into our area? Road 42 passes out of Able's positions and into no-man's-land in front of us. You're not suggesting a motorized column in no-man's-land, are you?"

"No," persisted Dusseau patiently, "but if we could get them that close, surely we could then hand-carry them the few hundred yards on into our positions here."

"Let's see if I understand you, Dusseau," I said, studying the map and stroking my chin in deep thought. "If we got the supplies as far as Able Company's location near the spot where Road 42 passes into no-man's-land and we then hand-carried them, the carrying party would have less than a thousand yards to travel?"

"That's the idea."

"But they would have to pass out in front of Able Company, into no-man's-land, until they reached our front, then they would turn and enter our positions from our front, and not from our rear."

"Right, Captain." Dusseau beamed with pride.

"Well, it sounds like it might work," I said. "But what happens if the party encounters enemy on their last leg as they are out in front of our positions? That could be quite dicey, couldn't it? I suspect that could ruin the day for the carrying party."

"Of course you are right, Captain. But just now there seems to be no contact with the enemy. They don't seem to be out front of us, do they?"

"No, they seem not to be around at the moment. Of course we could always send out a patrol to make sure before the carrying party is due to arrive. But how about coordination with the units on our left? Have you thought of that? Those roads over on the left must already be heavily used for supply lines for other units. You'll need MP clearance?"

"I'll check all that out with battalion and regiment. Look, Captain, this may well be a harebrained idea that could backfire, but I think it's worth a try. Anything is better than our present approach of hand-carrying supplies for hours and hours over the mountains and ridges for great distances from our rear—and at great peril for the carrying parties."

I had to admit that Dusseau made much sense. I agreed with him and gave his plan my OK. And it worked. The supply operation was undertaken as planned and carried off successfully, to the credit of all involved. As an added precaution we sent armed patrols to meet the motorized supply crews and escort the hiking carrying parties into our company areas. Dusseau's ingenious and imaginative approach was one of the many unique supply efforts of the war that, to my knowledge, has never been much publicized, if at all.

In the snug comfort of a rec room after the war is over, such an operation sounds like a snap. But under the stress and strain of the time, the uncertainty of an elusive and cunning enemy, and the burden of ponderous terrain and a threatening environment, it was anything but a leisurely and breezy stroll through the park in the merry month of May, as a certain song goes.

Ridge-running Operation "Killer" Continues

"Did the enemy again attack in your Hill 1126 positions?" historian Ryan wanted to know next.

"Not with any particular intensity. There was some patrolling by both sides, but about that time some major changes were taking place in Operation 'Killer.' "

I did not know it then, but high-level decisions were made to speed up "Killer" and carry UN forces to the 38th parallel. In our corps, our 2d Division was to lead the way as "the point."

Our battalion, along with rest of the 23rd, was pulled off of our positions around Hill 1126 and other positions occupied in the first days of March and we were moved by motor to assembly areas about fifteen miles west near the junction of Highways 42 and 442 at Sangdae-ri. We took over the 3rd ROK Division's zone and we were replaced by the 2d ROK Division.

I think it was about this time I heard that Colonel Chiles had relieved Col. Jim Edwards of the 2d Battalion. The development hit me with mixed emotions. I could not forget the wrongs I felt he had inflicted on my company at Chipyong, and yet I harbored some compassion for the guy. After all, he had quite a distinguished record, with many decorations to his credit. I preferred to believe that any deficiencies in his performance or personality were probably caused by prolonged frontline duty. Sammy, our S-3, told me that Chiles felt the poor guy was just worn out and had to have a break.

From the assembly areas about two miles or so north of Sangdae-ri we jumped off in the attack on March 6. Immediately we started climbing into high, rough mountains again, moving north at first, then northeasterly. My memory is that we met no resistance, and that seems to be borne out by the regiment's command report. Two days later we reached and crossed a valley with a road, if it could be called that, marked 6, and climbed again into the familiar high, desolate, and rugged mountains.

By the eleventh, attacking in a northwesterly direction, we had advanced about five or six miles and reached the valley running across our front from the southwest to the northeast, through which ran a service and farm road 442 to Hoengsong, some ten miles to our southwest.

At that point and time the 23rd was relieved by the 38th Regiment and we were motored over a several-day period to bivouac areas about ten miles southeast of Hoengsong, closing by the fifteenth.

March Bivouac in Reserve

"So the 23rd finally got a break?" Ryan asked. "How long did it last?"

"About two weeks."

"And was this one of the areas where General Almond made his command inspections?"

"Yes it was. You better believe it. We had a bit of a break in the weather. Spring was getting well underway and I remember our March bivouac as a period of generally sunny and warm days."

The 16-mm projectors were broken out, a large squad tent was set up as a "movie house," and the troops were able to see a flick or two. Kitchen crews located their messes in company areas and hot meals were served.

The engineers even arrived with their portable shower units and the men were able to wash normally and with hot water for the first time in weeks. But most important, for sure, to the higher commanders interested in troop readiness to resume the "momentum of the assault," the bivouac provided the opportunity for equipment rehabilitation and replacement. Therein lay the purpose of the command inspection—to see just what equipment was missing, or unserviceable, and needed repair or replacement.

Thus, one of our first orders was to "stand by for command inspections" and frenzied activity was the rule of the days. Company officers and NCOs had their work cut out for them. Equipment inspections were required at pup tents and elsewhere, first by squad leaders, then by platoon leaders, and company commanders.

Unit inspections were only the beginning of the process. Preparation of requisitions for submission to upper echelons then had to be completed by supply sergeants and officers. Busy, busy, busy were the troops, in a so-called rest area.

Following all this, and in time for replacement equipment to arrive, the Big A would come bouncing in with much flourish and fanfare and go marching up and down the ranks to see for himself just how well the unit leaders had done their work.

Always there was anxiety in the air before and during an Almond visit. Officers knew well that heads could roll if the Big A was displeased and, as stated, frantic measures, and sometimes deceptive

Bivouac area of the 1st Bn./23rd Reg. in a valley near Hongch'on in central Korea in midsummer 1951 during a rest period.

The staff of the 1st Bn./23rd Reg. with commander Maj. George Russell kneeling in front row with cane and author on far right.

ones, would be undertaken in efforts to insure that a rosy picture of preparedness was presented to the corps commander.

These were the elements, with all their advantages and shortcomings, of a General Almond command inspection, and they were events to be long remembered by all the participants.

Policing the Battlefield and MSR

While the 23rd was in its bivouac and "rest" area some six miles north of Wonju and southeast of Hoengsong in the last half of March, the regiment was given the job of policing the main supply-route, or MSR.

"What was your reaction to that assignment?" Ryan asked. "And who gave the order?"

"Oh, the order came from the Big A—he had a passion for conservation and reclamation of precious combat supplies."

"And you objected?"

"Not at all. I have always been most disenchanted with the pitiful supply attitude in the American army. In World War II, anywhere I fought, one could always tell where the Americans had been, as distinguished from other countries' armies, by the messy and littered battlefields."

Our national wastefulness has carried over into our military from when GI Joe left the farm or the city with very little dedication to conservation. Everyone knows it, and it had become not only a shameful disgrace, but also a combat liability of major proportions. "Big A" was one top general who also knew it, but, unlike many others, he set out to doing something about it.

General Almond required units in reserve, among other tasks, to scour the battlefields in search of useable American, or UN, military equipment. In the case of the 2d Division, the companies took turns roaming up and down the main roads and known bivouac or fighting areas and gathered up anything of possible use. Trucks would return to supply centers with oil drums, ammo crates, discarded clothing, and even small arms and other weapons. These were collected and reconditioned for re-use. I was not exactly an Almond fan, but I have always given him much credit for his supply discipline and salvage efforts.

"And did the troops accept General Almond's salvage program?"

"I think there was general approval. I don't recall any griping about it, unless a trooper was personally inconvenienced by having to leave his dugout or tent on a cold, windy, or rainy day to roam up and down a road or paddy. Some troops were warmly enthusiastic, others probably quite indifferent. GIs mostly do what they are told and are cooperative unless the task is so patently ridiculous as to generate reluctance or opposition."

"You say that salvage items even included abandoned weapons?"

"Oh yes, and often in staggering quantities."

"Why so?"

"Well, as I say, many soldiers are, or were in Korea, simply careless or unwise and left various items laying around when they moved out. They could be so worn out they were unwilling or unable to carry their full load, and to ease their burdens they would shed equipment along the way. Very often they would later regret it when they needed that extra pair of dry socks, blanket, or can of rations and did not have it."

By far, I think one can safely say that the biggest cause of equipment losses that necessitates energetic salvage operations where possible, is normal combat operations. A machine-gun or recoiless-rifle position is hit and the crew is wiped out. The dead or wounded are evacuated as the unit withdraws, leaving the weapons behind simply because there is no one to carry them. If the ground is later retaken, and the enemy did not elect, or have a chance, to take possession, the weapon may still be there and accessible for salvage.

Also, one must not overlook the mountains of equipment, weapons, vehicles, and other major items left behind by the ROK divisions in their numerous and almost, at times, routine bugout flights. By and large we were quite happy with the performance of the individual ROK soldiers in our American units, but it is no secret that the performance of the ROK units was another matter completely.

The ROK divisions were most unreliable and a source of constant worry and concern to Ridgway and others. As citizens of a new country, they lacked training, experience, and confidence in themselves as is also well documented by many writers. They repeatedly bugged out, and when they did so, they left most of their equipment behind. As the front moved again northward, much of that abandoned material was still around and was a target for salvage.

"How long did the salvage and MSR-policing project last?" Ryan next asked.

"We had our area rather spic-and-span by the time we returned to the line in April. I think we were the first to clean up after the long, hard winter, so there was much around. As supply discipline improved later, I guess there was less need for an intensive effort.

CHAPTER TWELVE

Ridge Runners to the 38th—Spring and Summer 1951

"Hey, Pratt, me boy, I've got more news for you—both good and bad. Which do you want first?"

It was George Russell, my battalion commander, greeting me as I strolled into his CP. The month of March, and our two week "rest" period with its command inspections and battlefield-policing operations, was drawing to a close. The rosy fingers of April dawns were just around the corner. Spring was in the air, if ever so faintly. For sure, we had seen worse days in the cruel winter just behind us. Still the war ground on.

Russell smiled as he saw the look of consternation blanketing my face. The last time he confronted me with a burst of good news and bad news was just after Chipyong. The good news, to him, was that we were going to continue our offensive, and the bad news was that our

238

battalion was not going to be allowed to spearhead the assault. I wasn't sure I could stand any more of his good news. His ideas of humor, if that's what it was, were not coinciding with mine.

"Relax, my exuberant company commander," Russell laughingly said, obviously enjoying my discomfort. "This time the good news is really good news. They're going to start R and R trips to Japan."

"Wow!" said I. "That is my brand of good news. When do I leave?"

"Not so dad-blamed fast, fellow. Not this morning. But within days. We'll let you know your quota. I'll probably have to let you be among the first, since you've been in Korea almost eight months. Not many chaps around with that much service here."

"Yeah, I know. Wonder why?"

"Can't imagine," Russell responded. "Guess not many have liked the accommodations here in Korea."

"And the bad news? Slip it to me gently. As bad as your good news is usually, Major, I'm not sure I can handle your bad news."

"Well, the bad news is not all that bad—although to you of faint heart it may be."

"Not sure I'm all that faint-hearted, Major. But on the other hand, I'll confess to not having your abundance of enthusiasm and exuberance. So what's the rest of the news?"

"Well, as you know, Operations 'Killer,' renamed 'Courageous,' and 'Ripper' are winding down, and Ridgway is replacing them with others."

"I'll bet," I answered with continued apprehension. "And I'll bet our good general has new names for them?"

"For sure," Russell agreed. "They are to be named 'Rugged' and 'Dauntless.' "

" 'Rugged' and 'Dauntless'? I wonder who dreams up all these names for operations?"

"Beats me," said Russell. "Probably some imaginative staff officer."

"What's the difference in the two operations?"

"Operation 'Rugged' involves a drive to the 'Kansas' line, which, as you can see," Russell explained, pointing to his situation map in the CP, "runs generally along the 38th parallel to our north in our sector here in central Korea."

"And 'Dauntless' ?" I asked.

"Dauntless, if we reach the parallel and it materializes, will consist of limited extensions into North Korea," added Sammy Radow, the operations officer, joining in the discussion.

"And of course, the jolly good news is that we will be in the thick of all this, I imagine?"

"You sure got that one right, Pratt. But that shouldn't surprise you. We're ending a rest period. Can't stay in reserve forever."

"No, unfortunately," I agreed. "When do we march? What're the details?"

"Probably tomorrow. The 23rd will entruck to assembly areas behind the marine division, just below the Hwach'on Reservoir. Our regiment will pass through and relieve the Marine 5th Regiment in the Ch'unch'on area."

"If the assault goes as planned, does that mean we will reach the parallel first among the UN forces?"

"We don't think so," said the S-2. "The offensive is already underway to the left and west. It looks like the honor of first reaching the parallel will fall on your old World War II outfit, Pratt—the Third Division."

With that and a few follow-up answers, the briefing broke up with company commanders winding their ways back to their troops for unit briefings and preparations for breaking camp.

On to the 38th Parallel

On April 1, the 23rd Regiment made a long, circuitous motor move up to our assembly areas near Hongch'on. Two days later our 1st Battalion, with the 3rd Battalion on our right, took positions on the Soyang River northeast of Ch'unch'on. We were back in combat and advancing with light or no enemy contact. The warmer weather beat a temporary retreat as cold days returned. There were more rough, rugged ridges to negotiate in the intermittent rain and sleet. Where oh where, we asked, were the warm sunny days of which we had gotten a glimpse while in bivouac?

By the ninth the battalion had pushed almost ten miles and my Baker Company was in position on an obscure Hill 663, only about three miles from the parallel. We were on the southern side of the reservoir. We noticed its waters were very low. I did not know that the Communist forces had just opened the floodgates a few days earlier to flood the river downstream as an impediment to the UN drive northward.

Should the UN Forces Recross the Parallel?

I didn't know it at the time, but our movement up to the parallel and just over had been the subject of careful, but highly controversial, consideration all the way from Ridgway to Washington and the UN. The political and diplomatic ramifications were immense, and far beyond the scope of the understanding and recognition of infantry company-commanders and their troops at the lowest command levels in the Korean War.

In recalling those days, however, it is interesting, I think, to consider the overall big picture into which our small combat units were fitted.

In passing, we can quickly note that national policy was not to spread the war any more than could be avoided and not to place the UN forces in Korea in too great risk. Great increases in the CCF forces in North Korea had been noted, and the Americans did not want to trigger an all-out Chinese offensive that could overpower the UN forces.

Adding to the uneasiness of American commanders was the continuing unreliability of the ROK divisions. We had the 7th Division on the right of our 2d, as right flank of the Eighth Army. On the army right were only ROK units. If they bugged out and fled in the face of a major CCF effort in the east, the Eighth Army would be in danger of being outflanked and cut off, with no assurance of an ability to withdraw if they needed to.

Numerous historians have pointed out how nervous our high commanders were on this April push to the parallel. We in the 2d Division, especially in the 23rd Regiment, which was to be the only unit north of the parallel, were in a particularly delicate situation. We protruded like a finger, far ahead of the general front line. Such a salient, in military operations, can be hazardous, since it is more easily nipped off at the base.

Fortunately, since there was initially very light enemy contact, we were not nipped off at our base. At times there was no contact at all. By mid-April the 23rd was about ten miles north of the reservoir, on the "Kansas" line.

On the twentieth my Baker Company advanced in combat formation through the little town of Yanggu at the upper end of the P'aro Ho Reservoir and started climbing the low hills about three miles north of the town. It was late afternoon. I was told to halt and take up defensive positions. To my rear I could see the village of Yanggu. Off to the right about a mile in the valley, I could see the winding Korean Route 31 heading toward us from the east and then bending northward. To our left rear were the waters of the reservoir and just beyond, on the southern shore hills, I knew Charlie Company was in position.

Still there was no enemy contact, at least none of any significance. Actually, enemy troops had been spotted by the forward platoons as we mounted and occupied our high ground, but they seemed to melt back into the brush and woods as we approached. At least they did not seem to make any particular effort to show hostility.

Advanced Outpost North of the Parallel

On the morning of April 21, I was ordered to begin patrolling into the areas forward of our positions. Sammy Radow was on the radio.

"How far should we go, Red 3?" I asked. "And what are our instructions if we are fired upon?"

"Do not engage the enemy. Carefully note positions and strength and withdraw," came back the answer.

"Roger," said I, indicating I had received my orders and understood them. I decided, as I now recall, that I would use good "ole" reliable Lieutenant Fenderson for this mission. His platoon had been in the lead during the attack, but in reserve since.

After I briefed Fendy, he moved his platoon out. Down the slopes they felt their way and into and across a small valley to our front. I watched nervously as they gradually disappeared into the woods beyond the valley clearing. Soon none could be seen, but we maintained contact as best we could by radio. The signals weakened, or disappeared entirely, from time to time. I knew this was because the patrol was moving up and down in gullies or ridges and that the transmissions would be blocked by the terrain.

After about an hour with no communications from Fendy, he suddenly could again be heard. I anxiously inquired as to his situation. He let me know that all was well, that they had seen no enemy but were on an enemy position that appeared to have been just vacated. He had seen dugouts and some trash laying around. Fendy asked whether he should continue forward.

I told Fendy that he should scout out the next prominent ground to his north, but to remain extremely cautious. I knew Fendy was getting rather far from the rest of the company and that if he did run into trouble and needed help it would be most difficult to respond quickly.

Again, we lost radio contact with Fendy and his platoon. From my map, I knew he must be dropping down into lower ground and that if that were so, communications should be possible again as he reached higher ground beyond. Sure enough, a few minutes later, Fendy's radio again crackled through to me and I learned he was on his second patrol objective. At that point Fendy reported he could see enemy on the next high ground to his north. Again he asked if he should continue.

"What are the enemy's activities?" I radioed to Fendy.

"They appear to be preparing emplacements and eating," was his answer.

"Do you think they have spotted you?"

"Negative," Fendy replied. "But if we continue to advance, they are sure to see us. What are our instructions? Are we to advance?"

"Negative," I radioed. "Note everything you can about the troops and positions, then disengage and withdraw, but carefully." I could almost feel the relief in Fendy's voice as he "rogered" my transmission. Fendy and his patrol returned safely without incident. I complimented him on a job well done.

Chinese Fifth Offensive: Rumbles in the West

Two days later, we were again ordered to send out patrols. This time Kotite's platoon pushed as far as the high ground on which Fendy had seen enemy troops two days before. From that hill, the tiny village of Sange Doe could be seen at the upper end of a three-mile valley running from the north shore of the reservoir. Busy enemy activity in and around the village was observed by the patrol and we reported that to the battalion S-3.

Later that day, I hiked back to the battalion CP about a mile behind us near the edge of the reservoir and the town. I was very concerned as to whether we were going to have to do more patrolling. I did not like the platoons operating so far from our company positions, especially with so much uncertainty about enemy locations and intentions.

"Relax, Pratt," Russell told me, "I don't think we are going to be ordered to do more patrolling. Quite the contrary. If anything, we are about to haul ass on the double."

"Really?" I said with both concern and, I thought, perhaps, relief. "Why?"

"Big things are happening. The big generals have been walking on thin ice for some days. All reports indicate a massive enemy buildup, and fear is that the Chinks might hit with a blockbuster at any minute. It seems that time has come. All hell is breaking out over in the west in the First and Ninth corps sectors. We might be facing one of the major Chinese offensives of the war." Later I was to learn that we were indeed on the threshold of a major enemy offensive that would become known as the Chinese Fifth Offensive to historians and official recorders.

"So what are my instructions?"

"Just sit tight for the moment. If there is a general withdrawal we will follow suit for sure."

I studied the tactical maps for some moments. We were the division right flank. To our right was the 7th Division and the ROK Corps beyond. The Marine Division was on our left, plus the ROK 6th Division north of Kap'yong.

"Do you think the ROKs are going to hold if they are hit?" I asked Sammy Radow.

"Who knows?" said Sammy. "If they do it will be a surprise, and if they don't, pity our poor tankers and the British and Canadians."

"Why pity them?" I asked again.

"Because they are in position just behind the ROKs. Our 72d Tank Battalion has been placed there as back up and support for the ROKs."

I studied the situation map for a bit. I could see Sammy's point. The Brits and Canucks were indeed in a tight and dicey situation if the ROKs bugged out. But then, so were we. What a weird way to conduct combat operations, I thought. Up and down the Korean peninsula like a window shade. There must be a better way to fight a war. One could only hope that someone would soon find it.

CHAPTER THIRTEEN

More Chinese Attacks and a Relief from the Lines

From the time the Chinese intervened in Korea in the fall of 1950 until the summer of 1951, about nine months later, they launched six major attacks, or offensives.

After the decisive Kunu-ri and Chipyong-ni engagements, until the cease-fire agreements of P'anmunjom in 1953, most of the fighting was concentrated in the high and remote central parts of the Korean peninsula just north of the parallel. These areas would earn their own identities, such as the Iron Triangle, Heartbreak Ridge, the Punchbowl, and some other labels.

The fifth of the six Chinese offenses was launched in late April of 1951.

Pullback from the 38th Parallel

As the Chinese Fifth Offensive burst out in the last half of April 1951, it exploded like a massive tidal wave and was felt most strongly in the western and left central sectors of the front. It hit the First and Ninth corps areas like the legendary ton of bricks, causing a general recoil all across the area. Our intelligence community was known to feel that the main objective was the retaking of Seoul, which the high command was determined would not happen.

The attack did not come down on us with any great force, except in the Kap'yong area southwest of Ch'unch'on. The attack did necessitate an eastern withdrawal in order to avoid an outflanking development.

At Kap'yong, the British Brigade, with the Australians and Canadians and Company A of our 72d Tank Battalion, were to catch the full brunt of the Chinese offensive in that sector. For three days around the twenty-fourth, they were to stand their ground against all the Chinese could throw at them. At one time their route of withdrawal was cut and they were, in effect, sliced completely off from all other units. Their stand, although too late to be decisive, was one of the most heroic of the war, and it contributed greatly to our own salvation in a way we did not fully realize at the time.

On April 23 Russell briefed his company commanders and told us we were to begin a retrograde movement, and that we would be leapfrogging with the 38th Regiment.

"We're going to start withdrawing tonight after dark," Russell explained. "All units should make their movements as quietly and quickly as possible so as not to alert the enemy of our relocating."

"What's the panic?" one officer asked. "We haven't been hit yet. What's the point of giving up all this ground that we have just taken with backbreaking effort?"

"Fear is, that if the western end of the front is pushed back very much we could be too far ahead on our end, and be outflanked. Anyone here want to be cut off and need reservations in a Chinese POW stockade?" No one answered that he wanted that.

"We just hope for now that the British and others with them around Kap'yong don't cave in, for our sake as well as theirs," Russell continued.

"Why for our sake?" someone asked. "They are pretty far to our left rear. If we withdraw southward along the Ch'unch'on-Hoensong-Wonju roadnet, how would the Kap'yong outcome affect us?"

"Because if Kap'yong falls," Sammy Radow chimed in, "the Chinese could sweep eastward right across our rear and cut us off at the pass just like a western oater movie." He pointed to his situation map to demonstrate his point. We got his message.

As it developed, the British and their team did hold out, and gallantly. The Kap'yong battle was to attract the personal attention of all the high-level commanders, and it would become one of the most heroic and astounding engagements of the whole war. Our division historian was to say: "For three days and two nights the British Brigade, reinforced by the 2d Division tanks, held the ground, battling with every ounce of strength they could muster and inflicting terrific casualties on the fanatic Chinese. . . . The stand enabled the flanking divisions to pull back and set up a new defense line."

On the twenty-fifth the 23rd RCT was ordered to pull below the parallel and the reservoir and hold while the 38th dashed back to the old "Cairo" line. Two days later, on the twenty-seventh, they moved on farther to the No Name line running roughly northeast from Hoenchon near Hangye. The following day our regiment began its general withdrawal to the No Name line, and by the end of the month the division, including the 23rd, was firmly in position there.

By then, the Chinese offensive had just about run its course, or at least we were so informed. Contact in our sector was light and sporadic. The intelligence reports were again describing the Chinese ability to mount a stinging attack but stressing their limited ability to keep it going.

The Chinese did not seem to have the logistical tail necessary to support their forward movements. It seemed that after an all-out effort their steam would run down in a few days, and that was what had again happened. All the reports indicated, too, that the enemy had not been very severely harmed and that they were still powerful and able to resume their offensive at will after a pause to catch breaths and replenish supplies.

A Period of Waiting and Watching

As April passed into May, we sat and waited for the next developments. There was much uncertainty concerning the enemy's intentions. It was also at about this time that Russell decided to give me a break personally. He strolled into my company positions one day with a couple of his staff officers and began speaking.

"Pratt," he said. "I plan to reassign you to replace my supply officer, the S-4."

His statement caught me by complete surprise.

"Is this punishment for something I've done? Or not done?"

"Not by any means," Russell hastened to add. "But I think you need a break, and I need a supply officer who has drive and performs."

"What's wrong with the one you've got? Doesn't he do that?"

"Yes, I guess so," Russell said, "but he's been evacuated. Has all sorts of medical problems. And I don't want to replace him with just any officer. This war is entering a new stage, where the emphasis is going to be on supply more than tactics. The terrain is getting higher and more rugged. It's going to be a real challenge to keep our line companies supplied in this defiant terrain, and success will turn on whether or not we are able to do so."

"But why me, Major?"

"I think, for one thing, that you have earned a much-deserved break. You've commanded Baker Company now since last fall. I don't have any other company commander who has so served for that long. The supply job will be less hazardous for sure. It will give you a chance to catch your breath. The job won't be as constantly tense as that of a rifle-company commander."

"But what about the 'drive' and a guy who 'performs'? Is that me?"

"Don't know," said Russell. "I think so, but I could be wrong. But you'll have a chance to show me. It's up to you."

"And you think we are going to resume the advance again?"

"Yes, that's the rumor. And into some of the most impassable areas in all Korea. Take a look at this terrain just in our path of advance from our present positions."

Russell pointed on his map to the central eastern sector of Korea, just above the 38th parallel. The elevation contour-lines were so numerous and close they were hard to differentiate from each other and seemed to run together in bunches. The region, we were to learn later, would become known as the Heartbreak and Pork Chop ridges and the Punchbowl.

"When do I make the move, Major Russell?" I asked.

"In the next few days. I'll let you know. For sure, before we go on the offensive again."

With that I had to be content. I had mixed feelings. For all of Russell's assurances that the change constituted an "advancement," I wondered if it wasn't just his way of silencing a constantly carping subordinate. I suspected he was weary of my too-frequent complaints about misguided ridge-running tactics that unnecessarily and uselessly wore down troops without accomplishing much in return.

A few days later, I bid my officers and men in Baker Company good-by as their commander and assumed my new duties as the battalion S-4 on the battalion commander's staff. I was to learn that the job was to be no snap, but, on the contrary, would be one of the most challenging in my entire military career.

The spring of 1951 was to be a major milestone in the waging of the Korean War. In the last half of April and May, respectively, the Chinese, with some help from the rejuvenated North Korean military, would launch what the historians and officials have termed the Chinese Fifth and and Sixth offensives.

These Fifth and Sixth offensives would be the last two major efforts by the Chinese. There they would be "checked," once and for all. Thereafter, more bitter fighting would follow in the highlands of central Korea just north of the 38th parallel, in the areas on and around remote Heartbreak Ridge.

The later fighting, however, almost until the signing of the P'anmunjom cease-fire agreements in 1953, would not result in any significant exchange of real estate or the location of the front lines, nor would it determine the final outcome of the conflict. That bloodshed was to determine only whether the Communists would seriously negotiate and, if so, just when the shooting would stop.

The fighting in April, May, and June of 1951 consisted, mainly, of a series of offensives and counteroffensives by both sides. The front lines moved forward and backward over the weeks without any particularly decisive effect. The troops began referring to the period as the "yo-yo" war—the up-and-down phase of the conflict.

The intensity of the struggle, overall, in that spring period, reached the highest level of the entire war. It did not necessarily exceed that of the 2d Division at Kunu-ri or of the 23rd Regiment at Chipyong, but the spring engagements involved not just a regiment or a division, but the entire Eighth Army from coast to coast and covering a much longer period of time—almost three months rather than only a few days.

Much had happened in the war in only a few months prior to the spring of 1951. The North Koreans had crossed the parallel in June. They were stopped around the Pusan perimeter for the summer. The UN troops had broken out of the perimeter and pushed into and almost completely through North Korea to, or near, the Manchurian border by winter. The Chinese had then intervened in force, and the UN and Eighth Army had withdrawn, and advanced, to its April 1951 positions roughly along the 38th parallel in the center and slightly below it in the west and above it in the east.

During the period, a series of command-designated "lines" were being used as UN objectives or as troop-location designations. The "Kansas" line ran mostly along the parallel, where UN positions were then located. Just to the north there were lines in the central areas of "Utah" and "Wyoming" near the "Iron Triangle," a sector between the towns of Ch'orwon, P'yonggang and Kumhwa. The "No Name" line ran below "Kansas" to the east of Hongch'on, and "Topeka" and "Lincoln" above Seoul ran eastward from Munsan.

As the early April days slipped by, the two adversary armies solidified their positions and tried to assess each other's intentions. Intelligence reports indicated a continuous strengthening of Communist forces all along the front, and especially in the western and central regions.

About this time the new army commander, Gen. James Van Fleet, arrived to replace General Ridgway, who had moved to Tokyo upon the relief of MacArthur. It is well recorded that General Van Fleet was convinced that the enemy would strike hard in the west with the objective of recapturing Seoul by May 1, an important day on the Communist calendar.

To block an enemy thrust in the west, Van Fleet had massed the bulk of his strength. There, in the I and IX corps were located the British Brigade, the U.S. 1st Cavalry, 3rd, 24th, and 25th infantry divisions, and the Turks. To their right in the central areas were the Commonwealth Brigade and the X Corps with the Marine Division and the army 2d and 7th divisions. ROK divisions were interspersed along the line, except in the extreme east, where only ROK divisions were positioned above the parallel to the coast just below the town of Kansong.

The Chinese Fifth Offensive

The Eighth Army's uncertainty concerning the enemy's intentions terminated in the late evening of April 22, just before midnight. At that time the CCF struck across almost the entire western half of the front. As expected by Van Fleet, their main thrust was toward Seoul, but considerable effort was also directed toward the central UN positions.

The offensive consisted of almost a quarter-million troops, perhaps even more. It was accompanied by the usual horn and whistle blowing, and beating of tin pans or buckets, and the firing of flares.

In the west, UN forces "recoiled" and withdrew to positions nearer to Seoul, where they stopped and held firm. In our central sector, withdrawals were also affected, except for the gallant stand of the Commonwealth Brigade and our 72d Tank Battalion at Kap'yong, to which I have already alluded.

In our own sector, and probably in others, withdrawals were made necessary not so much by enemy frontal pressure as by exposure of frontline unit flanks by the collapse and flight of ROK units along the sides. The unreliability of the ROK divisions, as elsewhere herein stated, has long been a highly controversial and a much-discussed subject in the war.

I am satisfied that many small-unit commanders will agree with my assessment that when assigned to American or other UN units as individuals, the Korean soldiers performed reasonably well, and in many instances with exceptional courage and efficiency. In their own organizations, however, with their own officers and leaders, it seems they simply lacked confidence and stamina and they fled in panic at the first appearance of the Chinese.

Many writers have detailed General Van Fleet's disenchantment with the ROK army. He visited our regimental CP one day soon after his arrival and assumption of command. I happened to be nearby, and could overhear his remarks to Colonel Chiles, and, I think, Major Russell and some staff officers.

"I don't know what the hell we are doing over here, 5,000 miles from home, with our men fighting and dying for a people who flee every time they see an enemy," the General was saying.

"It's not just that they bug out," Van Fleet continued, "but they invariably expose our flanks and endanger our troops. I don't know how long we can put up with this situation."

I later years I have learned that Van Fleet repeated his criticism in interviews after the war and elsewhere. I note too, that Clay Blair wrote much the same thing. As a veteran of the fighting in Korea, the matter has long given me much cause for thought, as I have tried in all fairness to objectively assess the extent to which the Korean soldiers should be faulted for their generally miserable performance in their own units.

For example, is it realistic and fair to expect any people to perform with distinction and perseverance in combat given the conditions that prevailed at the time in Korea, and the recent history under which the Koreans had lived?

Their history, over the centuries, was one mostly of domination and occupation by foreigners, for a long time the Chinese and, in this century, the Japanese. During all those years, the Korean people were never permitted to have their own leaders or to develop individual or collective initiatives. On the contrary, the policies of the domineering foreigners were to deliberately oppress the Korean people and to stifle indigenous creativity, imagination, or expressiveness. As with any occupied people, the goals of the occupier were subjugation, control, and submission.

Nor in the brief period after World War II until the Korean War was there much opportunity to overcome or reverse these debilitating conditions and attitudes. American involvement then is mostly a history of mismanagement, inappropriate continued use in high positions of cruel and hated Japanese officials, and U.S. ignorance and misunderstanding of the Korean people and their culture.

Under these conditions, the Korean soldier in the early 1950s could easily be likened to a slave just emancipated, inexperienced, uneducated, unskilled, uncertain, and quite insecure and bewildered. It may have been foolish to rely upon such a person as though he were experienced, confident, trained, and endowed both personally and as a member of a seasoned and free society such as ours. Such unrealistic reliance may well tell us more about ourselves than about the Koreans, whom many have bad-mouthed over the years.

Not that General Van Fleet was not justified in his dismay over the malperformance of the ROKs. To be sure their repeated collapses did greatly endanger the safety and welfare of Van Fleet's own forces, who were his concern and responsibility. But perhaps more weight and consideration should be given to the causes for the poor performance of the ROKs. There has been mucy recent evidence that our senior officials, encouragingly, now have a more enlightened understanding of Korea and its people, and that we can make due allowances for, and take actions to overcome, whatever limitations may yet exist in their will to fight for their country.

Logistics: The Science of Supply

It was about this time, at the height of the spring Chinese offensives, that I earned my spurs as the battalion supply-officer. I thought that leaving a line company might spare me the onerous burden of struggling up and down the continuous Korean mountain ridges. But it was not to be. I had not seen my last of those ridges by any means.

"Pratt, come over here. I have to give you a pep talk." It was my still-glorious leader, George Russell.

"You do?" answered I.

"Well, I think so. You're probably sulking because you are now only a staff officer and don't have your own command."

"Really? I don't recall that I have lost much sleep over that, Major Russell."

"Good. I hope not, because your work is now cut out for you."

A view of the 2 1/2-ton amphibious truck "DUKW" in use, as an alternate supply approach, on a central Korean river in midsummer 1951.

I was all ears and paying close attention, somewhat suspicious of what comments were to follow.

"Just because you're now on my staff," Russell continued, "don't think you are going to lie around on your fat ass. As I told you, just now I consider the supply slot my most critical staff position. We are going to win or lose from now on depending more on our ability to keep the line companies supplied than on tactics."

I ignored Russell's allegation concerning the configuration of my posterior, recognizing it as only a figure of speech and sure that none of us, with our rations and activities, could meet such a criterion anyway. If nothing else, the hills of Korea and the irregular meals were keeping most of us slim and trim.

"So any special instructions for me, Major?"

"Yes, the companies are complaining that resupply is their number-one problem. Either supplies are lost or the carrying parties cannot find them in their remote positions."

"And you want me to take a highly active role in steering the carrying parties to the companies?"

"That's it exactly. I think you should let your sergeant carry the load mostly in getting the supply convoys to us from the rear dumps—and you take a personal role with the carrying parties."

"That should keep me wide awake and alert."

"For sure. The parties are mostly ROKs and local civilians, as you know. Only a few GIs accompany them, and they seldom are much skilled in fine-tuning these tactical military maps."

"You can say that again, Major. But then I'm not sure I am much better. These maps seem to have been hastily slapped together, probably from aerial photos. I doubt there were ever any ground surveillance and sightings."

"We know that too, Pratt. But all the more reason for the best map reader available to go along with the carrying parties. You may not be perfect, but you're a damned sight more skilled as an officer and experienced CO than our enlisted troops."

I nodded my agreement. I was not seized with uncontrollable zeal for implementing Russell's instructions, but I recognized that what he said made much sense.

"And I guess you want me to start yesterday?"

"Right. Even now both Able and Charlie companies are stopped on position, unable to advance without rations, and they are both very low on ammo. So take all the time you want to map out your course of action, just so you do so immediately."

Russell added some remarks about my energy and reliability, which I recognized as the normal rhetoric by a good leader to inspire and motivate a subordinate.

I mulled over Russell's comments and instructions, then and in the following days and weeks while we remained on line. I tried my best to fully comply. As he had indicated, the job was to be full time and require more than maximum effort, however that could be done. In the process I was to log far more mountain miles under my combat boots than I had as a company commander. As a company officer, I usually remained on an objective once there, but in my new supply job I not only had to travel to one company's positions, but to the others as well, and usually not just once, but many times over the days.

In my Arlington rec room, historian Ryan decided to press a point.

"Did you find the supply mission to be much of a challege?" he asked.

"Yes, I think so, without any fear of overstating the case. The formidable terrain of central Korea presented resupply problems of a most extraordinary nature and made the supply of frontline units quite unlike any problems ordinarily faced by supply personnel in a routine combat situation—if combat can ever be considered to be routine."

Just finding a company in wild, mountaineous terrain, with countless gullies, draws, knolls, creeks, and other features, on maps that were new and strange, could be a chore of staggering dimensions even if this was being done in relative safety in the Rocky Mountains on a boy-scout outing. But in Korea in wartime, there was the added element of enemy troops who could be, and often were, anywhere and just over the next hill or around the next curve in the trail.

Very often the supply routes to frontline units would be up and over the mountains and ridges. At other times we resorted to the rivers, and even to the use of amphibious trucks and boats.

As the last days of April began to slide into the background, so did the Chinese Fifth Offensive. The corps intelligence summary reported "a distinct slackening of the CCF effort."

Once again, the enemy's inability to maintain the "momentum of the assault" became apparent, and after advancing to the limits of their logistical tail, their effort fizzled to a crawl.

"Pratt, I'm headed back to regimental CP," said Sammy Radow one morning. "Wanta go along?"

"Sure would," I hastened to reply. "Provided you're not gone too long. I have supplies to get forward as soon as they arrive from the rear."

"We'll be back in short order. Just want to see what we can find out about the situation across the front."

I jumped into the back of Radow's jeep and we were soon underway. At regiment, we confirmed that the CCF effort all along the front had slowed to a near stop, and that our high command was making plans for a counterattack.

"What's the code name for the counteroffensive?" Radow asked the regimental staff.

" 'Detonate,' " was the answer.

"Any idea of the details? Or when?"

"It will be an all-out effort to retake the ground just lost, and within a week or so—the twelfth probably, or thereabouts."

Notwithstanding the best laid plans of mice or men, or the high command, however, Operation "Detonate" was not about to happen, at least not just yet.

Passing the Time in Reserve

Early May found our division and regiment off the line and in reserve in the areas around Hoengsong, some twenty-five miles or so behind the Marine Division and the 187th Airborne Regiment. We were engaged in blocking and patrolling, mostly to the east and toward the ROK divisions' zones.

Additionally, with large numbers of replacements and new men, we carried out vigorous training in about every subject imaginable, from weapons to small-unit maneuvers. And of course, there were the ever-expected command inspections in all units. On the plus side, there were hot showers occasionally and hot meals daily—and even some nights with relatively sound sleep.

Several days into May, I strolled past the battalion commander's tent one rather dreary morning after a conference with my supply team. I heard a voice calling me and, turning around, spotted Lynn Freeman, the adjutant, heading toward me.

Freeman had been my exec back in Baker Company before Russell had tapped him for S-1 duties. Freeman was a quiet, pleasant chap, always courteous, thoroughly reliable, and properly military in his bearing and appearance. He reminded me of Alan Ladd, the actor. I often had the feeling he was looking for a tall ship to sail or a rampart to scale in some adventure-drama flick.

Regimental Briefing

"Captain Pratt, are you interested in a briefing at regiment for the battalion staffs?" Freeman asked me.

"Lynn, to ask the question is to answer it," I responded. "You know I never pass up a chance to get some inside scoop."

"Then stand by. The battalion CO and S-3 are about to depart. They've got room for one more in their jeep . . . told me to round up a volunteer if one could be found."

"You've just found one, and many thanks. I'll get my carbine and helmet."

When we arrived at the regimental CP, the briefing was just getting underway. We were all quite curious as to what might be in store for the outfit in the coming days. We knew that current intelligence reports had indicated that the enemy had all but disappeared from the battlefield, and in most areas was hard to find.

The briefing officer was a recent arrival and assistant S-3, Captain Albert Metts, a West Pointer. In the coming months, Metts and I were to form a close relationship and become warm friends. We were both from the South and shared what we considered new and enlightened views on social and other national conditions and problems. We were to have many interesting "bull sessions" over the coming months at times of lulls in the fighting or in our duties.

"First off, I should say," Metts began, "Operation 'Detonate' is off for now. We expect confirmation of that on the eleventh. The

The author (foreground, bareheaded) supervises the organization of carrying parties to high central Korean mountaintop positions of the 23rd Reg.

The 1st Bn./23rd Reg. supply team at positions in central Korea near high mountains that became known as "Heartbreak Ridge."

enemy is hard to find, in spite of numerous patrols by line units, but we know they're out there."

"In strength?" someone asked.

"Affirmative," Metts answered. "In fact, a most strong affirmative. Problem is, the weather is so overcast the aerial spotters are unable to keep track of them. But friendly agents confirm there is great concentration and intense activity just beyond our reach from present positions."

"What're their capabilities?" came another question.

Joe Waddell, the acting S-2, joined in.

"The enemy troops were badly crippled by their Fifth Offensive last month, but they are still around in strength and fully capable of launching another major effort."

"Will they?"

"Army is sure of it, but uncertain just when unless this weather clears and they can mount a more active surveillance effort."

"Where?"

"Good question, but it seems it will be in the central area where we will shortly be back on line."

"Oh? We're headed back for the lines?"

"Correct, and probably by the fifteenth or so," said Metts, casting a somewhat impatient glance at the chap who would imply such an implausible eventuality as our not returning to the lines.

"What's the basis for thinking the enemy effort will be in the central sector?"

"I'm not entirely sure, but we know that General Van Fleet has about abandoned his convictions that Seoul is now the main target for the CCF. Too much shifting of enemy forces to the east and central sector. And our divisions around Seoul have stopped him like a stone wall. Also, another interesting point—captured enemy have revealed that the destruction of the 2d Division is now a specific objective of the Chinese high command. We don't know whether to be concerned or honored."

While we thought about that, some additional information was dispensed concerning probable march times for relocation of regimental units from present reserve-training bivouacs to forward assembly areas.

"Any particular worries in all this that we should know about?" someone asked.

"Yes," answered Colonel Chiles, the regimental commander. "You should be aware that General Ruffner remains quite concerned that we are the right flank of the Eighth Army with only ROK divisions to our right to the coast. It's a setup very similar to the one the division was confronted with at Kunu-ri. Ruffner doesn't want to be another Keiser." I knew he was alluding to the Kunu-ri gauntlet disaster in November, when General Keiser was commanding the division.

"Isn't the army commander also worried about this?" Russell asked.

"Yes, he is. In fact, so is the corps commander. Almond has pleaded for help and been told that Van Fleet will probably pull the 3rd Division out of the I Corps around Seoul and move it to our zone if there is a need."

The last piece of information I received with more than a little interest. The 3rd Division was my old outfit from World War II, and I had tried to carefully follow its activities in Korea all the way from arrival, commitment, and withdrawal from the Hungnam beachhead in the northeast with the X Corps to the later relocation on the main front in the winter after the Chinese intervention. I welcomed the development of closer ties with the old "Rock of the Marne" 3rd Infantry Division.

Defense of Japan

On the way back to the battalion area Sammy Radow offered me an offical-looking document and asked if I wanted to browse through it.

"What is it?" I asked.

"It's part of the division intelligence report and it has some interesting analyses of high-level problems that we aren't usually aware of at our level."

"Like what?" I asked again.

"It points out that Ridgway in Tokyo is annoyed that he does not have authority to withdraw the Eighth Army from Korea at his option."

"Withdraw the Eighth Army from Korea?" I asked incredulously. "Why would he now want to do that after all the bloodshed over the past months to hold it?"

"Oh, the report doesn't say he wants to. Only that he would like the authority to do so if he deems it necessary to fulfill his primary mission."

"Well, aren't we in Korea his primary mission?"

"Not according to this annex."

"What is?"

"The defense of Japan."

"The defense of Japan? From what?"

"The Russians."

"The Russians?" I almost shouted with even more disbelief. "Do they really think the Russians are going to attack Japan?"

"Actually, not much, according to the study. But since there is always that possibility, it seems it must be taken into account and some kind of contingency plans drawn up."

We sat for a while in the jeep waiting our turn in a line of vehicles to cross a one-way Bailey bridge over a swollen stream. Finally I asked, "So Ridgway wants to defend with the Eighth Army without having to ask Washington first?"

"That seems to be about it."

"And there are no troops there now in Japan that could be used?"

"Well, the 40th and 45th National Guard divisions have recently arrived in Japan, but neither is very highly trained or combat ready just now. JCS has been secretly organizing some Japanese police forces into divisions of sorts, but they are not ready either. Report says that a serious Russian amphibious force would quickly overpower whatever defenses we could raise in Japan."

I pondered all this for the rest of our bouncy jeep trip. My efforts to read the report in the back of a jeep galloping over primitive road bumps weren't very successful. Then, as later throughout the cold war, it seemed to me we were excessively paranoid about Russian intentions and were seeing a Soviet threat behind every bush and ocean wave. After all, I mused, might not the Russians have justification for feeling defensive and suspecting the West? They had just lost millions of people and most of their country, and had been constantly invaded over the centuries by Tartars, Swedes, the French, and twice in this century by the Germans.

On the other hand, although we had been attacked by the Japanese at Pearl Harbor at the start of our World War II, we had never been seriously invaded in our entire history. Which, I often wondered, of the two countries was more justified in feeling threatened by the other? Of course I could never voice such thoughts while in the military for fear of being suspected of being "soft on Communism." Still, I often, but secretly, wondered through the years whether we were not overreacting to a Soviet threat that was more fancied than real.

As the years passed I was to grow increasingly dovish and disenchanted with the trillions of dollars we would spend on defense while almost destroying our country financially with a three-trillion-dollar debt to pass along to our future children.

Not that we should not have devoted reasonable efforts and money to remain secure and vigilant over the years, especially in our role as a superpower. Of course we had to do so. But how much was enough, and didn't we overdo it? I have thought so.

The events in Eastern Europe at the end of the 1980s would seem to vindicate me in that skepticism as the world witnessed the demise of Communist strength and the rise to power in Russia of a more accommodating leadership. Of course the Communist retrenchment could be moderated or reversed. Time will tell.

The Chinese Strike Again

We had barely returned to our battalion area when the electrifying news hit. It was May 16, and we learned that the Chinese had struck in full fury smack in the X Corps area in central Korea. The Chinese Sixth Offensive was in full swing.

The 9th and 38th infantry regiments of the 2d Division were on line and directly in the path of the main enemy effort. Early reports confirmed that the ROK divisions on the right were collapsing, as usual, leaving the right flank of the division fully exposed and vulnerable to encirclement.

Our regiment had already received orders on the 15th to relocate from our reserve bivouac-area near Hong'chon and to occupy defensive positions just to the northeast of Hangye, some twenty miles or so east of Ch'unch'on. Our 1st Battalion went into position on high ground overlooking the MSR about three miles northeast of Hangye with the 2d and 3rd battalions in defensive positions about five miles further up the road and to the right of the 38th Regiment.

On the eighteenth, the Chinese assault continued unabated. There was intense fighting throughout the area. On our left, the Marine Division was ordered back. Also the 9th and 38th regiments were allowed to retrograde to new defensive positions, leaving only the 23rd forward of the main line and protruding dangerously.

The enemy pounded across the front with all their usually employed weapons, sound equipment, and techniques. Nevertheless, almost nowhere did UN forces, other than the ROKs off to the east, fail to defend tenaciously and effectively. Again, the almost routine rearward relocation of units was not because of overwhelming enemy frontal pressure, but to avoid encirclement by massive numbers of the enemy spilling around the flanks.

Particularly devastating to the enemy in this period was our artillery fire. Ample supplies of ammo had been stockpiled for days in advance in anticipation of the next major enemy offensive, and all limitations on its use had been removed as the offensive got underway. As a consequence, barrages laid down by the division artillery during the height of the attack set division records for the Korean, and, perhaps, for any other war. Afteraction reports establish artillery rounds fired at over 17,000 on May 16; 38,000 on the seventeenth; and an awesome 40,000 rounds on the eighteenth.

Dicey Forward Reconnaissance

On the morning of the eighteenth, with the 1st Battalion in its defensive positions and the battle steadily intensifying all around, Major Russell directed that the S-2 and I go forward to scout for assembly areas in case the 1st Battalion was ordered to deploy up the road to support the 2d and 3rd battalions. Lt. Floyd Darmer, as I recall, was the acting battalion S-2 at the time.

We were a bit leery about motoring alone up the valley on the MSR in view of the uncertainty as to the tactical situation.

"Why don't we grab a couple of troopers to ride shotgun with us?" I said to Darmer.

"I'll second that—and then some," he was quick to agree.

"Who'll we get?"

"Dunno," he answered. "Hate to turn back to the CP. Why don't we get a loan from one of the line companies as we pass through their positions?"

"I think that's the answer."

Just then we were nearing Baker Company's positions near the road. I recognized Sgt. Charlie Frazier and Sgt. Harry Cole.

"Hey, Sarg!" I yelled. "We need a couple escorts to go along for added protection on a little reconnaissance forward. Can you and Frazer join us? You don't look very busy just now."

Cole studied me for a moment. I could see he was not overjoyed at the prospect of leaving the relative security of a spot where no firing was taking place. Still, I knew he would think twice before turning down his former CO.

"I guess we can come along, Captain. Never like to say no to an 'ole' CO like you. Stand by for a sec while I let the platoon leader know we will be gone."

In short order Cole and Frazier returned and clambered into the rear of our, by now, crowded jeep. In another short order we were underway and grinding ourselves up the road. Traffic, strangely, had seemed to disappear. We had the road to ourselves. I thought that odd. We were on the MSR—the Main Supply Route—and behind two full battalions somewhere up ahead. Ordinarily the road should be busy with supply, command, and other vehicles or weapons carriers.

The road was rough and primitive, never much to begin with, but now even more chopped up by continuous heavy military vehicles over the weeks. Like most Korean countryside roads, it was filled with chuckholes and ruts from the current thaws and rains in spite of the engineers' diligent efforts to keep the supply routes passable and operable.

Our road wound along up a valley floor as most country roads did, and no doubt still do, in Korea. On each side the terrain rose steadily to the hills and low mountains in the background. Rice paddies and other farm fields were scattered about and stepped upwards as the ground rose in elevation.

As we rounded a bend, the sound of intense small arms and rumble of occasional explosives grew louder a mile or so ahead. Still, we were the only vehicle on the road. Following some groans from Darmer or the troopers after a particularly rough stretch, someone suddenly spoke.

"Captain! Up ahead there! On the side of the road. There are several moving figures. They don't look like friendly troops!"

I motioned to the driver to stop and reached for my binocs. Training them ahead, it took only a moment to confirm that the quilted-looking figures were not GIs but Chinese.

"Christ, Darmer," I said. "Those guys are enemy. But what the hell are they doing here? This is the MSR. We know damned well we've got two whole battalions ahead of us. Listen to all that firing. You're the intelligence officer. Tell me what this means."

Poor Darmer looked helpless, terrified, and confused as he tried to comprehend what he was seeing, or find an explanation.

"Then those Chinks are in behind the frontline battalions?"

"It sure seems so."

"Have they seen us?" asked one of the NCOs.

"I think so. They are looking our way, but they are not aiming their weapons this way. They're just standing there and watching as if to see what we are going to do."

"What are we going to do?"

"Get our butts out of here for starters—if we can," I answered and indicated to the driver to turn the vehicle around, but slowly and cautiously as I kept a close eye on the enemy troops ahead.

Prisoners of War—Briefly

As the driver completed his turnaround, he kept the jeep in low gear with the engine barely at an idle.

"Keep it slow and easy for a bit," I told the driver. "If we immediately make a dash for it, it may encourage them into firing, and we are badly outnumbered."

"Roger, Captain," the driver answered and moved to comply.

"My God," suddenly said Darmer. "There are more enemy just over to our right there by those bushes," he added and pointed them out to the rest of us. "Now what?"

"We've got no choice," I said, growing more apprehensive by the second with growing doubts that we could get out of this situation. "Just keep the jeep moving as you are," I told the driver. "So far they are not showing any hostility, for some reason."

We continued to move, crawling along at no more than five or six miles per hour. The first enemy we saw, now behind us, were slowly disappearing into the distance as we moved. We watched the enemy in the brush alongside the road, but now noticed more enemy troops on the left-hand side of the road as well. Some of them were walking toward the road and us.

"Should we make a fight for it?" someone asked.

"That might be one of the bravest things we could do," I said, "but for sure also one of the dumbest—suicidal. We wouldn't stand a chance. We're badly outnumbered and they would cut us down instantly. Just bite your tongue and keep your hand on your weapon."

We had gone only about another few feet when about a hundred yards away and ahead we saw up on the road, as well as along the sides, at least some forty to fifty enemy troops moving around as though to take or scout for firing positions.

Near-panic gripped us all. Our only avenue of escape was clearly cut. Now we had enemy troops, in paralyzing numbers, on all sides. We were at their mercy and under their full control. We were all alone, far from friendly forces, and completely surrounded.

"What should I do, Captain?" asked my driver. The poor trooper was the picture of dismay and despair. His voice was shaking and trembling. For lack of a better solution at the moment, I told him just to continue moving as he was doing and for no one to make any sudden or alarming move that might trigger any of these Chinese into hostile action.

"We'll just have to do what they say," I told the group. "They probably don't speak English, so if any of you see them motion instructions, make damn sure we obey. Otherwise it's sure suicide."

I did not relish the prospect of spending the rest of the war in a Chinese POW camp, but felt it might be better than being dead.

"Above all, guys, keep it cool. Don't give them any reason for thinking we mean them any harm," I cautioned.

Our jeep continued slowly forward—or "rearward"—toward our own rear areas. By now we had arrived at the Chinese on the road and awaited some indication from them as to what we were to do. At that point it seemed certain that we were to be captured, if not shot, and I think we had all resigned ourselves to that eventuality—at least I had done so.

As the jeep moved and no Chinese trooper approached us as though in charge, we slowly glided past the ones on the road and nearest our vehicle. We were careful not to exhibit our weapons or indicate hostility in any way.

The Chinese soldiers simply stood and watched us as we passed by. Some touched the jeep. We all donned our warmest, friendliest, and most placid countenances. One of the NCOs extended his hand with a pack of cigarettes, which turned out to be a smart move. The nearest Chinese troops hesitated, then took the cigarettes as others nearby pressed in curiously to see what had been offered. It seemed to divert their attention.

I looked into the faces of a couple of the troops and they stared back at me. I tried to smile and act peaceful. I thought a couple smiled back, but mostly, under the quilted hoods of their uniforms, their expressions were blank and showed no emotions whatever.

Still we had no instructions, gestures, or indications from the Chinese through whose midst we were passing. No one seemed to be in charge or willing to assume any initiative. It was almost as though they were stunned or were walking around in an air of uncertainty as to who we were, or what they were to do even if they determined that we were the much-despised capitalistic warmongers they were supposed to eliminate.

Gradually, as the Chinese continued to watch, we eased past the last of the soldiers and reached a stretch of the road where we could see no sign of life nearby or out to our front—that is, toward the rear. Bit by bit, as we glanced backward, we could see the last of the Chinese fading into the distance. Some were standing in the road, still watching us. Others were moving about as though we had never been there. It appeared we had cleared the enemy-occupied area and there was nothing or no one to prevent us from moving out smartly.

"Driver, throw this thing into high gear and haul ass and fast," I said. The driver lost no time in complying.

On our return to the battalion our every thought and word was on the incredible and terrifying ordeal we had just experienced. To say that we had had a close call was simply a masterpiece of under-statement.

We tried to rationalize. It was all like a dream. All of us had assumed we would be captured at best, if not eliminated on the spot, but we could not explain to ourselves or each other just why the Chinese had remained so passive and simply stood by as we drove to, through, and away from them.

In endless contemplation thereafter, we concluded that the Chinese who had failed to restrain us when they had already as a practical matter captured us were just as surprised at seeing us as we were at seeing them. It must have been, we decided, that they lacked specific instructions as to what to do under such an unexpected development and no one among them was able to take the initiative and confront Americans, whom many would not have seen or con-fronted before at close hand. There may have been no officers or senior NCOs among them. By the time that the Chinese came to their senses, we were gone. There might have been hell to pay for some poor NCO or other junior leader for letting American prisoners slip from their grip.

Upon returning to the battalion, we made haste to report our amazing adventure and close encounter to Major Russell. He was in his CP with aides dashing about and map boards at the gallop with fixed bayonets.

"Major Russell," I gasped, rushing up to him, "you wouldn't believe what had just happened to us."

"I might, Pratt, but not just now. We have deep trouble on our hands, with two of the companies locked in a fierce fire fight."

"But, Sir," I persisted, "you just almost lost two of your staff officers and three EM."

"Perhaps so," Russell added, "but right now we are near to losing a hell of a lot more. Give me a break, Pratt. Let it wait for now."

With that I had to give up. Actually, Russell was quite right. Hairy as our adventure might have been to us, in the overall situation it must be characterized as relatively trivial, no matter how bizarre. I think in the end, our dedicated commander must have writen off our story for the most part as unbelievable, or at least grossly exaggerated. For sure he had little time for such docudrama at the moment of our return. Russell had his hands full with more than any battalion commander deserved.

"Pratt," he said, "we can get back to your problems later. Just now, two of the companies are under attack, but worse, it seems the rest of the regiment is cut off and in serious danger of annihilation."

"You mean the 2d and 3rd battalions?" I asked.

"That's it. The rest of the division on the left has pulled back. The ROKs on the right have collapsed and the regiment is out on a point."

"Why?" I asked. "Why aren't they permitted to withdraw?"

"They are. The order has just been given by Ruffner."

"Shouldn't it have been given earlier?"

"Colonel Chiles thinks so. He has been pleading for permission for hours, but was denied."

"Denied? By whom?"

"Corps commander. Almond was not convinced the situation was serious enough."

"But he's now convinced?"

"Apparently so."

"And now they are pulling back?"

"They are trying—have started. But it seems the Chinese have circled around and cut the road to their rear."

I looked at Darmer. We were on the same wavelength. We knew we could tell them something about the Chinese on the escape road out if anyone were inclined to listen to us. The only road out for the two battalions was the one we were just on, now swarming with Chinese and on which, but for the grace of God or someone, we would have been captured. But all seemed now too busy around the CP for us to try again to bring up the subject.

The May Massacre and Hangye Gauntlet

What was then developing, of course, was the well-documented engagement of May 17–19 on the road north of Hangye, during which the 2d and 3rd battalions of the 23rd had to fight their way to the rear and out of an entrapment because of an enemy-cut road to their rear.

The division historian at the time would refer to the engagement as the "May Massacre." Others would refer to it as the "Hangye Gauntlet." Call it what one may, it was an ordeal for the 23rd Regiment not much unlike the slaughterhouse at the Kunu-ri "gauntlet" of S. L. A. Marshall only four months earlier, which almost wiped out the division.

The Chinese forces that Darmer and the NCOs and I had seen on the road behind the two battalions had been vastly strengthened and reinforced. After we had been allowed to slip through them, they completely sealed off the road and awaited the arrival of the withdrawing battalions. When the battalions started back, belatedly, the Chinese were ready, and all hell broke loose.

The battalion commanders, Jenson and Richardson, with tanks of the division's 72d Battalion, banged away repeatedly at the Chinese roadblocks. Colonel Chiles, with a leg shell-fragment wound, characterized the Chinese resistance on the roadblock as continuous and fanatical. Convoys of vehicles on the road were stopped and fired on by Chinese from the flanks. Gridlock to the extreme prevailed, and it was more paralyzing than a 1990 Washington, D.C., I-495 beltway blockage after the collision of two or more eighteen-wheelers.

By a series of skillful infantry maneuvers and with superb support from the armored cannons of the tankers and constant air and artillery missions, the battalions finally managed to extricate themselves. By May 19 they had passed through our lst Battalion in its covering positions on the outskirts of Hangye. At the end of the day all battalions, including the French, were in new defensive positions on the high ground south and southeast of Hangye. That was the point of maximum CCF advance and we were to withdraw no further.

The 3rd Infantry Division to the Rescue

An extraordinary example of battlefield mobility was occurring during all this fighting with the relocation of the 3rd Division from the west. The army commander had finally given in to the pleas of General Almond and had ordered the 3rd reassigned to the X Corps. The 3rd would go into position to the right of us and in the area left empty by the collapse of the ROK divisions.

In a remarkable and speedy display of mobility, the 3rd Division had moved almost all the way across Korea under cover of darkness. The problems of maintaining secrecy for such an enormous amount of armor, vehicles, and troops must have been challenging almost beyond description. I heard many words of praise for the division and its commanders afterwards.

The arrival of the 3rd Division was most comforting to the 2d, with its exposed flank to the east. An encounter with my old unit, the 7th Infantry of the 3rd, was not long coming. It was on a road some miles south of Hangye on a late afternoon shortly after our regiment had relocated to its new defensive positions just south of the town. I had stopped for some reason, and, glancing up, saw a jeep with the 7th Regiment bumper markings, strange to our area until then. There were a couple of tired-looking junior officers in the vehicle.

"Hey!" I shouted to them. "What outfit you fellers from?"

"Seventh Regiment," came back the quick answer with some obvious pride.

"Seventh Regiment? What division is that outfit in?"

The two looked at each other with much impatience that a fellow officer in the American army would not know that the 7th was in the 3rd Division.

"The 3rd Division," one answered in a tone that implied, even if it did not say, "you dummy."

"Third Division?" I continued, baitingly. "Is that division here in Korea? I thought the 3rd was doing garrison duty back in the noncombat zone."

By this time I could see the two "cotton balers" were reaching the boiling point and about ready to come out of their jeep at me. I decided the time had come to defuse the situation; that is, if I wanted to keep my scalp. I approached their jeep and smiled.

"Relax, guys. Just needling you. You're in my old regiment from the big one some years back. No one need tell me about your 'Rock of the Marne' and its combat record." With that they looked at each other and then also broke into a smile.

"You had us fooled there for a moment. We thought you were looking for a fat lip."

"No way," I replied. "We've all got enough to do over here without fighting each other—especially on as stupid a subject as whose outfit has it the roughest when we all have it so rough. Just damned glad you've arrived."

With that we parted company. We were to see much more of the 3rd in the coming weeks and months. There was yet to be much bloodletting, and no one could object to spreading it around with some equality.

A couple days after my encounter with the 3rd Division officers, I wandered into the CP.

"Stand by for briefing, Pratt," Radow greeted me.

"Roger, Sammy. Am standing by. Something brewing?"

"Always," Radow said. "Corps Commander has concluded the Chinks have shot their wad and Van Fleet says now it's time to launch Operation 'Detonate.' "

" 'Detonate'? You mean we're now to go back on the offensive?"

"That's it."

"Great guns. Up and down, back and forth. How can we go on the offense so quickly after fighting so desperately to keep the enemy off our backs just three days ago at the Hangye gauntlet?"

"Well, that's for smarter guys than me to decide, but reports are that the CCF paid a ghastly price for it's Sixth Offensive, just over. They lost whole corps and tens of thousands to UN firepower."

"But haven't we, too? Our regiment has many wounds to lick and heal."

"Yeah. True. But the rest of division and corps are apparently in much better shape. Everyone's getting replacements tonight. Big guys think now it's time to strike, and hard. Better get your logistical plans buffed up, Pratt."

"Roger, Sammy." And off I went. Clay Blair was to later describe the period just ending:

... the week of May 16 to May 23 had been one of the most remarkable episodes of the Korean War—another magnificent victory. Nick Ruffner's 2d Division had withstood a savage pounding by most of two

CCF armies (six divisions) and with scarcely a pause had launched a vigorous counterattack.*

The UN Counteroffensive

The X Corps commander, General Almond, reported on May 20 that the tide had begun to turn against the enemy, and three days later the army commander ordered the implementation of "Detonate." The X Corps jumped into the offense. By the twenty-fifth, it was clear the enemy was withdrawing rapidly. The X Corps continued in its drive northward with the Marines and the 187th Airborne Regiment spearheading.

In the last days of May, elements of the 2d Division passed through the 187th and our regiment reached the old "Kansas" line, roughly, in our central sector, along the 38th, more than retaking all the ground lost in the Chinese Sixth Offensive of a few days earlier.

We were well along on the last great push northward by the UN, and another major milestone in the war. On the twenty-seventh the regiment reached Inje, some ten miles north of the parallel and above the reservoir with only scattered enemy resistance and at times no contact at all. The lst Battalion went into position in some rough low mountains overlooking the town to its northwest.

All battalions continued their slow and careful move northward through rough, mountainous terrain. By June 4 the lst Battalion was in position on the east-west road connecting the main artery north from Inje on our right and the road north from Yanggu, about ten miles to our west. I remember recalling on that date that it was also the June 4 anniversary of the entrance of my 7th Infantry Regiment into Rome in the aftermath of the Anzio beachhead breakout seven years earlier, back in 1944.

The stage was set for the additional moves northward for limited distances in the weeks to come that would result in the historic and agonizing engagements on Bloody and Heartbreak ridges, at the Punchbowl, and elsewhere later that year and into 1952 and 1953, until

* Clay Blair, *The Forgotten War* (New York: Time Books, 1987), p. 897.

the cease-fire agreement. The ground we were on would not again be occupied by the enemy.

It is recorded that at this point Generals Van Fleet and Almond wanted to continue the pursuit of the enemy forces and complete the operation. General Ridgway in Tokyo, no doubt operating on instructions from Washington, directed that the Eighth Army and X Corps stop and go on the defensive, at least for the time being.

A contemplated marine landing at Tongch'on well up the east coast and about due east of P'yongyang and a dash by the 187th from Inje to Kansong below Tongch'on were cancelled.

With respect to the 2d, it was decided it had sacrificed enough and had earned a long respite. Accordingly, it was ordered into reserve for remanning and other purposes.

On June 5 we were relieved and began withdrawing to our reserve assembly areas around Hongch'on. The relief of the division from the lines was completed by the twelfth.

The division historian was to write that the 2d had killed more than 65,000 enemy troops and that the reserve period was to be "the longest non-combat period enjoyed by the division since its arrival in Korea and it was the unanimous opinion of all that no division deserved it more."

CHAPTER FOURTEEN

Summer Bivouac—a Respite and Breather

When not devastated by war, Korea is one of the loveliest countries on planet Earth. Its beauty is spectacular and breathtaking.

The country's soaring and majestic mountains form a panoramic backdrop for picturesque scenes from almost any angle or viewpoint in the land. There are endless valleys carpeted with paddies of waving rice plants and dotted with quaint and fascinating villages with "Papa-sans" in their distinctive and traditional native dress, with pipes and hats.

Korea in Magnificence and in Shambles

Snowcapped peaks mirrored in the reflective waters of the inland lakes, rivers, and reservoirs could well deceive an American visitor into thinking he or she is viewing the Grand Tetons in Wyoming. Or, traveling along the rocky coastal roads with countless coves and inlets, especially around Koje Do or Mokp'o in the south, one might imagine he or she is at Midway Point on the Seventeen Mile Drive at California's Pacific Groove area.

Modern urban areas transform smoothly as the tourist moves around into peaceful and colorful rural settings. From one end to the other in Korea, the landscape and scenery today and throughout most of history is the stuff of which tourist brochures and picture postcards are made. Pastoral land- and seascapes and inviting outdoor scenery abound. Korea's designation as the "Land of the Morning Calm" is well deserved and most understandable, to which just about anyone can attest who visits the country in these last decades of the twentieth century.

But it has not always been so. By the summer of 1951 and just a year after the North Korean invasion across the 38th parallel, Korea lay in shambles. It was broken, bleeding, and smouldering. As the war juggernaut rolled south almost to Pusan, then back to the far north, again south of the parallel, and then for months seesawed up and down, almost everything and anything in the country was destroyed. After a year of bitter fighting, Korea had suffered much the same fate as the Italian boot, and other areas, in World War II.

The movement of armor and other heavy military equipment had destroyed almost every road in the country until they were rebuilt by the engineers. Almost nowhere did any bridge remain standing. Factories, power plants, and other industrial facilities and community structures such as hospitals, schools, and administrative buildings were bombed into oblivion with only hollow walls, if anything, remaining. Most towns were but ghosts of what they had been to their former occupants.

Worst off of all were the people of Korea, who by the millions had been burned or blasted out and dispossessed of their homes. They were living, or existing, in caves, tents, cardboard boxes, lean-tos, or even open fields in their efforts to survive, and for the most part, starving and suffering horribly in the process.

Beauty in the Bivouac

In the midst of and in spite of all this, in June of 1951 our division settled in its reserve positions around Hongch'on in relatively pleasant circumstances. Hongch'on is smack in the center of the Korean peninsula, about fifty miles due east of Seoul and about thirty miles south of the 38th parallel.

Being near the 38th parallel meant that the climatic zone would be temperate and the summers from warm to hot. In Korea, the summers are also extremely wet with torrential rains through most of the summer months.

The 38th parallel of latitude, just to our north, circles the globe and passes through or near San Francisco, Saint Louis, Washington, D.C., Lisbon, Athens, and Izmir, Turkey.

As pathetic and devastated as were the conditions generally in Korea in June of 1951, it was possible in our bivouac valley to almost forget, for a few days at least, that we were in a war zone and in the midst of widespread hardships and destruction. Tents were set up. Kitchens were cranked into action and hot meals were served. There were even PX supplies of candy, snacks, toilet articles, and assorted other goodies.

Promptly in our "rest"-area bivouac there were engineer-operated showers again at the streams and in the evenings the 16-mm projectors were unpacked and movies were shown to the troops. It was not very difficult to imagine that we were on field maneuvers in the back hills of any one of many military reservations back in the States.

Activities in the Bivouac

One day in mid-June, I strolled routinely into the battalion CP after completing some of my supply duties and ambled up to ever-active Sammy Radow.

"What's in store for us, Sammy? How long is this good life going to last?" I asked.

"Not sure, Pratt, me boy, but looks like around a month at least."

"Wow!" I shot back. "Sounds too good to be true. Are the troops to just lie around in the sacks and live it up?"

"You don't believe that any more than I would. You've never seen a time when troops were permitted to do that?"

I had to admit that I had not. Rest from combat never meant complete idleness, from my experience. "So what's in store?"

"Starting tomorrow, the fifteenth," Sammy continued, "there are intensified training programs to implement. Lots of new replacements arriving again. So companies will cover the spectrum of training subjects."

"The usual close order drill and athletics?"

"Oh, much more than that. Division and regiment have ordered heavy training on crew-served weapons, communications, field fortifications, and night attacks. Also supply discipline is to be especially stressed. Higher-ups are POed that too much equipment is being left around. Falls into enemy hands and then gets used against us."

"We don't want to overdo that aspect of the operations. If troops get too conservation-minded, I might be out of a job."

"And that would break your heart wouldn't it, Mr. Supply Officer? You might even then be sent home."

"No command inspections?" I asked.

"Of course. To ask that question is to answer it. In fact, our battalion and the mortar company are slated for one on the eighteenth. But first, on the sixteenth, day after tomorrow, the command is to spend the morning practicing for a parade. Must get all men and equipment shined up for that."

Sammy was right. On the afternoon of the sixteenth the regiment passed in review before the corps and division commanders with Colonel Chiles and newly arrived Col. James Adams in attendance on the reviewing stand. Few knew that Adams would shortly be taking over command of the regiment upon the reassignment of Chiles. The band sounded rusty, but still great. Award and decorations were passed out for those still around to receive them. Some recipients were absent, recovering from wounds. Many, sadly, were also absent because they were no longer listed among the living.

Carrying parties departing supply dumps in central Korea in summer of 1951 en route to remote troops' positions several hours away.

A forward landing strip and supply dump of the 2d Infantry Division in Korea in the summer of 1951 near Wonju and Hongch'on.

Improvised troops' "showers" in reserve positions in central Korea in the summer of 1951. The safer engineer-run showers were not often available.

X Corps commander Maj. Gen. Edward Almond, the "Big A," arrives at the bivouac positions of the 23rd Reg. in central Korea for a command inspection.

Troops of the 1st Bn./23rd Reg. stand "at ease" for a command inspection by the corps commander in central Korea in the summer of 1951.

Supply-carrying parties of the 1st Bn./23rd Reg. prepare to depart for the six-hour climb to frontline positions on Heartbreak Ridge in late summer 1951.

The exigencies of combat often called for unorthodox and ingenious displays of creativity, but they usually accomplished the desired purposes.

A trooper from the 23rd Reg.'s positions on Heartbreak Ridge monitors the progress of a patrol entering the Punchbowl far below.

Heavenly Contacts

On Sunday, June 17, church services for all faiths were offered for the first time in many weeks. I had passed the chaplain, Father Woods, the previous day, somewhere in the bivouac area.

"Are you going to be at services tomorrow, Captain Pratt? It will be a good influence for the men."

"I'll try, Father, to be with you, although, as you know, I am a Protestant, usually."

"Yes, I know. But you are welcome among us Catholics, too."

"I understand and appreciate your graciousness. I fear, though, that I must go to the rear on a crash-supply mission. We have big command inspection coming up. Gotta make sure there are no shortages of equipment."

"Of course. But join us if you can."

"I will, but if I can't perhaps you can put in good word for me to that big commander eternal in the heavens."

"Naturally, I will do so," said the chaplain. "But am sure he would rather hear it from you direct."

I thought that a retort I could not top and decided to quit while I was not too far behind. I saluted the chaplain, made my farewells, and stole smartly away. I could hear him chuckling behind me.

The good chaplain and I had engaged in similar exchanges on previous occasions as related. He quite correctly never gave up in prodding me to attend his services. Actually, I usually did when I could and felt guilty and remiss when I did not.

As we underwent our command inspection on the eighteenth, the rest of the regiment conducted training in small-arms firing, platoon and company firing problems, tactics, dismounted drill, bayonet drills, marches, and proficiency tests on 60-mm and 81-mm mortars and heavy machine guns. It was clear that we were off to a flying start in our "rest" period to insure that the division was whipped again into the most combat-ready condition and as quickly as possible.

Later in June the regimental battalions, including the French, participated in larger unit exercises with our supporting 37th Field Artillery Battalion and the tankers. The training continued through June and well into July. On several occasions, to the delight of the troops and with much pushing and shoving for best positions, the USO field shows visited the division units in their rest areas. Included among the USO shows was the renowned "Camel Caravan" group.

More Action or Cease-Fire?

One day in early July on a trip to the regimental CP area, I chanced upon the acting S-3, lst Lt. Hershel Chapman, who had once been one of my officers in Baker Company, and the newly arrived TI and E, or troop information and education officer, lst Lt. Thomas Waddell. Waddell was soon to become the regimental intelligence officer, or S-2.

"Things seem awful quiet around this valley just now," I ventured, as I approached the two sitting at a field table in the S-3 CP tent. "Is the war over and someone forgot to let us know?"

"There's a joker in every crowd, Captain Pratt. You trying to be him?"

"Sort of, I guess. Anyway, what gives these days? Is anything of import happening?"

Both of these officers were in spots where they could be expected to possess up-to-the-minute information on conditions, and lots of it. They both started talking at once, then looked at each other, laughed, and Waddell deferred to Chapman.

"For our part, Captain Pratt, we are headed in a few days, probably midmonth about, back to the lines. We're going to relieve the 5th Marine Regiment on the 'Kansas' line up above Inje, just north of the parallel."

"And then? Another major offensive?"

"Doesn't seem so, although there's likely to be aggressive patrolling beyond the 'Kansas' line and some adjusting of frontline positions. For sure, the top command at present is in a period of contemplation."

"Contemplation? Is that the correct word to use? It's refreshing to learn that someone over here in Korea is doing some thinking. Other than us, of course."

"Well, it's about as good a word as any. The question pestering Washington and Tokyo is whether there is much to be gained, and many more lives to be lost, by continuing to attack. The public shows signs of tiring of this war."

"So do we strike tents, quit, and go home?" I offered in an effort to show lightheartedness.

"Wouldn't we all like that? Actually, the next moves seem to center around efforts to arrange a cease-fire. There's been talk of meeting somewhere up above Seoul with the Communists' representatives."

"Really?" I said excitedly. "Any progress?"

"Well, yes," Tom Waddell joined in. "There is to be a first meeting in Kaesong in the next few days, I think the tenth. Adm. Turner Joy is Ridgway's rep."

"What're the prospects for results?"

"Big question. Word is that there are many issues to be ironed out."

"Such as?"

"Where will cease-fire line be drawn? Along present positions, or do we pull back to the 38th, as the Communists are demanding, and give up lots of real estate north of the parallel our guys fought and died to win? Also, we want some guarantees before we stop fighting about the release of POWs now rotting away in Communist camps. How soon will there be a real exchange of POWs?"

"By George, the matter does get complicated, huh?"

"You bet," added Chapman again. "Even the place where they are meeting is highly controversial."

"Why so?"

"Because our side wants a truly neutral meeting place."

"Isn't Kaesong in neutral territory?"

"It was, but the Communists moved in with armed troops. UN people entering the area must pass through Communist checkpoints and people arriving by choppers are escorted to meeting places by Communist armed guards. The Communists are even keeping out the Western press. The place is anything but neutral. It's strictly under the control of the Communists."

"Then why doesn't our side tell them to shove it until they shape up?"

"Van Fleet was in here few days ago and said Ridgway sure wanted to do so, but is under much pressure from Washington not to take any action that would jeopardize chances for a cease-fire.

Anyway, even if talks are started, guesses are they could go on and on, from past experience with communist negotiators."

"In the meantime, war goes on, I suppose?"

"That's about it. But not with too much vigor, it seems. Everyone at the top seems to want to hold casualties to a minimum with public support evaporating back home."

"And I know of no one around here who wants to be the war's last casualty," I felt impelled to add.

And so the war would roll on for almost another two years. And little did we suspect on that pleasant and peaceful summer day in our bivouac valley how heavy the casualties and bitter the fighting were soon to be.

During the second week in July, I wandered again one morning into Sammy Radow's "war room" tent in response to a notice of a staff meeting by the battalion commander. We had just observed Independence Day a day or so earlier with athletics, movies, a band concert, and some other diversions.

While waiting for the staff and others to assemble, I perused Sammy's sitmap with UN and NKPA* and CCF forces all lined up, opposing each other as reflected by neat little map symbols along the "Kansas" line just north of the 38th in our central zone. I noted our global location, about five miles northeast of Hongch'on off the MSR, to be at longitude 127°, 55' east of the prime meridian at Greenwich, and 37°, 34' north of the equator, with a magnetic compass deviation of 6° west off true north. What priceless information, I thought, if I were sailing a boat down the center of our central Korean valley. The problem was, I wasn't sailing. So what was the use for such information? Perhaps the artillerymen needed it in their fire-direction centers.

A New Regimental Commander

While prognosticating on possible uses for my newfound informational treasures I heard a rustle of activity behind me and someone saying we should take our seats. A moment later an officer barked us

* North Korean People's Army.

to attention and in walked the regimental commander, Col. Jack
Chiles, with a tall, slender bird colonel in tow.

"At ease, gentlemen," Chiles ordered as he reached the front of
the group. As we settled and sat waiting, he continued.

"There is some changes in command coming up that I want you
to know about here in the 1st Battalion as well as the rest of the
regiment. I will be leaving shortly for rotation back to a new assignment in the Pentagon. Upon my departure, our exec, Frank Meszar,
will assume command, but only temporarily. He too is due for rotation,
and when he leaves your new regimental CO will be Col. James
Adams," he said, pointing to the new colonel by his side. Chiles added
some comments about Adams' background. Then, after some intro-
ductions all around, the two with their aides departed, leaving Major
Russell to complete the briefing of his staff on other matters.

Most of us greeted the news of Colonel Chiles' departure with
mixed emotions. Chiles had not been a bad commander at all. In many
ways we considered him to be better than average, and, in fact, he was
to go on and finish his career with the two stars of a major general—no
doubt helped immensely by his wartime command experience as our
regimental CO.

A big, big strike against Chiles in the 23rd Regiment, probably,
was first a general feeling of much resentment by some regimental
officers that he had been crammed upon us as a "teacher's pet" of
General Almond, and at the price of the forced reassignment of our
popular and well-liked Paul Freeman.

In fairness to Chiles, it can be said that such a situation placed
him in an untenable and certainly not a very envious position as a new
commander. Freeman was highly respected and extraordinarily
capable and, quite simply, a hard act to follow, no matter how well
qualified his successor. Nevertheless, the departure of Chiles, for these
reasons among some others, was not the cause of great moaning at the
bar among the rank and file insofar as I could determine at the time.

A Battalion Staff Briefing

Russell then called on Radow and the acting S-2 to brief us on
what to expect when the division returned to combat to relieve the

marines on the "Kansas" line about midmonth. We learned that on line we would again have the ROK divisions on our right to the east coast, one ROK division on our left, and the 7th U. S. Division beyond. We were to go in at just about the places we had been a month before when relieved by the marines—on the mountain mass between valleys leading north from the towns of Yanggu and Inje just over the 38th and above the Hwach'on Reservoir.

Russell then called on his other staff officers for contributions to the briefing session. Finally, he glanced in my direction.

"What have you got in the logistical department, Pratt, for the good of the order and the enlightenment of the command?"

"Well, Major, I think I have some info, generally good. Most of our requisitions for clothing and weapons and other equipment have been filled. Supply-wise I can report we are ready for combat, or substantially so. But a special note, over and above the PX supplies, is that we are going to start receiving Cokes and beer. The ration will be one each per day per man. That's a first in combat in this or any other war."

"I don't see how we have fought the war thus far without those essentials," Russell responded with a wink at others in the tent.

"But that's not all," I hastened to add. "The bigger and almost unbelievable news is that we are, starting today in this battalion, going to get our ratio of ice cream. Some will greet this with disinterest likely, but for others it should be a big moral booster."

"You have to be joking, Pratt," said one officer. "How the hell they going to get ice cream here in central Korea in midsummer?"

"No joke, good buddy. The quartermaster people have portable freezers and storage fridges, gasoline-powered, and they will roll them around, rotating from unit to unit. The ration won't be enormous—not like a commissary of supermarket back home with all the half-gallon cartons one wants. But will be at least a taste of one cup about once a week."

"And the team will be in our area tonight?"

"That's an affirmative. We can expect the troops to be drawing cards for each other's minute share. Or trading their beer or Coke ration. But at least there will be a taste for real ice-cream lovers after all these months. A nostalgic reminder of home."

"And what's our illustrious administrative officer have for us?" asked Russell, turning to Lynn Freeman.

"Also good news. R and R to Japan is to be stepped up. Everyone is to get at least one R and R trip during their tour in Korea. Many of you are already due and can be sent away just as rapidly as the battalion commander and I work out a schedule."

With so much good news, it seemed there was little else to say, so the meeting broke up. There were troops also to be briefed and there was balancing to be done as to what extent good news outweighed, if it did, the less-than-sought-after communiqué that a return to the lines was just offstage.

CHAPTER FIFTEEN

Return to the Front and a New Job

The "Indianhead' Division Returns to the Front

"Coffee? Soft drink? Beer? Water, Tom?" I asked my interrogator in my rec room on that March evening in 1988 in Arlington.

Tom Ryan, the staff historian from Eighth Army Headquarters in Seoul, waited to answer until the roar of a string of military choppers passing overhead disappeared in the distance.

"Nothing at the moment, Mr. Pratt." Tom Ryan was a most circumspective person and had not yet began addressing me more informally. "But what're all those helicopters doing on your rooftop? Are you conducting a private little war here in South Arlington? Do you have your own heliport?"

"Hardly, Tom. I would laugh at your response, but we here don't think it very funny."

"They must be military? There were so many just now, and huge. They actually shook your house to the foundations. Is this a frequent or common occurrence?"

"Sad for us to say, it is," I answered. "Often daily. Sometimes hourly. And in flocks."

"Are they on maneuvers here in the capital area?"

"No, no. They are based down at Fort Belvoir, some twenty miles south, at Davidson Field. Among other things, they provide chopper support to and from the Pentagon."

"You mean the Pentagon is under attack?"

"Well, yes, but not the way you might be implying. There is no shortage of people out to get the Pentagon, or its occupants—the media, the Hill, taxpayers, the peace movements, and many others. But there's no military assault around there, at least just yet, and the passengers on the choppers, ordinarily, are not troops heading into combat."

"Then why are the choppers buzzing around?"

"Many local residents and taxpayers ask the same thing. The Pentagon people would describe it as 'administrative support' for various governmental activities."

"Such as?"

"Oh, congressional requests, diplomatic missions. Sometimes to bring in military people for holiday or other observances at Arlington Cemetery, the White House, or the national monuments. But the joke among the locals here when they look up at a string of choppers passing low overhead is that the generals and admirals must be going to lunch or some other place nearby that they want to reach without fighting local traffic gridlocks in the metropolitan Washington area."

"Why are they so low, almost skimming your rooftop?"

"To avoid confrontations with the swarms of commercial jets and other traffic in and out of National, Dulles, and Baltimore International airports in the immediate area. Word here is that the choppers must stay under about 500 feet, but to us below their flight path it often seems they are much lower."

"And their flight path is through your kitchen?"

"Almost so, it seems, as you can see and hear. They are supposed to follow I-95–I-395 inside Arlington—to and from the Pentagon heliport."

"And that's just outside your front door?"

"Right. We are exactly three houses from the interstate, which accounts also for the constant hum of eighteen-wheelers and other traffic you hear."

"Gets wearisome?"

"You can believe that."

"Then why do you stay?"

"What else is a body to do these days? It's the price of living in an urban area, I suppose."

"Perhaps you are right," agreed Ryan. "We have some similar rackets around us where we work, play, and live in Korea, but perhaps it's unavoidable with military activities. But let's get back to the war in Korea. You're going to cover now the return of the 'Indianhead' Division to the front lines in July 1951?"

The War Continues for the "Indianheaders"

"Yes, our time had come. All good things must end, so the expression goes, and so did end our relatively pleasant and certainly not very hazardous stay in the summer bivouac-area around Hongch'on."

On July 12, advance elements of the 2d Division began moving out to relieve the Marine Division then on positions roughly the same as those occupied by the 2d a month earlier, when the 2d was relieved.

All regiments of the 2d took their positions and by the 15th the relief had been substantially completed. Our 23rd Regiment again occupied defensive positions on the mountainous mass to the northwest of the MSR running north from the town of Inje.

Punchbowl Defensive Positions

During the last two weeks of July, the regiment's battalions improved defensive positions and conducted continuous patrolling into a broad valley just to the front that would become known as the "Punchbowl."

The Punchbowl would become well known to us and to the home

folks back in the USA. We were to be quite active there, and later in the war, when the peace talks would collapse, the marines would experience some particularly heavy fighting in and around the Bowl. Their fighting there, in the shadows of the high ground to the immediate west, which would become known as Heartbreak Ridge, would be the subject of a Hollywood film of the same name.

The Punchbowl was, and is, a broad valley, roughly 7,000 yards from north to south, and 5,000 yards from east to west, or vice versa. Through the Bowl passes an east-west portion of Korean Highway 453, which runs down to Inje, fifteen miles to the south and about three miles north of the 38th parallel.

Most of the Punchbowl had been filled with tiny villages or clusters of farm dwellings and rice paddies before the war. Near its center are several rises in elevation, including Hill 525, which was to figure repeatedly in combat patrol and other activity. In the northern half of the Bowl, there was an abandoned airstrip for light planes just on the edge of the village of Songhwangdang.

Upon returning to the line, the defensive positions of the 23rd Regiment were on the high ground to the east, southeast, and south of, and overlooking, the Punchbowl opposite the Heartbreak Ridge high ground to the west of the Bowl. The regiment would remain on those positions for the rest of July and almost all of August, during which time position improvements would be made, and vigorous and continuous patrolling would be carried out, mostly into the Punchbowl.

On the fifth of August, I accompanied the ration and supply column from the battalion CP up into the high ground around Hill 793 near the northern edge of the Bowl. Hill 793 was to serve as a patrol base for many of the forays down into the Bowl. The view of the Bowl from that location was spectacular.

Two of Baker Company's officers saw us approaching and came forward to receive their supplies. They never missed an opportunity to needle their former company commander.

"Well, well," one said. "If it isn't none other than the supply officer himself, leaving the safety and plushness of his bivouac down below to join us peasants on the lofty peaks."

"Right," I shot back. "Gotta get out and see how life is on the other side of the tracks. What are you chaps doing to earn all this gourmet chow in C-ration cans we're bringing up to you? Just sitting around on your cans?"

"Of course. Very boring. In desperation, to break the monotony, and to keep the battalion CO happy, since he ordered us to do so, we cruise down into the Bowl with some regularity."

"And what have been the results of that cruising?" I asked, getting a little more serious.

"Well, mixed. Two days ago patrols from Charlie Company and the French Battalion went into the Bowl near Hill 525, without any enemy contact. They found some houses with booby traps and burned the houses. But yesterday, when one of our platoons went down to scout Hill 525, they came under fire from a dozen or so enemy at the crest."

"So what did the platoon do?"

"They withdrew as directed."

"And then?"

"The battalion commander ordered the whole company to go down, encircle the hill, and take prisoners."

"And did they?"

"No. The enemy dubbed their boots and withdrew smartly. They apparently had had enough when confronted with a whole company."

"So? No prisoners? Mission a failure?"

"Not completely. The patrol covered the hill with antipersonnel mines and returned. A little later the French set up an ambush a short distance away, but nobody came. So they too withdrew."

After some more words, I too withdrew and started the long hike back down the hill into the valley below, where our battalion CP was located. A refreshing difference in the supply trails on the hills leading to the Punchbowl area positions, as contrasted to those in earlier weeks further south, was the absence of enemy troops behind the lines to ambush the carrying parties.

The frontline positions in late summer of 1951 were relatively stable, and units were tied in with each other and connected. This made it difficult for the enemy to infiltrate through the lines and circulate into the rear areas.

A Period of Probing and Patrolling

The rest of August continued to be a period of relative quiet in the 23rd Regiment's area, during which we and the enemy mostly probed each other's positions. It was a time for the two sides to feel each other out and assess relative strengths, positions, and intentions.

Numerous patrols were sent into the Bowl, sometimes without incident, and at other times came under fire from mortars or small arms. On August 26, a Baker patrol pushed as far as the village of Oryu-ri on the western edge of the Bowl, where it contacted an enemy patrol in the same area and withdrew after a short exchange of fire.

On the nineteenth, twenty-fifth, and twenty-eighth of August, Able Company positions on Hill 793 were probed by the enemy who also withdrew after learning that the area was occupied by our troops.

Relief by the Marines and Repositioning

In the last days of August, the Marine 5th Regiment relieved the regiment and the battalions of the 23rd and began a generally westward relocation to the southwesterly edges of the Punchbowl, and below some of the highest terrain, some five miles to the north, which would become known as Heartbreak Ridge.

While the 23rd had been patrolling the Punchbowl from its positions on its southeasterly rims, the division's 9th and 38th regiments had not been idle to the west. Those units had been for most of the month of August engaged in bitter fighting to take, lose, and retake, again and again, a series of ridges and high ground identified on the map as Hills 983, 910, and 773, which would become known as Bloody Ridge. The 23rd was being moved around and into the area to join in that continuing struggle.

Promotion and a New Job

It was about this time in the late summer of 1951 that Major Russell motioned to me one day to come near and lend an ear.

"Pratt, there's some news just in that will shock you, I imagine."

"Don't know that much of anything these days would shock me, Sir. Unless you say the war is over."

"This will, I assure you. I've just been advised that on the latest DA* list you've been promoted. You're now a major."

"Well, that is a bit of a shock," I had to agree, but not entirely unexpected, and certainly not unpleasant.

"You can shock me like this anytime you wish, Major." I had almost six years in grade as a captain, which made me quite senior. With combat time thrown in, I knew that I must be ripe for advancement, if the experience of others could be taken as a guide.

"I don't have any other shocks like that, Major," he replied, with deliberate stress on the "major." He knew it was the first time I had been so called, and he was enjoying my reaction.

"But there's one thing lacking, it seems to me," I said.

"Yeah? What's that?"

"You're being left behind yourself. Would be nice to see you sporting some silver leaves. What's the status on your own promotion to light colonel?"

"Never mind. I understand it's in the mill. Should be forthcoming pretty soon. Anyway, you've now got to have a new assignment."

"You're right, I suppose. Haven't had time yet for me to think of that. What am I now to do? You don't need a major for a supply officer, do you?"

"Hardly at all. Nor can I keep you as my exec, since Radow's promotion had also come through and he has asked for the exec slot. You are to go to regimental staff now."

"To regiment? What am I to do there?"

"Colonel Adams wants you as his exec."

"His exec? Why? He doesn't even know me that well. I doubt he remembers ever talking with me."

"Perhaps not, but Al Metts knows you and has put in a good word."

"But why exec? That's a light-colonel slot. Why such a big jump so quick?"

"Don't get the big head, me boy. I don't think the regimental CO is excluding all the rest of the officer corps just for you. It's simply that

* Department of the Army.

rotation is being stepped up and most of the light colonels are going home. There is no one around to fill the job, so you are it."

"So when do I leave?"

"I'm going to pick a new supply officer to replace you. As soon as you think you have broken him in, you'll be free to take off and report in to Colonel Adams. Work it out with my new exec, Sammy Radow. Thanks for the fine work you've done for me, and good luck on your new job."

Within several days I had completed the turnover of my duties to my replacement and made my farewells. In due course, after some delays in traveling due to rough roads and flooded streams from the midsummer flash thunderstorms, I arrived at the regimental CP and sought out the regimental commander. I found him conferring with some of his staff and waited until he had finished. He glanced up and saw me, whereupon I saluted as smartly as I could.

New Duties, New Ridges

"Colonel Adams, I am Major Pratt from the 1st Battalion and reporting for duty. Do I understand that I am to be your exec?"

Adams smiled warmly, returned my salute, and extended his hand.

"That's right, Major Pratt. We've been expecting you."

I was much pleased with this first contact with the regimental commander. I was to find my relationship with him to be pleasant and rewarding. Adams, I would learn, was another rather remarkable officer and combat commander. He was tall, slender, and exceptionally agile. He could take off up a hill like a deer, and keep it up all day with hardly a pause for breath.

Adams also took his job quite seriously. I had the feeling that combat command was a new experience for him, and one that he accepted with much gusto and enthusiasm. He literally radiated energy. It was as though he had a new and enjoyable toy out of which he was determined to get the most he could. One could readily see that he greatly relished his responsibilities. He showed that he was determined to keep constantly on top of the situation in his regiment and personally direct its operation to the maximum extent practicable.

Adams told me to relax for a bit until he had finished with some items at hand, after which he would fill me in on his ideas of how he wanted me to operate. I assumed he would advise me, as the executive officer, that I would run the staff for him, especially in his absence, as is the case ordinarily for an exec. But he had other concepts of my duties.

"Pratt," he began a bit later, "as you know, an exec is in general the chief officer for a military staff. He is to supervise, monitor, coordinate, and be responsible for administrative and supply matters, leaving the commander free for operations and command."

"Yes, Sir," I answered. "That's the way I understand it, and I'll try to do my best for you."

"Well, not so fast. Of course I expect that, too, but in addition, or even more so, I want you to be my alter ego and command backup. I need a second set of eyes to keep track of the tactical situation and I want you to help me in that way."

"I'm not sure just what you mean, Colonel Adams," I replied. "How, or why, am I to do that?"

"Well, I don't sit on my duff all day, but still, we are spread over such a wide area, and in such unbelievably rough and remote terrain, that I find it simply impossible to cover all the areas every day that I want to."

"And how am I to fit in?" I asked probingly, while at the same time highly suspicious that I knew all too well where Adams was leading. Upon learning of my promotion and reassignment some days earlier, I had been reveling with the expectation that henceforth I might have life easier. I viewed my ridge-running days up and down the high ground as terminated, for all practical purposes. I envisioned myself as leading the life of the "rear echelonner," off the very forward front lines, and near the field kitchens, with hot coffee and chow and, most likely, a dry place to sleep at night.

"You're to fit just like a well-tailored glove, Major Pratt. You and I shall consult daily, or as often as possible, and plan our schedules with a goal of one or the other visiting every regimental battalion every day. It would be physically impossible for only me to do it, and not sure even that we both can do it, but at least we can try."

"Right you are, Colonel, we can certainly make a big dent in your objective," I said, trying to sound cooperative and enthusiastic, but thinking to myself, "Damn! There goes my life of ease hanging around the regimental CP and the hot meals and other perks."

"But if I'm away from the CP most of the time, you're not concerned that the administration may go to pot?" I ventured.

"Not really. We've got quite a strong staff now. Al Metts is a real doer as the S-3, and with powerhouses Joe Hannover as S-1 and Tom Waddell as S-2, the staff will almost run itself without any supervision. Anyway, it's a risk I am more than willing to take if it will get me a much-needed helper like you to stay in close contact with the frontline units. I have to use my staff officers where I think they will do the most good, and this is how I think you will do the most good."

And so it was. For the rest of my time in Korea and all around the coming Heartbreak Ridge miseries, I was to spend the bulk of my time continuing my high ground and ridge-running activities. The combat man's "life of Riley" for me was yet to be realized.

CHAPTER SIXTEEN

Wartime Administrative Roadblocks

One bright day soon after assuming my new duties of the regimental exec, I was confronted with a combination administrative-tactical situation requiring remedial action of some kind.

It all happened in the 3rd Battalion sector, high up in the mountains, about the time the 23rd was shifting westward away from the high ground overlooking the Punchbowl. We were en route to join in the Bloody Ridge fighting, then in heavy progress. Some of our own line companies were already thick in the fighting and getting more heavily involved by the day and hour. Thus far, however, the 3rd Battalion did not seem to be in direct contact with any enemy forces.

Self-inflicted Wounds—What to Do?

As I approached the battalion CP, I noticed in the "aid station" nearby two men on litters, apparently awaiting evacuation down the hill by bearers.

"What's the problem with those troopers?" I asked one of the medics at hand.

"Gunshot wounds, Sir," the fellow answered.

"Gunshot?" I replied with surprise. "How so? I understand your battalion has had no contact with the enemy for the past day or so."

"That's correct, Major," the fellow continued.

"Then how can they be gunshot wounds?"

"Self-inflicted, Sir," the soldier continued, looking a bit sheepishly at first me and then his companion.

I looked down at the two soldiers. Both of them avoided my gaze. They had guilt written all over their faces. Both the men had bandages on one of their feet.

"You mean these men deliberately shot themselves in the feet to avoid combat?"

"Oh, I didn't say that, Major. We don't know. They always say it was an accident, and we don't have any evidence to the contrary."

"So they are promptly evacuated and for them the war is most likely over?"

"We guess so. At least I've never known them to come back. Might even have a permanent disability, for all we know up here on the lines."

"You talk like it's a common occurrence," I added.

"Well, it seems to be, more and more, especially if the fighting is ferocious, or about to be."

I left the medics at the casualty point and searched for someone from the battalion commander's staff. I found either the executive or the operations officer, as I recall, and asked if they were aware of the fact that they were incurring casualties from self-inflicted wounds.

"Oh, yes. We know about it. Isn't exactly new. Has been occurring off and on over the weeks, but at a stepped-up rate lately."

"Aren't you concerned about it? Does the CO know?"

"Yes, Major, on both counts," he continued. "Battalion CO is furious. We know these guys are simply trying to avoid combat. It's not fair to the rest of the guys for them to get away with it."

"Then why do they get away with it?"

The officer looked defensive in the face of my questioning. He paused with a wrinkled brow for a long moment and then said, "Well, it's a tough problem to control. We can't avoid evacuating them and they know it. After all, they are wounded and require medical attention and recuperation. Few, if any, will return. And they know that, too. They always claim that their wound is caused by enemy action, or, if there is no combat firing, they will say it was an accident."

"And we don't try to prove otherwise?"

"How? They are certain to make sure they are all alone when it happens. At the height of a fire fight, there is no way to tell whether a bullet wound in the foot, or lower leg, or hand, is from an enemy gun or one of our own. If there is no fire fight anywhere near, then the wounded soldier will claim he was cleaning his rifle, pistol, or some such, and it discharged accidentally. In either case, he gets evacuated and avoids further danger and frontline agony."

"And these guys will go that far, shooting themselves, to avoid staying on the lines in combat?"

"Some will, as you can see."

I was not really much surprised by what I was being told. I had knowledge of such developments as far back as World War II in Italy, Alsace, and elsewhere during cold and miserable weather and heavy fighting, when men become most depressed. It's at such times that the weakest among us turn to other and more cowardly, if drastic, methods to escape from their obligations and duties as military men.

I was most concerned about the reported high incidence of SIWs, or "self inflicted wounds," as they were medically and administratively categorized. I determined to explore what might be done about them, not only as a matter of command efficiency, but also in fairness to the great majority of soldiers who were doing their duty courageously, if reluctantly, and not resorting to such foul and disgraceful means of avoiding their responsibilities as combat soldiers.

As soon as I had an opportunity, a few days later, I approached the regimental adjutant, Maj. Joe Hannover, the staff officer responsible for administration.

"Joe," I said, "are you aware of any increase in SIWs?"

Hannover's eyes rolled upward as he let out a long "whe-e-e-e-w."

"Boy, am I ever," he answered. "Yesterday alone, as the fighting has stepped up, there were eight."

"Is that a record?"

"Not necessarily. I would have to review the casualty statistics.

But it might be. They've been running high and peaking in times of hardest fighting."

"But it is a continuing problem?"

"Certainly is."

"And aren't we doing anything about it?"

"Not much we can do. We can't assume the SIWs are deliberately shooting themselves, although everyone around knows almost for sure that they are the ones pulling the trigger. Nor can we establish that in action the wounding is not done by the enemy. We have to have witnesses, and the guys make sure they pull it off when no one else is around. They get behind a bush, or in a ravine, or in darkness, and do the foul deed. So it's their word against ours, and they are entitled to the presumption of innocence until the government proves otherwise."

I knew, being fresh from law school just before shipment to Korea, that Hannover was absolutely right on that point.

"Actually, these guys, in fact, if not as proven, are guilty of willfully avoiding combat—a court-martial offense, punishable by death in wartime. And without witnesses, the government is unable to establish that, so the guys get off scot-free."

Rewards for Misconduct

"Not only that," continued Hannover with disgust literally dripping from his every word, "they will eventually get out with an honorable discharge with full VA medical attention for life guaranteed. If there is a lasting disability, they will also be entitled to a pension, or disability compensation, probably for life also. They will also get the GI-Bill educational or other benefits."

"That's it?"

"Not by any means is that it. There's more to turn your stomach. If they claim the wound is by the enemy, which also will stick unless the circumstances indicate otherwise, they will wind up with a Purple Heart award for wounds in combat, and probably the cherished Combat Infantryman's Badge for satisfactory performance in combat. They will return home as war heroes in every sense of the word."

"Why did you use the phrase, 'unless the circumstances indicate otherwise'? What circumstances?"

"Well," Hannover explained, "there have been some instances where the SIW victim claimed enemy action caused his wound, but we learned from his platoon leader, or others, that there was no enemy fire anywhere in the area near the wounded soldier. Usually when we so learn the soldier has already been evacuated and is long gone—perhaps even back in Japan in a hospital and out of our control forever."

"So you can't confront him with his phony statement?"

"No, but we can administratively change his medical status from WIA, to SIW, which denies him a Purple Heart."

"But in many other cases you can't do that?"

"Not if there is as much as a single enemy-rifle shot somewhere near him. He is sure to claim his wound is from that enemy shot, and how can the government disprove it even if he were returned here for a hearing?"

Hannover was, of course, more than right. To return a soldier from Japan or the States to Korea for a hearing, long after an event, and after any possible witnesses are long since unavailable due to combat exigencies was out of the question. And the soldiers wounding themselves knew this. They were getting away with it with impunity almost without exception, and even worse, their buddies could see that they were doing so. The likelihood existed that with the wrongdoers' successes, others would most likely follow suit and were doing so, judging by the accelerated rate of SIWs. The matter simply could not be ignored.

A Drastic Remedy for an Urgent Problem

"Joe," I said to Major Hannover, "we cannot overlook this. Something must be done. The matter calls for some kind of action."

"I certainly agree," he said, "but what can we do? Aren't our hands tied?"

"To a certain extent, yes. But I've been pondering. There are some measures we can take to see if there aren't some improvements.

"First off, I am going to draw up a memo to all units, calling attention to the severity of the problem, and we can float it by the CO for his approval. We can require that it be read to all platoons at the lowest level, and that commanders certify back to us when that has been done. That will at least let every man in the regiment know that we know what these guys have been doing, and that we are not fooled by it.

"Also, in this memo, we will outline what action we are henceforth going to implement; namely, that when a man passes through the regimental medical collecting point for evacuation, he will then and there, before departing, be court-martialed on the spot."

"Court-martialed? For willfully avoiding combat?"

"No, that's too involved and we could never get away with it. There's not enough, or even no, evidence, as we have discussed. But we can charge and convict the guy in a more informal summary court-martial with circumstantial evidence of careless discharge of his weapon. That's an actionable minor offense. Certainly not what is deserved, but at least some action that may, when word spreads, throw a fear into others who might be contemplating shooting themselves. Also, since the wound is caused by the victim's own misconduct, it may save the country a bill for the rest of the guy's life if it results in a permanent disability."

"Well," said Hannover, "I think it's worth a try, Sherm, even though such a process might never pass muster by the civil libertarians of this world back in the States."

"Nor do I, Joe, but these are desperate times, with desperate events, and they call for somewhat desperate, or at least drastic, action. At least, we owe it to our good soldiers to give it a try. Every guy we lose wrongfully through his own felonious and gross misconduct creates a vacancy in the frontline ranks and places his remaining buddies in jeopardy. I don't think we can justify our existence here in regiment unless we do all possible to remedy the situation."

"One other thing," Hannover added. "How about the Combat Infantryman's Badge for satisfactory combat service? What should we do about that?"

"For sure, it should not be awarded to anyone evacuated with an SIW. We sure as hell can't call that service 'satisfactory.' And I think you should review past orders to see if the CIB has already been awarded to men later evacuated with SIWs. If so, let's revoke the awards. We're authorized to undo what we have done if later circumstances so dictate, are we not?"

"Absolutely," Hannover agreed. "We'll have the personnel officer do so forthwith."

And the adjutant did. In short order the proposed memorandum went out to all subordinate battalions and separate companies in the regiment, and certificates were returned verifying that it had been read to all members of the regiment. The results were little less than astounding. SIWs as a cause for medical evacuation all but disappeared during the remaining few weeks that I was to spend with the regiment before my rotation later in the year.

Whether or not our measures to reduce SIWs ever resulted in later complaints by the individuals concerned, or anguish from the ACLU or others of like mind back home, I have never been able to learn. Certainly, it has always seemed to me, no one could possibly object to our somewhat less-than-orthodox procedures if it resulted, as it apparently did, in the correction of a grave and unacceptable injustice to those conscientious and loyal men of our regiment who were being wronged by the misconduct of relatively few. Every wrong in life cannot always be corrected by adhering to the letter of the law or rules. Few would contend that the end always justifies the means, but sometimes the end justifies some slight deviation from the ordinarily prescribed means. At least it seemed to me it did in our situation there in Korea, in combat, where we had to resort to whatever practical recourse might be available to us.

Shortly after assuming my new duties as Regimental Exec, I made an unusual acquaintance. I encountered a Greek soldier that I have always felt was in the category of people dealt with in the *Reader's Digest* series of years back when the magazine had a regular feature titled "The Most Unforgettable Character I Have Ever Met."

It happened one day in late summer of '51 when I was bouncing along a road in central Korea roughly southwest of the mountainous mass soon to be known as Heartbreak Ridge. In a rather lonely and isolated road stretch I spotted a chap with his jeep and driver, who signaled me for help. I could see by his uniform and vehicle markings that he was not American.

"What's the problem?" I asked him.

"Just gimme a coupla aspirin. I already got a Purple Heart."

American casualties in the Korean War exceeded 50,000 killed and over 100,000 wounded. With such heavy losses, the award of Purple Hearts for wounds from enemy actions became almost boring, as reflected by the Mauldin World War II cartoon above.

"I'm out of petrol," he answered in good English but with a strong foreign accent. "Could you spare some?"

"You're in luck, fellow," I answered him. "I have my spare can in the rack, and I can give you half or so of it. By the way, with that accent and uniform you're not American, are you?"

"No," he said. "I'm Greek. I'm with the Greek battalion."

"Really? That's good to know. I knew there was a Greek battalion here but have never run into them. Are you with an American unit, or does your battalion fight alone?"

"No, not alone. We are part of the 1st Cav–the 7th Regiment. They call us their fourth battalion."

"Yeah, I understand," I responded. "We have the French battalion as our fourth battalion in the 23rd Regiment."

As my driver unbuckled the jerry can and began transferring the fuel to the Greek's jeep tank, we continued our conversation.

"What are you doing along this road? Are we in your sector?"

"Not exactly," he answered. "I've been back to check on some of my men who were wounded. I'm a platoon leader."

"Have you been here long?"

"Since the winter. Came with the battalion as a sergeant."

"Did you come straight from Greece?"

"Oh yes. We are all volunteers and carefully selected."

"Is this your first combat?"

He laughed.

"Not exactly. I fought in the Greek Civil war against the Communists in '46 and '47, and before that during the big war with the guerrillas in my country."

"Don't you think you have had enough of war?"

"Yes, I do. But we Greeks believe strongly in this Korean War and that communism must be stopped here."

I felt awkward when hearing his comments. I knew that most Americans were a great deal less convinced that the Korean conflict was a necessary war for the United States, and I remembered our French General's chiding back at Chipyong-ni.

"Where are you from in Greece?" I asked the fellow.

"I doubt you will know if I tell you, unless you have been to my country. But I come from the southern tip of the Peloponnisos. From an area known as Mani in the Morea. Does that mean anything to you?"

"No, I guess not," I confessed meekly, hating to show my ignorance. "Does your home area have any claim to fame?"

I could see the guy was warming up and thoroughly enjoying his chance to respond to my questions about him and his country.

"Any claim to fame? We think so. Our Mani area is the only part of Greece the Turks were never able to conquer in their four hundred years of control before our war of independence in the 1820s."

"Why was that?" I asked, sure that he would have an answer to his liking.

"Partly because of the rugged terrain where I grew up. But more so," he said with his pride clearly showing, "because we are among the toughest and most independent of the Greeks." I suspected that there might be Greeks from other parts of the country that might argue with him on that point, but for sure I was not going to do so.

In later years I would greatly expand my knowledge of the Greeks through research and otherwise. I would learn how ferocious and fearless they could be in fighting for their independence or another just cause. In Korea their remarkable combat record became legend. They were repeatedly decorated and prevailed again and again when assigned the most difficult missions. Clay Blair and others were to write glowingly of their conquests in Korea and picture them literally as fighting tigers. There is no shortage of stories that they frequently spurned artillery or other fire support in favor of close hand-to-hand fighting with bayonets or otherwise.

But then the same can be said of many of the other UN forces that fought with us in Korea. My fellow Americans may well resent my saying so, but my impression has been that overall and generally the other non-Korean troops engaged the Communists with much less uncertainty over the reasons for their being there than did we Americans.

My Greek acquaintance had his gasoline, and the day was passing. We both had chores to do.

"What's your name, in case we cross paths again?" I asked as we prepared to part.

Again he laughed. "You think you can remember a Greek name?"

"Probably not," I admitted. "But try me."

"My first name is Spyros. But I will write out my full name for you."

He did and handed me a paper. From it I read: "Spyridon Alevizakos."

"Thanks for not asking me to say that," I told him, as we waved and drove off our respective ways.

I was later to learn that the guy stayed almost another two years in Korea, unlike us Americans, who rotated after about one year. He continued to fight courageously and doggedly, and in addition to decorations from his own government and the Koreans he was awarded the Bronze Star with V by the United States after leading his platoon on an attack against a heavily fortified enemy-held hill. He was wounded seventeen times by machine guns, grenades, and bayonets.

After the Korean War, this remarkable Greek studied in London and obtained one Ph.D. and then another later in America. He served with the United Nations as a roving Ambassador, obtained American citizenship, and now resides in New York. He is in every respect one of the most unforgettable characters that I have ever met.

CHAPTER SEVENTEEN

Bloody and Pointless Fighting—Stalemate

As the month of August 1951 rapidly slipped into history, the 23rd Infantry Regiment repositioned itself to the southwestward edge of the Punchbowl as its positions were again taken over by the 5th Marine Regiment. The 23rd's new mission was to aid in the bitter fighting for a group of hills to become known as Bloody Ridge.

With these activities and engagements, the stage was being systematically set for one of the most costly and tragic battles of the Korean War. It would be on a remote section of inconspicuous and unheard-of high and rugged terrain just above the 38th parallel in central Korea. It and the fighting there were to be known through history as the Battles of Heartbreak Ridge.

Taeu San and Hills 1179 and 1059

As a preliminary to Bloody Ridge, in the closing days of July, following the 2d Division's return to the lines, several fights had taken

314

place. They were mostly by the 38th Regiment, but aided by the 9th and one battalion of the 23rd, to capture the small village of Taeu San and Hills 1059 and 1179, key features on the western slopes of the Bowl.

Fighting for these objectives by these 2d Division units had been bitter. The resistance by NKPA units was stubborn and tenacious. Overcast weather made adequate fire support all but impossible because of restricted visibility. With the clearing of weather on the twenty-seventh, however, observation was again possible and massive artillery and mortar barrages on the enemy positions were ordered.

By the twenty-ninth, a stubborn enemy was overpowered in close hand-to-hand fighting, and all objectives were in the possession of the division.

Bloody Ridge

In July, Maj. Gen. Clovis Byers had replaced Gen. Edward Almond as the X Corps commander. With the capture of Taeu San and its nearby dominant hills, one of the new corps commander's first orders was for the 2d Division to continue its assault and to capture the next terrain in line. That terrain consisted of another group of high peaks identified as Hills 773, 940, and 983. This cluster of "hills," each about a half-mile apart in a general east-west line, were located some three miles west of the southern rim of the Bowl and they overlooked the MSR from Yanggu to the south.

These hills were to become known as Bloody Ridge. The struggle to capture them would occupy most of the attention of the 2d Division for all of August and for several days in early September.

The battle for Bloody Ridge would go on and on in high elevations and in wet, difficult weather. Day by day, ground would be taken, lost, and retaken—only to be lost again as a ferocious enemy fought hard to retain his advantage and keep open and operable his lines of communications and control. Casualties would mount. Hearts would break. Blood would flow. Enormous amounts of ammo would be expended.

The Communist defenders of Bloody Ridge were determined that it was not to be taken. But the troops of our regiments, not to mention probably every senior commander from General Byers on down, were just, or more, determined that Bloody Ridge would be captured.

Finally, on the fourth of September, with the 23rd Regiment poised to attack the ridge from the west, the troops of the 9th suddenly, after much prolonged and intense fighting, moved with little opposition to the top of Hill 940 and the enemy withdrew. They were fleeing in near panic to escape entrapment.

The long, torturous struggle for Bloody Ridge had ended. The regiments paused to consolidate, shift, or exchange positions, and catch their breaths. For the next several days, 2d Division activity consisted mainly of tank and artillery support for the ROK divisions attacking on other high ground just to the west.

The stage was now set for the next and major milestone in the Korean War; the struggle for the cluster of peaks within sight of Bloody Ridge and only a couple of miles to the north. That cluster consisted of Hills 851, 894, and 931. They ran in a north-south line about two miles due west of the Punchbowl and they were within a rifle shot of each other.

These peaks and the ridges that interconnected them, like many others in central Korea, were high, extremely remote, rocky, and rugged. As stated, this terrain would be written in history books and in the blood of the 2d Division, and other units to follow, as "Heartbreak Ridge."

Tom Ryan waited again for the roar and telltale thump, thump, thump of another string of chopper blades beating the air over my house to subside. As the sound gradually faded into the distance near the Pentagon heliport a half-mile or so away, he roused himself into a questioning position.

"You said some moments ago that the fighting on Heartbreak Ridge was to be costly, and also tragic. What did you mean by that?"

"Well, costly, as is so well known and widely written and recorded just about everywhere, because of the ghastly loss of life in our initial struggle to take the ridge and in the heavy and repeated fighting to occur there for almost another two years, until a cease-fire agreement was finally reached at Panmunjom in 1953."

"And of course those developments were also tragic."

"Yes, in every sense of the word. But especially so, I have always felt, because of the seemingly pointlessness in the heavy loss of life and the painful sacrifices made there. Even after the price paid in lives and blood, there was no really significant change of positions, nor did it seem to have been the factor that most influenced the pace of the cease-fire negotiations, although some may disagree with me on that point."

The pace of cease-fire negotiations in the long months after they began in mid-1951 did not seem to be closely related to either the tempo of the fighting along the front or the exchange of real estate there. On the contrary, both sides finally agreed to a cease-fire only after other issues, particularly the exchange of prisoners, were resolved, as any student of the Korean War knows well.

Mainly for these reasons, I have never considered the fighting in central Korea above the parallel to be particularly decisive or influential in the outcome of the war, sad as it is to say in deference to the brave souls who perished in those hills.

The attacks on the hills of Heartbreak Ridge began on September 13 and 15 by the 2d Division's 9th and 23rd regiments, respectively. The attack routes were, generally, from the east and up the more rocky and abrupt rises of the hill mass. The enemy's supply routes were up the western side, which rose more gradually and thus was easier to negotiate.

The principle hills of Heartbreak dominated the Mund-ung-ni and Satae-ri valleys and from their peaks the Punchbowl and Hill 1179 could be seen off to the east.

The struggle for Heartbreak would stretch for what would seem an eternity until October 22, when the division would be relieved by the 7th Division. During the fighting all elements of the division would become involved at one time or another, and often all at one time.

The fighting for and on Heartbreak and its comprising hills, ridges, and approaches, would be much like that for Bloody Ridge just before, except that it would be far more intense and at greater cost. There would be attacks and counterattacks. Terrain features again would be taken and lost as before, and retaken and relost. Blood would continue to flow and men would go down for the count by the hundreds. The weather would continue to be sometimes sunny but also rainy, overcast, and steamy and miserable for sweaty, exhausted, and suffering troops.

Logistical support problems multiplied and compounded. The elevation was so high where most frontline combat companies operated that helicopters could not operate effectively. The air was so thin the blades could not take their "bite," and the choppers would be unable to rise to the hilltops, or hover, as is their custom. This prevented, ordinarily, the use of the choppers for resupply, medical evacuation, or tactical fire support.

The marines are known for their perseverance, and they were slow to concede the limitations of the choppers, among other items. One day when I was checking frontline positions of a battalion in an area previously occupied by the marines, I noted a startling pile of choppers in a ravine just off a clearing on a ridge.

"What on earth are all those choppers doing up here lying in a pile?" I asked a battalion officer near me from the rifle company in position there.

"They were here when we relieved the marines, Sir."

"I know, but why? Any word on how they wound up in this mess?"

"Yes, some of the marines explained to us as we relieved them. We had the same question."

"And their answer?"

"They said the choppers crashed when they attempted to land or hover to pick up wounded. Each time a chopper arrived, it would fall and crash."

"But so many? After one crashed, couldn't they get the word?"

"Apparently not. As you can see, there are three choppers there. I guess it took that many to convince them the chopper can't operate at this high elevation."

The marines thus, like us, were compelled to hand-carry their wounded to lower levels, where medical-evacuation helicopters could remove the wounded. Such hand-carrying, however, was always a tedious, time-consuming, and laborious operation involving large numbers of men who could far better be utilized in manning frontline positions in support of their buddies.

The fighting itself in the Heartbreak engagement was an agonizing ordeal and a holocaust defying realistic description for the gallant men involved. Actual events of that nature can never be reproduced in totality or even significantly by the printed word. Writings can, however, often help convey a limited impression and partial picture of past events.

The command report for the 23rd Regiment for the period, prepared by Al Metts and signed by Col. James Adams, is on file at the U.S. Government Archives Record Center at Suitland, Maryland. It contains graphic entries that give some idea of the difficulties and pain experienced by the men of the regiment in their awesome assault on Heartbreak Ridge. Extracts at random from the regiment's command report include the following:

. . . on 14 September during the morning hours the enemy placed heavy mortar and artillery fire on the units of the 23rd. . .

. . . L Company attacked on the finger leading to the ridge between Hills 931 and 851. . . at 1425 hours the company encountered fire from numerous machine guns placed in bunkers . . . at 1715 hours E Company was moving slowly forward . . . and F and G Companies received heavy mortar fire. . . .

This was the beginning of the bitter, vicious struggle for the ridge line between hills 931 and 851 and the hills themselves which became known as "HEARTBREAK RIDGE."

I company advanced slowly, foot by foot, meeting heavy small arms and automatic weapons fire from enemy located in bunkers to the North, West and East . . . I Company established defensive positions and estimated it was facing two enemy battalions . . . the terrain was very steep and difficult to negotiate . . . at 1615 hours E and F companies were placed under heavy enemy mortar fire . . . E Company was surrounded and fire was placed on it from all four sides. . . .

G Company began the attacks on "Heartbreak Ridge" on 16 Sept. . . . progress was slow . . . heavy enemy small arms and automatic weapons fire . . . I company renewed its attack at 0630 hours . . . moving against very heavy machine gun and small arms fire from enemy located in deep bunker positions . . . the enemy launched a counter attack . . . coming down from Hill 851 . . .

. . . at 2300 hours the enemy again placed extremely heavy mortar fire on the 3rd battalion positions and launched a two platoon probing attack on the L company positions. The enemy attack increased in size during the night. . .

The probing attacks against C Company developed into full scale assaults at 0300 hours on 17 September. . . . The enemy's persistence had diminished C Company's ammunition supply, and his mortar fire had dispersed the lst battalion carrying parties, so that the defenders, ran out of ammunition and in some cases were overrun . . . I company immediately began to receive machine gun fire from the North. . .

At 1000 hours on 18 Sept "C" Company jumped off in a determined effort to recapture the knob from which it had been previously driven. After a three hour fire fight, against small arms and mortar fire, C Company secured this high ground. . .

From midnight until dawn on 20 Sept the enemy made almost continuous probing attacks . . . on the 2d and 3rd battalions . . . at 1030 hours G and B companies launched a joint attack . . . before either company had advanced more than 200 yards, they met extremely heavy small arms, automatic weapons, mortar and artillery fire. . .

. . . after attempting to push through this curtain of enemy defensive fire, both companies found it too costly and withdrew to their original positions. . .

At 0545 hours on 22 Sept, the lst battalion launched an attack from the South on elements of the 13th NK Regiment defending the 931 hill mass . . . attacking forces pushed stubbornly forward, against the desperate enemy, who employed small arms, automatic weapons, mortar fire and grenades. . .

. . . the enemy resistance was so fanatical that he placed his defensive mortar fire on his own positions and defended his bunkers to the last man . . . the attacking troops gained the top of the south knob of the 931 hill mass only to be driven off four successive times by the intense mortar fire. . .

2d battalion jumped off at 0545 hours to attack the 931 hill from the North . . . leading elements were immediately halted by the intensity of the enemy defensive fires which made it almost impossible to move forward in the rugged terrain . . . E company continued the attack . . . knocking out one bunker at a time . . . the company reached the base of the north knob. At this point the intensity of fire became so great the company was forced to pull back . . . at 1425 hours the enemy launched a company size counter-attack.

During the night of 22-23 Sept the 2d and 3rd battalions repulsed repeated enemy attacks until daybreak . . . the lst battalion engaged the enemy on the ridge for the remainder of the day assaulting hill 931 four times only to be driven off each time by the determined enemy defensive fires and grenades. On the fifth assault, at about 1750 hours, three men succeeded in reaching the crest of Hill 931 by using bayonets and hand grenades to drive off the defenders. . .

And so goes the 23rd Regiment's Command Report for September 1951, and well into October, page after page with similar entries. But perhaps more succinct and to the point is the following excerpt by a division historian.* It describes a climax in the Heartbreak Ridge fighting by my own former battalion, the lst of the 23rd, but it can easily be applied to any of the other companies or battalions of the 2d Division during this critical and ghastly period of the war:

> Desperate to end the continual fighting, the First Battalion of the 23rd again forced its way up the slopes of Hill 931. There it grappled with the enemy, cut into his ranks and inflicted severe casualties. . . .
>
> A company found itself within 50 meters of the crest. It called upon every reserve of energy and courage it had and flung itself upward but was battered back. Again and again it tried to make the grade in spite of mortar, grenade, and bullet it crept and crawled forward only to be shoved down again.
>
> A fourth assault met with failure and summoning unbelievable guts the dauntless men moved out again and by sheer dint of courage scaled the peak. 931 had been taken. . . .
>
> . . . the anticipated enemy counter attack came at 0220 hours the 24th. Maddened, screaming, animal like, the North Koreans charged the positions in mass, hurling grenades out of the night and directing their murderous fire into the bunkers they had built and knew so well.
>
> It was too much for the thinned, battle weary men to resist and at 0330 hours the remaining few were forced from the crest. At 0445, with A company again in the lead, the First Battalion counter-attacked . . . the fighting continued throughout the day . . . until nightfall . . . during which they turned back countless enemy probes. . . .
>
> . . . the heart-rending story was repeated in the sector of the 9th . . . for eleven days the two regiments had given every ounce of energy and reserve they possessed to take their objectives. . . .

The fighting on Heartbreak Ridge ended for the 2d "Indianhead" Division by October 22, 1951, at which time the division was relieved

---

* From an uncopyrighted and out-of-print book titled *The Second United States Infantry Division in Korea 1950–1951*, by Lieutenant Clark C. Munroe, with illustrations by Captain Byron Smith and Private First Class Robert C. James. The book shows no printing date but includes a foreword dated 15 November 1951 and a publisher; Toppan Printing Co., Ltd., Tokyo, Japan. The book is understood to have included contributions from numerous anonymous individuals.

by the 7th Infantry Division. The division had captured Heartbreak and accomplished its mission.

There was to be, as is well recorded, later fighting in the area, often bitter, in the almost two years before the cease-fire agreement went into effect. Heartbreak, mostly, would be retained by the UN, however.

Today, the approximately mile-and-a-half-long ridge generally straddles the southern edge of the demilitarized zone, or DMZ as it is called, that separates the South Korean and UN forces from the Communists. Heartbreak's northernmost peak, Hill 851, lies smack in the middle of the two-mile-wide DMZ; the main or middle peak, Hill 931, is at the southern edge of the DMZ; and the southernmost peak, Hill 894, is about 400 yards within UN-controlled, or "South Korean"– held, territory.*

The Fighting Continues

Sadly, the fighting and bloodletting in the Korean War did not end before or with the capture of Heartbreak Ridge by the 2d "Indianhead" Infantry Division. It continued elsewhere and thereafter for almost two years until the cease-fire agreement was finally reached at P'anmunjom in July 1953.

As the 2d struggled for Heartbreak, the marines on our right pounded away, with mostly new men, it is reported, and pushed on through the Punchbowl to capture the high ground beyond to the north. That terrain now forms the southern edge of the DMZ in that sector.

It was at that time, during the height of the bitterest fighting, in the fall of 1951, when Al Metts, Sammy Radow, and I left on rotation for the States and new assignments. For us, direct involvement in the war, or "police action" as it was to be disengenuously referred to by apologists for long after, was over, but not for many other poor souls

* For a detailed and precise account of the Heartbreak Ridge fighting, the reader should refer to *Heartbreak Ridge, Korea 1951,* by the late Arned L. Hinshaw (New York: Praeger Publishers, a division of Greenwood Press, 1989).

Reviewing stand for the X Corps commander, Maj. Gen. Edward Almond, at a 2d "Indianhead" Infantry Division parade in the late summer of 1951.

Troopers of the 2d Bn./23rd Reg. ponder possible enemy attack routes on Heartbreak Ridge just east of the Punchbowl and north of the 38th parallel.

Trench positions and bunkers of the 23rd Reg. near Heartbreak Ridge above the 38th parallel. The edge of the Punchbowl can be seen at the right center.

A trooper of the U.S. 2d Infantry Division adjusts the trip wire for a night flare used to warn of approaching enemy troops.

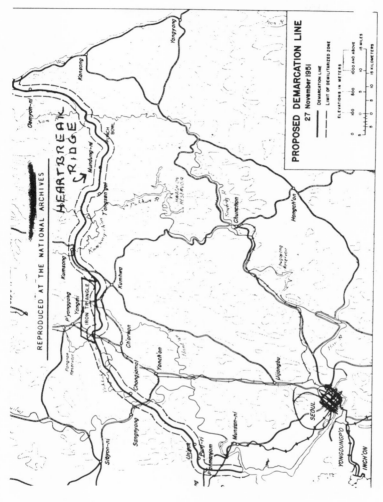

PROPOSED DEMARCATION LINE
27 November 1951

DEMARCATION LINE
LIMIT OF DEMILITARIZED ZONE

ELEVATIONS IN METERS

100   500   1000 AND ABOVE

0   5   10   15 MILES
0   5   10   15 KILOMETERS

The Korean DMZ as proposed at the earliest armistice talks in 1951 and which was little changed in the two more years of fighting before the cease-fire agreement in July 1953 at Panmunjom. From the U.S. Army official history of the Korean War.

23rd Regimental executive officer Maj. Sherman Pratt (center, bending over) inspects defensive positions on Heartbreak Ridge in the fall of 1951.

Defensive bunker on Heartbreak Ridge of the 23rd Reg. As opposing forces decreased their maneuvering, defensive positions resembled those of World War I.

155mm "Long Toms" of the Arkansas National Guard fire support missions behind the 2d Infantry troops on Heartbreak Ridge in the late summer of 1951.

A "chopper" pickup pad behind Heartbreak Ridge in the late summer of 1951. Such rapid evacuation of wounded in the Korean War saved many lives.

23rd Reg. Majors Sammy Radow, Sherman Pratt, and Albert Metts at the Pusan Rotation center en route to the U.S.A. upon completion of duty in Korea.

who remained, or arrived in the many more months later before the cease-fire.

Over to the west in the I Corps area led by my old 3rd Division commander of World War II, Lt. Gen. John "Iron Mike" O'Daniels, the 3rd Division and lst Cavalry and others were to be heavily involved in Operation "Commando." They would be subjected to ferocious enemy attacks on "Old Baldy" and other key terrain. Their historians would describe that fighting as the most bitter of the entire war. Whether it was *the* most bitter, we in the 2d might or might not agree, but there can be no denying that the struggle there was fierce and bloody.

In fact, the lst Cavalry Division would be so severely hit it would be withdrawn and returned to Japan. The lst Cavalry would later be replaced by the 45th National Guard Division from Oklahoma, which had been in Japan for about a year.

Aggressive patrolling and sometimes intense exchanges of fire and artillery barrages by ground forces and periodic massive bombing raids by the fly guys would be the rule of the period throughout the following months.

A year after Heartbreak, in October 1952, exceptionally heavy fighting erupted in the Iron Triangle area south of P'yonggang in the 3rd and 25th division sectors. The CCF suddenly mounted a major aggressive effort and overwhelmed the 65th Puerto Rican Regiment. Some of its positions and others were lost. As a consequence of sorts, the 65th was broken up soon thereafter and its personnel were absorbed into other combat units.

Even as late as the spring of 1953, only weeks before the cease-fire, intense fighting recurred. In the last days of May, for reasons not entirely understood by the UN command or Washington, it is written, the Communists launched powerful offensives along most of the front lines. During these periods blood continued to flow mercilessly and the names of Old Baldy and other insignificant hills, such as Jane Russell, Pork Chop, White Horse, Pike's Peak, to name but a few, became known to the American public back home.

As the casualties continued, sometimes in grisly numbers, public support for the war on the American home front, and elsewhere worldwide, steadily eroded. The "police action" became an issue in the presidential campaign of 1952, during which Eisenhower made his much-publicized and attention-getting declaration, "I shall go to Korea."

The Elusive Cease-fire Agreement

Talk of a cease-fire in Korea began as early as May 1951, when the war was less than a year old. After some preliminary shadowboxing by both sides, delegates met at Kaesong, a supposedly neutral area, on July 10. The UN delegation was headed by Adm. Turner Joy.

Both sides in the controversy had apparently reached the conclusion that all-out victory was not possible at a price they were willing to pay in lives and national effort. But both sides wanted an end on their own terms.

As the talks began, we were in our summer bivouac around Hongch'on, and as word reached us hope was high that the fighting would soon be over. It was not to be, however, as is, of course, well known.

The peace talks would be stretched out for almost two years, notwithstanding repeated resumption of strong hostilities first by one side and then the other, apparently aimed at persuading the other side to negotiate and make desired concessions. The talks would be adjourned in seemingly hopeless disagreement, then resumed, then again broken off in bitterness and frustration, over issues on which neither side would yield. The scenario would be repeated time and again.

The earliest disagreements surfaced over the question of Kaesong as a negotiating site; whether all armed forces should be withdrawn from Korea, and when; the exact location of the cease-fire lines; and even the width of a resulting demilitarized zone that would separate the two opposing forces.

The Communists first opted for the 38th parallel as a cease-fire line but finally agreed to a line essentially where the fighting forces were in fact located. They also abandoned an earlier demand that the UN pull back from the Punchbowl, Heartbreak Ridge, and certain other terrain features after the UN negotiating team agreed to give up territories further east and north near the coast and at Kumsong. It was also agreed that the Communists would withdraw from Kaesong and the talks would be moved to P'anmunjom, as the UN desired.

By the end of 1951, most of the items on which agreement was necessary, including the location of the DMZ, its width, and many related factors, had been agreed to. There remained only the questions of enforcement measures for the cease-fire and the exchange of POWs.

The cease-fire enforcement provisions, including inspections, rotation of troops, buildups, reprovisioning, surveillance, and related items, were to be worked out after bitter bargaining and gives and takes. The single issue of POW matters was to be almost unresolvable and, more than any other issue, would cause the war to continue for almost another two years.

As many of those who were alive at the time or who pride themselves as students of the Korean War will recall or know, the exchange of POWs, or more precisely, just which POWs, was an issue on which the the two sides differed strenuously. The matter was to bog down over whether POWs, mainly those held by the UN, should be forcibly or voluntarily released and repatriated.

It is not the purpose of my narrative here to treat in depth this question, in which I had no direct personal involvement and which transpired for the most part after I left Korea. It might be helpful, however, in order to set my remarks and experiences into some sort of context, to comment briefly on the POW controversy.

Disagreement on the POW issue had a major impact on the settlement of the war, delayed the cease-fire agreement for an extended period during which additional tens of thousands of lives were lost, involved fundamental and philosophical questions of morality and justice in the treatment of people and their human rights, and profoundly affected the lives of thousands of the victims of the fighting who wound up as prisoners on one side or the other.

In the early months of the cease-fire talks, both sides made efforts to tabulate the total number of POWs. Lists were inaccurate, and varied as time passed. Initially, the Communists admitted to having only about 12,000 UN POWs, of whom a little more than 3,000 were American. On the other hand, UN figures on POWs listed a little over 130,000, of whom about 20,000 were Chinese and the rest a mixture of

North Koreans and South Koreans impressed into service by the North Koreans.

The CCF position was that there should be a full and complete swap of POWs. The UN, however, with the strong support of President Truman, did not want any POWs held by the UN to be compelled to return to Communist control, where they might be punished or even put to death for political reasons.

When early polling of the POWs in UN control indicated that almost half of the POWs did not want to return to Communist control, to the stunning embarrassment of the Communist regimes, the talks again broke down and were recessed indefinitely in April 1952. Thus the cease-fire was pathetically delayed for many months on the single issue of POW exchange.

Hawks versus Doves

Many writers have pointed out how greatly divided were the senior American officials all up and down the chain of command during the long period of negotiations at P'anmunjom.

Military "hawks" on the ground and in the Far East, such as Generals Mark Clark, Van Fleet, and Ridgway, generally tended to take a hard line at the negotiating table if permitted to do so. They favored military pressure as the most practicable measure to deal with the "treacherous" Communist foe. They resisted concessions and surrender both in substance and as a negotiating tactic.

Top officials in Washington, however, especially the president, wanted the fighting over. They clearly showed symptoms of acute dovishness. So, it seems, also did the public in poll after poll. The terrible and continued carnage was not acceptable politically or as a matter that advanced or coincided with what growing numbers of the public perceived to be in the best national interest.

Further exasperating the negotiations were several developments that caused widespread concern and embarrassment to the administration in Washington, as well as to field commanders.

The first of these, peaking in early 1952, consisted of charges before the UN, which were denied, that the Americans were using germ warfare in Korea. That warfare, it was said, consisted, among other things, of air-dropped, bacteria-infected fleas, lice, ticks, and other bugs on the civilian population of North Korea. The Russian delegate to the UN even presented "exhibits" to support the charge and the Chinese publicized taped "confessions" of American POW pilots who admitted to participating in such airdrops.

During this period the Chinese also launched their infamous and cruel, but incredibly successful, "indoctrination" of POWs program. With the program and implied threats of murder and physical torture, the Chinese obtained "confessions" from American POWs that they were the dupes of imperialistic warmongering capitalists. The confessions were then used in a worldwide propaganda campaign to generate opposition to the UN presence in Korea. As a result of the brainwashings, or other causes, twenty-one Americans refused repatriation when the exchanges at last were undertaken in 1953. These developments did not help the UN cause or the quest for peace.

Perhaps the most successful of all Communist efforts to embarrass and humiliate the UN and the U.S. and undermine military efforts in Korea occurred at the POW camp on the island of Koje off the southwest coast of the Korean mainland. There the Communists organized and carried out riots with deliberate and carefully planted agents. The inmates actually captured an American general in charge who entered the compound in the naive belief he could consult with the Communist POW leaders.

The POWs on Koje "tried" their captive general, sentenced him to death for "atrocities," and released him only after he signed confessions they later used for propaganda purposes. Almost a full American division was dispatched to the island to restore order—a division that could better have been used to help the troopers' buddies on the front lines.

CHAPTER EIGHTEEN

At Last, the End

The Cease-fire Finally Arrives

By the spring of 1953, after long months of no progress at the P'anmunjom talks and continued blood flowing and periods of no P'anmunjom talks at all, a series of events occurred that caused a resumption of negotiations and final agreements.

The newly elected, but not yet seated, President Eisenhower had made his visit to Korea as promised in late 1952. Upon assuming office in January, one of his first acts, with his newly appointed and hawkish Secretary of State, John Foster Dulles, was the initiation of a period of diplomacy that became known as "brinkmanship."

Early brinkmanship acts of Eisenhower and Dulles created a worldwide impression that the Chinese Nationalists might, with American support, be allowed to invade China from Formosa, that atomic weapons might be employed, and that military actions might not be restricted to Korea. About the same time, in Russia, Joseph Stalin died. These events apparently persuaded the Communists that the time had come to end the Korean fighting. At any rate, within days after Stalin's death the Russian foreign minister publicly stated that differences between the Korean adversaries might be resolvable by negotiation. Similar peaceful overtures were made almost immediately by North Korean and Chinese leaders. Washington responded favorably, but with suspicious caution.

Although massive UN air raids and a general Communist offensive occurred thereafter, the delegates returned to P'anmunjom and, on July 27, 1953, signed the armistice to stop all firing in Korea by UN and Communist forces, effective at 10 P.M.

Even Syngman Rhee's last-ditch effort to derail the cease-fire failed. Rhee wanted to continue the war to unify all of Korea and had threatened not to join in the cease-fire and to fight on alone, if necessary, with his ROK divisions. He had turned loose thousands of POWs at the last minute, to the displeasure of the Communists and to undermine the POW exchanges. But when another massive Chinese assault came late in June and many of his ROKs collapsed and fled requiring the U.S. 2d and 3rd divisions to stop the Chinese, Rhee came into line and all outstanding issues were resolved.

Thus the Korean War, at long last, it seemed to those directly involved and at home in America and other countries represented there, came to a halt.

The long fighting was at an end. Observers, historians, philosophers, military strategists, statesmen, johnny-come-latelies, Monday-morning quarterbacks, and simple people on the street could begin the task of deciding whether the result was worth the effort.

It was a question not likely to be soon answered, if ever. Nor was it, as the French General Monclar vainly hoped, a great and historical effort by an international body that might become the struggle to end all wars. We would see proof of that all too soon in yet another bloodbath, with less than desired results, just to the south elsewhere on the Asiatic mainland in Vietnam.

No narrative by me, or any others for that matter, about the Korean War could be complete without at least some mention of a hapless group of people whose miseries far surpassed those of us on the front lines. I refer, of course, to the prisoners of war in the Communist camps to whom I have alluded several times herein.

To be sure, history is not without its gruesome records of how the victors down through the ages have treated the troops of the van-quished opponents. In antiquity they were usually placed in slavery until they died of mistreatment and overwork. Very often they were simply put to the knife or sword and killed. The Crusaders in the twelfth and thirteenth centuries, on their marches to the Holy Land, rounded up the armies of Islam by the thousands and chopped off their heads until the fields east of Constantinople "glowed red with rivers of blood," as one historian phrased it. And so too have the Moslems slain the infidels in their pathways. The "Hordes of Genghis Khan" wiped out whole civilizations on their sweep down from the steppes of Asia.

Even in our own national history, there is no lack of incidents concerning the deplorable treatment of prisoners. The slaughter of Indians in the plains wars is well documented, as are the mass deaths that occurred in the Confederate prison at Andersonville, Georgia, and the Union prison in Maryland, just south of Leonardtown near the mouth of the Potomac. There, just off State Highway 5, a visitor can view the marker at the location of the Civil War camp containing a seemingly endless roster of the Confederate soldiers who died while imprisoned there.

While the treatment or fate of our men in the Communist camps during the Korean fighting may differ in some respects from that of many others down through time, it was no less disastrous individually, if not collectively, for most who survived only temporarily, if at all, as POWs there.

Many knowledgeable and capable authorities and historians have written on this subject, but perhaps the most graphic and sobering description is by none other than General Mark Clark. The general should have been well informed on the matter. He was top commander out in the Far East in the closing days of the war. In his book *From the Danube to the Yalu,* General Clark devoted a whole chapter in his book on the conditions inside the Communists' prison camps operated and run by the Chinese leaders then in control. He wrote that the full story of the shocking treatment of prisoners became clear through interrogations aboard troop ships as the repatriated men were brought home.

In a speech prepared for delivery to the United Nations, General Clark spoke of "10,032 individuals whose murdered bodies stand as mute witness to the savagery" inside or en route to POW camps. The speech was never delivered to the UN because the administration felt it would simply give the Communist delegates an opportunity to tell "their side" of the story, which "we knew would be a fabric of lies, distortions and propaganda." The speech was released for publication, however, and contained the following grisly details, in part:

We find the identical criminal pattern in Korea that was evidenced in the communist massacre of Free Poland's Officer Corp in Katyn Forest . . . there were calculated killings targeted upon our military personnel, often committed while the individual prisoner's hands were bound behind his back . . . many variations were introduced which would have paled torturers and inquisitors of past centuries. In some instances gasoline was poured over the wounded and ignited by either grenades or matches. In other cases, helpless men were tortured by bamboo spears until God granted merciful death to terminate [their] agony. . . .

[Early in the war] . . . when the recapture of Taejon appeared imminent, the communists determined that prior to withdrawal, mass liquidation would be the fate of the prisoner camp . . . groups numbering from 100 to 200 each were efficiently removed from their cells at night; hands tied behind their backs, bound to fellow prisoners, transported to selected sites, dumped into open trenches and summarily shot . . . examination of the bodies revealed that most had been beaten and mutilated prior to execution . . . of the thousands only six survived . . . three civilians, one ROK Army soldier and two Americans. . . .

The seriously wounded were left on the field and often killed either by concentrated small arms fire, bayonetting, or a combination of both . . . Many marches were made under severe climatic conditions. . . Prisoners reported marching in bare feet until the flesh ripped from their toes . . . guards took shoes and other articles of clothing from the prisoners . . . stragglers were clubbed or kicked when they fell . . . men who could not continue were left to die . . . repeated witness accounts testify that prisoners were pushed off cliffs . . . starving prisoners were desperate to the point of hunting down dogs or other animals along the route north. . .

Once men arrived at permanent prison installations, conditions were no better . . . there were no medical facilities, heat or blankets . . . the death rates soared. Causes of deaths, as reported by prisoners and accompanying medical officers, included: lack of attention, malnutrition, dysentery, pneumonia . . . approximately 1,600 men died in a ninety day period in one camp alone.

Aside from the physical mistreatment of prisoners by the Communists, which included beatings, forced marches, crowding, unsanitary conditions, and lack of food and clothing, General Clark reviewed the mental torture the prisoners experienced, which became known as "brainwashing." This brainwashing, achieved by a calculated, diabolical, and cruel manipulation of the prisoners' minds, resulted in numerous acts of seeming disloyalty. Equally or more serious, it also caused countless numbers of POWs to simply give up psychologically and physically and go off in a corner by themselves and die, or, if they survived, they were converted to a point of view very sympathetic to the Communist cause.

General Clark describes how the Communist plan and technique for brainwashing and controlling men's minds involved a process wherein prisoners were quickly segregated. Prisoners with any leadership propensities, who it seems amounted to only a handful, were whisked away by themselves. The remaining 95 percent were then subjected to "discussion" groups, which the Communists set out to manipulate like so much putty in their hands. In due course, the objective was to destroy the mind—to discourage and eliminate individual thinking or resistance and to create guilt complexes on the part of the prisoners for becoming unwitting tools of the capitalistic warmongers who were responsible for the war.

This Communist technique of brainwashing was surprisingly successful. The record shows that it caused great doubts among our prisoners as to the justification and moral right of our being in the war. As a result of the brainwashing, many prisoners became dupes of their captors and signed confessions of wrong conduct and guilt that were used by the enemy for propaganda purposes, to the embarrassment of the UN and America. Other prisoners, as reported by General Clark, simply surrendered in captivity and ceased to be a problem for the Communists.

The success of the brainwashing and its impact on our men became such a serious problem that it resulted in the adoption of a new code of conduct for our fighting men and commanded the attention of military commanders and psychologists who conducted studies and lectured troops on the subject.

In one such postwar lecture series at the Brooks Army Medical Training Center at Fort Sam Houston in San Antonio, Texas, army psychiatrist Maj. William T. Mayer periodically detailed the techniques of Communist brainwashing in the POW camps and the results. Major Mayer was a member of the U.S. Armed Forces Joint Committee Assigned to Study the Behavior of U.S. POWs in Korea. His words are startling, disturbing, and yet fascinating. I think they warrant consideration, in part, by the reader here.

> We entered our study of brainwashing with some very definite ideas of our own as to what brainwashing was all about. We were surprised to find, contrary to our beliefs, that it was not a system of torture, or punishment, or degradation, or brutality. At least not on the surface—or initially but the results of the experience was all of these.
>
> Brainwashing was simply aimed at destroying the will to resist—both on the battlefield and in captivity, and, generally, in the Cold War. . . . The first step used in the POW camps was to carefully and systematically segregate the prisoners upon arrival. By close observation they identified the "reactionaries," that is, anyone with any indications of leadership because of rank, actions, intelligence, personality, religious beliefs, ethics, or other characteristics. Such people can easily be spotted in any group of prisoners around the camps. Those people were promptly rushed off to other camps. We found that this class of prisoner, who might display initiative or independence, comprised only 5% of the prisoner population! Only 5%, believe it or not!

Major Mayer then explained to his listeners how the Communists, once a group was thus segregated, could then easily control and mould the remaining 95 percent who were unresisting, easily persuaded, and compliant. He said the objective at the outset was to make each prisoner feel isolated from the rest of his group, which is so important in a dictatorship.

> The communists knew that every counter revolution must begin with a conspiracy, most often between only two people. So if the conspiracy can be stopped at the beginning—at its very start—you have a form of social control that cannot possibly be achieved by machine guns, slave

camps, or torture—or any other form of coercion. The communist aim was to separate each man and place him in a cell of his own making.

The communists created this form of isolation and confinement by cultivating informers—a very common practice in communist or totalitarian societies. Kids reporting on parents; students on teachers; workers on bosses. In our society this is a lowest form of conduct. Those who rat are not respected but are rejected and looked down on. But in a communist society it is considered a civic duty. In the POW camps our men were encouraged, and rewarded, for informing on others, and it was made to appear harmless.

Major Mayer told how their studies revealed the Communists' clever and smooth approach. They told our men not to worry; that the purpose of informing was not to hurt anyone; that the American informed on was not going to be thrown into a hole or have his fingernails pulled out or be beaten up. The men were told that the Communists simply wanted to counsel the wrongdoer, take him aside, explain that he had done wrong, and not to be afraid, but that he should confess. The counselor would say, in essence, "In our society if you make a mistake, and confess it, and repent—criticize it—don't repeat it—that's all we ask." The major reported that most POWs did so. They felt there was no harm to anyone. The Communists let them off the hook. Everyone profited by it, and the informers were rewarded with extra favors, candy, cigarettes, and such things so important to deprived men in long confinement.

Under the informer system, informers grew by leaps and bounds. Within the first year of captivity every group of ten POWs had at least one informer among them.

"Now just look around," Mayer told his listeners, "If you knew that among the people sitting here at least one was considered a reliable and calculated informer, what would you do? You would clam up. You would not be sure who you could trust, so you would trust no one. You would decide you cannot fight the whole world so you would not fight anyone. Least of all would you undertake to confide in or conspire with anyone with the idea of escaping or causing problems for your captors."

Major Mayer next described how the prisoners thus converted by the informer system into passive, suspicious and insecure individuals were then primed and ready for the group-discussion sessions. He said the sessions would begin innocently enough by encouraging all prisoners to open up and talk about anything that came to mind.

The early discussion sessions would be painless—for about a week— subjects could be anything the prisoners wanted to talk about. Then the discussion leader would turn the subject to the prisoners' selves. Their concerns, misdeeds, guilts, embarrassments, or problems. As prisoners revealed more and more of their less colorful backgrounds, they turned more and more inward and increasingly isolated from all outside their group.

Concurrent with the discussion sessions and to better exploit and capitalize on their progress in steadily eroding the prisoners' morale and confidence, the communists made diabolic use of the mails. They withheld mail that would lift a prisoner's spirits, and delivered that which would be demoralizing. Although the wife, or other close one on the home front, may have been writing regularly with loving, caring, and treasured information and news, those letters would be withheld or destroyed. Finally when a disheartening letter arrives, written at a time when the kids were sick, the car broke down, and the writer simply let it all spill out, that letter would be delivered. As would the ones from the bill collectors, or the "Dear Johns," or other tidings of bad news.

The major explained how the mail approach was designed to further the objective of creating an attitude of discouragement, despair, and depression, an emotional vacuum, and a willingness to forsake ideals and home-front loyalties and just resign and surrender. The prisoner then was ready for discussions as an unresisting and compliant listener on subjects of the leader's choosing.

At this point the discussion leader started talking about politics, history, and many other related subjects. His task was not difficult since he talked to the 95 percent least educated and knowledgeable prisoners. The average educational level of the rank and file trooper in Korea was only about the 9th grade. The leader told his audience just to listen to the communist side of the story—that's all. "You don't have to agree. Be neutral if you want. But listen. That's fair isn't it?" It was not difficult for Americans to agree to fair play. So they listened.

The leader then started talking about capitalistic industries. On and on he would lead the "discussion." He would talk of the DuPonts, the Rockefellers, the Carnegies, and how they made their money from the sweat and brow of the working people at long hours in sweat shops. He also talked of the illegal use of the 7th Fleet without a UN sanction and how the UN negotiators at P'anmunjom were dragging out the war so that war profits could continue back home. He even had up to date copies of the *Wall Street Journal* showing earnings by industries engaged in war production.

The communists usually did not try to convert our men to communism. "Just listen to our side. If you think it has merits, go home when the war is over and tell our side of the story," they would say. They would harp on the ghettos in large American cities, on Southern sheriffs with guard dogs, on unemployment, cops shooting down demonstrators and homelessness and many other social problems in the capitalistic societies.

Finally, the major continued in his lectures, after the prisoner is softened up with the informer program and mentally unable to withstand weeks of political indoctrination, self-isolated and in a state of near psychological paralysis, his will to resist collapses and he surrenders—mentally, physically, and totally.

Men with minds broken simply gave up while prisoners of the communists. Men died in large numbers in the camps—4 out of every ten—38 percent did not come home. That's the highest number in any camp, in any foreign war, in which we have ever fought. But the reasons why they died in communist camps are particularly disturbing. They often died because of the effects of indoctrination, or brainwashing, the failure of leadership and even worse, at the hands of their own despirited and mentally stunned fellow prisoners.

The psychological surrender in Korea was not precisely like other forms of surrender. It is more elusive, and hard to pinpoint. But it was widely fatal and killed many troops. The surgeons called it "give-up-itis." Sounded harmless to many. But the kid who had it, typical of many others that died, could not tolerate the isolation from other soldiers imposed by the brainwashing techniques. He simply crawled off into a corner. Brooded. Cried. Threw down the dirty ole food that even if dirty could have kept him alive, pulled the blanket over his head and within 48 hours he was dead. Dead! Not starved; not psychotic; not diseased; but dead. And hundreds of others died in the same manner.

We heard also of the instance, all too typical, when a soldier had been thrown out of his hut with others, by two soldiers in the bitter cold and he soon died. We asked other soldiers there if they had done anything to stop the two from throwing out the soldier. They said no. We asked why. Their startling answer: "Because it wasn't any of our business." A solemn example of the dramatic success of communist brainwashing techniques for isolating, demoralizing and distorting civilized ideals. Such was the agonizing experience of our POWs in the hands of the communists in the Korean War.

Certainly the long-range effects of the Communists' physical and psychological treatment of our POWs in Korea is difficult, if even possible, to ascertain. Many, almost half, never returned, as pointed out by General Clark, Major Mayer, and others, because they died in the camps either directly or otherwise from the effects of brainwashing. Others who did return may be scarred forever with guilt complexes for the things they may have done while under the coercive influence of their Communist captors.

While it is my strong belief that the Korean War should not become our "Forgotten War," which to a large extent it has, and that there are lessons to be retained by the bloodshed in the Pusan perimeter, and at Kunu-ri, Chipyong-ni, Heartbreak Ridge, and elsewhere, it is even my stronger conviction that we should remember most of all the suffering of those who were imprisoned, mistreated, and killed by the Communist enemy.

It is on that note that I think it appropriate to end this narrative of one soldier's experiences in that struggle. It was the only instance in history of an army taking to the field in combat to enforce the will of an international body created to maintain peace and order on this planet.

It remains to be seen at this writing at the beginning of the 1990s, after Operation Desert Storm in the Persian Gulf pursuant to United Nations resolutions, whether for any longer the Korean War will be the only such international action in history.

Famed "Willie and Joe" cartoonist Bill Mauldin at the Korean War vets' reunion in Arlington, Virginia, in July 1990 (author rear, second from right).

EPILOGUE

Some Afterthoughts—Farewell to "the Land of the Morning Calm"

Upon rotation from Korea and Heartbreak Ridge in late 1951, with Al Metts and Sammy Radow, my relationship of sorts with Korea ended.

For my part, like many other vets of that or other fighting then or at other times or places, I had a decision to make. Do I return to civilian life and leave the military and the war behind, or should I best stay in the army if it will have me?

For me, the decision was not difficult. The army folks said I could stay, at least for the time. So I stayed. I had by then twelve years' service, which meant only eight to go for twenty-year retirement if half pay, rather than three-quarters, was acceptable. I have never regretted my decision.

I had several more interesting assignments after Korea before

345

retiring in the early 1960s. I've always treasured those assignments as rewarding and unique educational experiences.

First, I served as a public information officer at the Nevada atomic proving grounds for the 1953 exercises conducted jointly by the Atomic Energy Commission and the Department of Defense. Those tests of eleven "detonations" were some of the most extensive ever carried out, although in later years they are all but forgotten.

The 1953 nuclear tests included the first live TV coverage of an atomic explosion and involved the destruction of a specially con-structed civil defense village to determine the effects of nuclear weapons on a typical community. The final "shot" was from the army's 280-mm, double prime-mover artillery piece, which has been the only atomic round ever fired and detonated by this country, and probably any other, from a military launcher.

Later, I was privileged to serve for three years in Iran with the then very small military advisory mission. That post was during the hectic days of the militant prime minister Mohammad Mosaddeq and the volatile expulsion of the British from the Iranian oil fields on the Persian Gulf.

Duty in the relatively primitive country of Iran was not exactly plush or posh. At first I had resisted the assignment, preferring a more glamorous and easygoing location, such as Germany. But I've since felt that its value was almost beyond description in widening my background, understanding, and perspective in view of subsequent developments there with the ousting and death of the shah in the early 1970s, the taking of our diplomatic hostages by the ayatollah during the Carter administration, and the Iran-Contra affairs of the Reagan years in the 1980s.

Finally, just before retirement, I again fell fortunate, upon return-ing from Iran, to an assignment of extraordinary prestige for me from the Arkansas poor country and a mere doughboy for the roughest years of my military life. Through a series of unexpected breaks I was nominated and accepted for an assignment in the Pentagon in the secretary of the army's Legislative Liaison Office.

Legislative liaison officers for the military services, as with other federal agencies, provide a link, sometimes necessary, to the law-making body of the government. The tens of thousands of inquiries, and "contacts" per year between the defense department and the

Congress is an enormous business. Some of this activity is unavoidable and involves contracts, material procurement, construction, or responses to citizen requests for help.

Much of the military-liaison effort, however, and a part that could likely be abolished without any harm to the national interest, is devoted to pushing for a service pet-project or weapons system based on claimed need, or caused by interservice rivalries and bickering over slices of the defense budget.

My duties as a liaison officer, in addition to a share of the above, included a unique responsibility not shared by my colleagues. I was the unit advisor for a specially organized army reserve unit on Capitol Hill. The unit had been activated by Secretary Wilbur Brucker in the Eisenhower administration in response to requests from senators and representatives who wanted to maintain their active status in the reserve components but could not do so when in Washington and away from their homes and local military training centers.

The special congressional reserve group met weekly in one of the Hill office buildings in early morning and sessions consisted of briefings by senior army officials from the secretary and chief of staff down. To minimize possible public criticism, the members received no "drill" pay, but only retirement points, and every effort was made to avoid the appearance of special or plush treatment not afforded other reservists.

Notwithstanding those precautions, when word of the unit spread in Jack Anderson's column and elsewhere, President Kennedy's secretary of defense, Robert McNamara, ordered it and similar air force and navy units disbanded in the early sixties.

My congressional reserve "troops" had included such notables as Senators Jacob Javitts (N.Y.), Henry "Scoop" Jackson (Wash.), Strom Thurmond (S.C.), Ralph Yarborough (Tex.), House Speaker Carl Albert (Okla.), and many other members of Congress and senior reservists on their staffs.

In the Pentagon liaison assignment I had been honored to serve under Maj. Gen. John "Mike" Michaelis, who had commanded the 27th "Wolfhound" Regiment of the 25th Division in the earliest days of the Korean War in the Pusan perimeter. Michaelis had gained national recognition after wide publicity and almost daily coverage by correspondent Margaret Higgins of the *New York Herald Tribune*.

In the army liaison office I served directly under Medal of Honor holder Col. Keith Ware of the 3rd Division in World War II, who signed my last army efficiency-report upon my retirement. Later, Colonel Ware, then major general, was killed in Vietnam when his helicopter was shot down. My understanding is that he had the somewhat dubious distinction of being the highest-ranking casualty of the Vietnam War—an honor, no doubt, that he and his family would have been quite willing to forego.

My confrontation with the Communists in Korea was to be the last major one of my lifetime—at least to date. The three engagements after my retirement, and meddling in law in and out of the government, were all minor in comparison to Korea. The first one, an eight-month overland struggle through African sand and jungles in a Fiat Spyder sports car from Cairo to Cape Town I consider that I won. At least I reached my objective and as far as I have been able to ascertain, it has been the only such feat on record.

The other two confrontations were a skirmish locally with a political opponent and one with the IRS over a trivial disagreement. I came out second best on both occasions. While both losses were disappointing, neither was worth anguishing over. After all, every election must have a loser, and who ever wins with the IRS? I like to think I fought the good fight both times, even if I lost.

Korea's destiny since the dissolution of our "relationship" in 1951 has been mixed and certainly more turbulent than mine.

On the plus side, South Korea has prospered economically and has become one of the world's leading exporters, especially to the United States. Hyundai cars, Samsung electronics, and numerous other product names have become almost kitchen-familiar words in American society.

Korea's GNP has grown steadily since the war. As with most of Western Europe, reconstruction, growth, and development have proceeded rapidly, and today it is difficult to find any evidence that the country once lay in shambles from an almost totally destructive war.

Socially, too, Korea has advanced to a degree that would be the envy of many a developing country. Medical care and other social services have been greatly expanded, and illiteracy has been practically eliminated.

Korea as a nation and Koreans as a people are certainly more familiar to Americans than ever before. The location of the Olympics in Korea in 1988 helped to familiarize people everywhere with the faraway "Land of the Morning Calm" or the "Hermit Country," as it was once called by the world's chancelleries.

Additionally, today more than a million Koreans live in the United States, few of whom ever appear on welfare or in the courts for wrongdoings. The long-existing and well-established Korean work ethic insures that Korean people become hardworking, productive members of American society and an asset to the country. American respect and admiration for Koreans has steadily grown as the century nears its end.

In Korea, the demographics have undergone revolutionary changes. From a country with most of its people engaged in agriculture at the time of its liberation from Japan at the end of World War II, Korea has become today a largely urbanized society. Over 75 percent of its people live in cities, and almost 25 percent in Seoul alone. This remarkable transition in the last half of the century has brought about profound changes in attitudes, employment, political participation, and many other areas of human activity. A casual stroll through any first-class library index will reveal many works by prolific writers who itemize and articulate in detail on this phenomenon.

Probably Korea's greatest single and most frustrating problem and challenge lies in the political arena. Here the country remains in turmoil and agonizing instability. Korea struggles to reach an acceptable level of peaceful democratic maturity but that objective seems to steadily remain just beyond reach, as though someone or recurring events continue to move back the goalposts.

Particularly painful to Koreans and to the international community that supports and is sympathetic to them is the fact that the country is still divided politically and geographically.

After almost forty years, since the cease-fire of 1953, the country remains split at the DMZ. The northern half contains a third of the population and a government that calls itself the Korean Democratic People's Republic and continues to be controlled by the Communists; the southern half of the country is controlled by the Republic of Korea.

All efforts to date to terminate this unnatural, illogical, and counterproductive division of the country have failed.

Whether the startling collapse of Communist regimes in Eastern Europe and the cooling of the cold war with the U.S.S.R. in the late 1980s will increase the chances for reunion of North and South Korea remains to be seen. Most observers seem to hold out little prospect for such a development soon, and especially so long as the aging Communist leader, Kim Il Sung, remains alive and in control of the north.

At this writing, however, it appears there may be some basis for optimism that the north and south may at long last be headed toward an end to their almost total division. On May 17, 1990, the news services carried stories that North Korea was signalling a readiness to talk as the remains of the first U.S. servicemen to be repatriated at long last was getting underway.

The North Korean ambassador to the United Nations, Ho Jong, was reported as saying his government would like to discuss with U.S. and South Korean officials replacing the 1953 armistice with a permanent peace treaty. The news items further reported that although much suspicion existed on both sides, the apparent change in the North Korean position seemed to be caused by the late easing of the cold war elsewhere, and to counter recent overtures by the Soviet Union to improve its relations with South Korea. One can only hope fervently, in the interests of Korea as well as her supporters, that these gestures bear fruit.

Within the Republic of South Korea, there has been greatly increased political interest and expression since the days of liberation. This citizen involvement, more often by students or other youth groups, including the Communists, has often been violent, however, and has resulted in much instability and turmoil. This is reflected in the numerous changes of government that have taken place by other than peaceful and orderly transitions.

Since liberation and the establishment of independence in 1948, the country has experienced no less than six republics and numerous other interim governments incidental to the establishment of the republics.

The first republic, under President Syngman Rhee, lasted until

1960, at which time public pressure resulted in elections and the installation of the Second Republic under Prime Minister Chang Myon.

Student demonstrations and demands grew under the Chang government and with the North Korean threat ever present a group of military officers used the occasion to carry out a coup in 1961 and seized control. The coup established a military-civilian coalition government under army Gen. Park Chung Hee, who remained in power and ruled with a strong hand for slightly more than two years.

In 1963 the military junta returned the government, ostensibly, to civilian control under the Third Republic. Many of the military leaders, however, including Park, simply retired and retained control as civilians. The days of the Third Republic ended, and the Fourth Republic was begun in the early 1970s, when General Park declared a national emergency followed by martial law and imposed rigid government control over almost all aspects of Korean society.

The Fourth Republic was brought to a shattering close in 1979 when Park was assassinated by the former head of the Korean CIA. In the aftermath of the Park assassination, a military coup, headed by Gen. Chun Doo Hwan, took place and the Fifth Republic was established. Chun gradually took firm power and held it, more or less, first as an active and then as a retired general, for almost a decade in the face of growing public opposition.

In February 1988, following a vigorous campaign and an election in the preceding month, the successful candidate, Roh Tae Woo, was sworn in as Korea's new president and the Sixth Republic came into being. Roh had won not a majority, but only a plurality of 40 percent of the vote. At this writing, the Roh government remains in power.

Throughout Korea's six republics from 1948 and to date, demonstrations, riots, and similar public unrest have been the order of the day. Before, during, and after each election or change of government, massive outpourings of youth and others, often but not always students, have filled the streets, college campuses, and other places with endless confrontations with the police and the military forces. In some years, the total number of demonstrations in all parts of the country has reached into the thousands, with sometimes a heavy loss of life or numerous injuries.

One of the most controversial and bitter demonstrations during the post-war period occurred in the city of Kwangju in southwestern Korea in May of 1980, when the populace joined students and literally took over the city in defiance of authorities. The incident is known as the Kwangju Rebellion, and to this date is used as a *cause célèbre* by opponents of anyone in public life who is known or suspected to have been a party to the government's action to then restore the city to government control.

The Kwangju takeover ended only when the government sent in crack military units, who were repelled and then reinforced by additional regular troops. In the slaughter in a week of fighting, several hundred, or thousand, people were killed, depending upon whose version is to be believed.

Another incident of public defiance of the government that cannot completely escape attention occurred as recently as 1987. On that occasion students entered and took over control of the Seoul Catholic Cathedral as a sanctuary from pursuing police. Only the intervention of the American ambassador seems to have prevented the government from storming the cathedral by force to eject the students, who later left after negotiations.

There are, unfortunately, endless and additional examples of the turbulence under which the Korean people have lived, even after the ending of fighting from the 1950–53 Korean War, in their quest for a truly meaningful and secure democratic society. For an excellent and very recent recap of the extent and nature of this unrest, and the performance of the several republics, I would direct the interested reader to the quite scholarly and learned work of Dr. David I. Steinberg, *The Republic of Korea, Economic Transformation and Social Change* (Boulder, Colorado, and London: Westview Press, 1987).

Whether the governments of Korea or its students and other citizens were justified in their actions during these turbulent periods, or to what extent, is a most difficult matter to ascertain.

Civil libertarians and liberals would most likely come down hard on the side of the demonstrators, especially if far from the scenes of conflict and snug in their rec rooms back in the States or elsewhere. They would argue that students, laborers, and other protesters had no other effective recourse to bring about needed changes in the governmental structure, liberalization, and progressive social change, to end brutal governmental repression and bring about other pressing reforms.

Hard-liners, on the other hand, would and do argue that strong governmental action, including even military-coup takeovers at times of governmental impotency, was necessary and unavoidable in the face of the real and ever-present military threat from the Communist North Koreans across the 38th parallel and the DMZ.

One writer has justified the government's suppression of civil liberties as a national defense measure not unlike or nearly as severe as our own incarceration of the whole Japanese population in World War II, when our mainland, unlike Korea, had not even been invaded.

Other and more sophisticated arguments for and against the students and the government's positions can be made, but they are beyond the scope of my brief recap of my own personal wartime experiences or these few thoughts thereafter.

The objective observer is surely hard-pressed to fairly assess the relative merits of the two opposing positions of the government and its critics. My feeling is that the case for the demonstrators has been significantly weakened by the continued violence and demonstrations, even as late as May of 1990, under the Roh government, which is considered by most observers to be the most progressive and liberal since the liberation of the country after World War II.

American news sources carried reports on May 10, 1990, of renewed and widespread clashes between radicals and police in a dozen Korean cities and of attacks on, and burning of, American facilities.

This continued violence occurred even after President Roh had apologized for the Kwangju killings, as had been demanded for many years by the demonstrators, but refused by past leaders. It also happened at a time when "the country has been moving, however slowly, toward democracy" and "in an era of reform," as Peter Maass reported in a byline article on the latest clashes in the *Washington Post.*

These developments seem to indicate that significant numbers of Koreans are not yet willing to trade Molotov cocktails and violence for more peaceful and democratic methods of the ballot box. One can only speculate on the motives of these radical Koreans and whether the best interests of Korea are really their concern.

* * *

As political events inside Korea percolated and ebbed and flowed over the past decades, the country and its people have made news repeatedly, in both related and distinctly different ways and over a great variety of issues. Some of these have constituted milestones in the growth and development of the country and in its relationships within the family of nations.

Some of the post-war developments involving the United States and Korea, or their people, seem to be the consequential progeny of a "war" that was never officially declared, or formally ended. Today there is merely an awkward state of flux with only a P'anmunjom cease-fire arrangement in existence. Unfortunate incidents have occurred during that protracted period, to the embarrassment of both countries.

Some of these developments seemed to have been the direct outgrowth of the unique relationships that germinated during the fighting and grew thereafter as the two countries and their peoples undertook to build and strengthen mutually satisfactory contacts in diplomacy, commerce, national defense, and many other areas. Other "irregularities" seem to be simply a product of an ongoing struggle during the cold war period between two widely separated political philosophies, each jockeying for better positions.

Probably the most severe post-war strain in relations between the United States occurred in the early and mid-1970s and briefly recurred in 1984. American public opinion about Korea then dropped to an all-time low. It was sensationally reported over that period by the media as major news events that certain U.S. defense industries were involved in bribing Korean officials, and a Korean in the United States was accused of channeling as much as a million dollars a year for several years to members of Congress, and other high government officials, in return for actions favorable to Korea.

In a banner headline across page one of the *Washington Post* on October 24, 1976, the paper proclaimed: "Seoul Gave Millions to U.S. Officials." *Post* writers described how Korean businessman Tongsun Park had "dispensed between $500,000 and $1 million yearly in cash, gifts and campaign contributions to U.S. Congressmen and other officials during the 1970s" and that Park had also financed Korean intelligence operatives in the United States during the period.

The *Post* writers reported that the activities were financed "chiefly by commissions extracted by Tongsun Park and the South Korean government from U.S. rice dealers making federally subsidized rice sales to South Korea under the Food for Peace program" and also from "other funds . . . siphoned off from charitable foundations ostensibly promoting closer cultural ties between the U.S. and Korea."

In the protracted and widespread publicity of these events the Reverend Sun Myung Moon, of the Unification Church, and his top aide, Col. Bo Hi Pak, who I mention elsewhere, were frequently reported as constantly involved, indirectly or otherwise, in providing funds for businessmen Park and as having close ties with the Korean CIA in both countries. In the wake of our own Watergate affair, the media promptly labeled these Korean-American exchanges as "Koreagate." Following the revelations of these maneuvers, some people went to jail, including members of Congress. Some were humiliated, defeated in later elections, or otherwise discredited. Insofar as is known, those particular unorthodox activities were promptly discountinued or at least sufficiently curtailed.

Unacceptable as were the activities of Koreagate participants, it seems from available information that the Koreans involved were not motivated by greed or a lust for personal aggrandizement, except for Tongsun Park perhaps, to some extent, who was said to have lived in lavish style. On the contrary, it could be argued that they were driven by a patriotic desire to further the best interests of their own country by currying favors from their superpower sponsor at a time of great national peril and with a continuing Communist invasion threat breathing down their necks.

In short, it might be said, while not overlooking the old adage that the road to hell is paved with good intentions, that the Koreans of Koreagate meant well, but that they were naive, clumsy, misdirected, and amateurish. An observer, in passing judgment on Korea and Korean participants of Koreagate, might want to consider the thoughts expressed by the *Washington Post* in an editorial headed "Korean Bribery," on October 27, 1976. The *Post* editor put it this way, in part:

> . . . no doubt South Korea, watching the United States . . . disengage (from) . . . Vietnam . . . could not help wondering whether the United States might go on to disengage from its other Asian-mainland outpost on the Korean peninsula. This is presumably the prospect which

prompted Koreans to start taking out insurance in Washington with under-the-table payments and other favors. Yet the tactic is utterly unacceptable . . .

But the editorial continues:

Americans ought to reflect, somberly, on the fact that what the Koreans evidently have been doing in the United States bears a sharp and painful resemblance to what the United States has done in Chile and various other countries: to contaminate, with secret money, the internal political processes of another state.*

Several years later another unsavory incident to sour Korean-American relations occurred. On April 21, 1984, the *Washington Post* reported that the FBI, the Justice Department, and the IRS were investigating charges that the Bechtel Corporation, a large San Francisco conglomerate, used a paid consultant "to bribe South Korean officials between 1978 and 1980 to obtain nuclear power plant construction contracts" in violation of law. *Post* writer Mary Thornton reminded readers that Reagan cabinet secretaries Caspar Weinberger and George P. Schultz held top positions in those years at Bechtel. Both officials denied they had any knowledge of bribery payments, and it seems it was never established that they did. Nevertheless, the matter received prolonged news converage at the time, to the embarrassment of high officials on both sides of the Pacific, and Washington was filled with the sound of raised eyebrows.

As a reminder that the Korean War is not exactly concluded but continues in a cease-fire status, but, we hope, with decreasing inflammability with the thawing in the cold war, there was the incident in 1968 of the capture of the intelligence-gathering ship USS *Pueblo* by the communist Koreans.

The North Koreans, on January 23, claiming the *Pueblo* was within their territorial waters, surrounded the vessel about twelve miles from the coast, boarded it, killed one crewman and wounded several others, and forced the ship into the port of Wonsan. The eighty-three officers and crewmen were held for almost a year, tortured, and forced to sign confessions of their guilt. After lengthy

* ©The Washington Post. Used by permission.

negotiations at P'anmunjom, the United States, in a written document, apologized, admitted it had violated North Korean waters, and gave assurances that it would not do so again. Although the United States immediately repudiated the document, stating that it was false and signed only to obtain the release of the crew, the North Koreans released the Americans, but not the ship, on December 22.*

The capture of the *Pueblo* raised many questions in the United States. The public asked why such vessels in dangerous waters were not better escorted or protected, why reinforcements were not more readily available at the time, and about the conduct of the military personnel in captivity and many other related matters. Left unsettled to this day is whether the *Pueblo* was actually inside North Korean waters either before or at the time of its capture.

The seizure of the *Pueblo* could have triggered a resumption of the Korean War fighting in some form or at least air or navel raids on North Korean targets. Perhaps President Johnson would have so reacted had he not been so preoccupied with the aggravating war to the south in Vietnam then in full swing. In retrospect, doves will be pleased with the outcome whereas hawks perhaps were not.

An irony of the *Pueblo* incident is that it is so little known or remembered today. Although the American hostages taken from our embassy in Teheran involved barely half the number of people that were held and brutally tortured from the *Pueblo,* the Embassy incident seems to be much more readily recalled by most Americans. But then perhaps that is understandable. After all, the Korean War itself has become known to many as "the Forgotten War," so it can hardly be surprising that subsequent events incidental to that war are also little remembered.

In the period surrounding the 1988 Olympics, the United States and Korean governments struggled with the awkwardness of Korean demonstrations against the U.S. and our servicemen stationed in Korea.

The question of how long U.S. military forces will remain in Korea continues to be controversial and unanswered. Members of the

* For a detailed background of the *Pueblo* incident from the perspective of the ship's commander, see Commander Lloyd M. Butcher, USN, *Butcher: My Story* (New York: Dell Publishing Company, 1970).

Congress have long demanded that our military presence in Korea be terminated, or at least sharply curtailed. When President Carter suggested a cutback during his administration, opposition here and in Korea was so intense it forced him to retract and drop the matter.

Now, with the easing of the cold war, the issue of American military presence in Korea is again on the front burner. On February 1, 1990, the wire services reported that Korean officials had reluctantly reversed their long-standing opposition to U.S. troop withdrawals from Korea but wanted the troops to be noncombat units. It seems they still want to retain the combat unit which, essentially, is our only combat division there, the 2d Infantry Division.

There was also the news story in March 1990 about the South Korean discovery of a Communist tunnel under the DMZ and of abuses of human rights by both the North and South Koreans. On April 11, 1989, the *Washington Post* carried an article by Fred Hiatt describing in stark detail the harsh life, hunger, and rights abuses in the north.

A month earlier, on March 11, Hiatt wrote in the *Post* of the brutal military practices in the South Korean military that drove many to suicide.

I have had my own share of contacts, even after retirement, that reminded me there was still a Korea around and that it had problems and people interested in solving them. In 1962 I worked for a while on the faculty of the Military Assistance Institute, an activity in Arlington, Virginia, that briefed military officers bound for advisory duty overseas in numerous host countries.

Our faculty members at the institute made a practice of taking their student officers to the various embassies around town for familiarization with and briefings by the military attachés of the country for which they were headed.

In my visits with my American students headed for Korea, I worked with and became closely acquainted with a young Korean army major for whom I developed great admiration and respect. This major was energetic, sharp as a tack, clean-cut, and impressive, and spoke flawless English.

This Korean officer literally worshiped America and Americans, and was yet faithful and dedicated to his own country and to his mission. We worked together in the interests of our respective countries as a smooth and mutually respectable team. I had the greatest of confidence in this fellow and considered him to be absolutely above reproach morally and ethically. I thought him to be as splendid a representative of his country as could be expected.

This Korean major at the Embassy of Korea was named Pak* Bo Hi. In due course he was rotated back to Korea at the end of his Washington tour and retired, or left the army. A few years later I had the distinct pleasure of attending a concert by the Korean Orphans Choir in Constitution Hall in Washington. It was one of the most beautiful, harmonious, and melodious presentations of a young people's choral group that I have ever heard.

The program of the orphans choir was varied and included not only Korean folk songs but even American traditional and gospel numbers. There were solo numbers by preteen girls. The hall was overflowing and many in the audience were in tears, so touching and emotional was the performance by those little Korean orphan children.

The advance man and publicity director for the choir for its U.S. tour, I there learned, was my friend and close acquaintance, former Major and later Lt. Col. Pak Bo Hi.

Still later, some years after the Korean children's-choir tour, I again noted Pak's name in the headlines and was reminded just how much Koreans can be active, energetic, and involved. He was deeply engaged in promoting Christianity and fighting Communism. He was, and still is, I understand, the top assistant to the Korean minister Rev. Sun Myung Moon, head of the Korean Unification Church, which was later to become highly controversial and often in the news.

As with most ethnic groups in the United States, public opinion of a particular group and, perhaps, its country of origin can be heavily influenced and colored by the activities and news coverage of certain individuals from that group that are in the United States. This is no less true for Koreans and Korea.

Thus American perceptions of the Korean War and whether it is better forgotten and was a futile or worthwhile undertaking for this country or whether or not the best interests of our country are served

---

* The Korean name Pak is very common and in English is often also translated "Park."

by continued close association with Korea since the war can depend to a large degree on the public's opinion of only a few individuals who may be Koreans. The Reverend Moon and Colonel Pak seem to be such persons. They have been, not always to their liking, as with Pak's kidnapping in 1984 and Moon's imprisonment over tax problems, highly profiled in the national news for many years. To what extent their activities, other than the above, are approved by the public and have improved and harmed Korean-American relations is a matter of much debate and uncertainty.

Both Moon and Pak can be said to be products of the Korean War and its consequences. Moon was born near Pyongyang in 1920 during the Japanese occupation of the country and witnessed the Communist takeover at the end of World War II. Pak was born later, in 1930, near Wonju, also during the Japanese era, and had reached adulthood when the North Korean forces crossed the parallel in 1950.

Both men witnessed the near total destruction of their country and the heartbreaking suffering of their people as a result of the Communist invasion. They felt during most of the years after the Korean War that the Communist threat was ever present, real and not apparent, at the very border of their country. Even today with the thawing of the cold war, they warn that the danger to South Korea has not entirely abated.

Both Moon and Pak are devout Christians and products of missionary churches established in Korea mostly by American Catholic and Protestant efforts. They emerged from the Korean War as avid anti-communists, decrying its atheistic and totalitarian philosophy and goals. Both men developed an affectionate admiration for America and its democratic ideals, and by the 1960s they had settled in America.

The Reverend Moon set about to initiate various anti-communist causes, and he established the exceptionally energetic and successful Unification Church. The movement soon attracted large numbers of converts, but it became highly controversial nationwide. The media soon labeled the church's followers as "Moonies," and the movement was charged, as viewed by many, with excesses of brainwashing, propagandizing, reorientation, indoctrination, evangelism, and even mental and physical coercion.

In the mid-1980s Moon was indicted, tried, and imprisoned for income tax evasion by not reporting as income monies received from his church activities. During most of this period, Colonel Pak, as stated, was closely associated with Reverend Moon and served as his chief aide.

I have long had mixed feelings or doubts about the justification for the attacks on the Unification Church and its founder and the prosecution of Reverend Moon. I don't think I could ever be a Moonie by persuasion, but the whole affair has smelled to me of hypocrisy and a double standard. Most of the tactics Moon and his people are accused of to attract and hold adherents are the same, more or less, as are used by almost every major established religion nationally and in the world. I think most of his critics have been institutional religionists, of many faiths, that feel threatened by Moon's successes in winning away from them their own members.

Coercion of course would be beyond acceptable limits, but I have never seen or heard of any source that could establish with reliable certainty that such methods were in fact used by the Unification Church. My acquaintance with Pak would lead me most strongly to believe they were not.

With respect to the use of church, or other, funds or the equivalent for personal purposes and not reporting them as income in violation of law or the IRS code, I suggest that such a charge could be made against almost any church, business, political, or other leader at any time. Why Moon and not many others? Wasn't his "prosecution" really persecution? The dividing line between the acceptable and the illegal here is very fine indeed. We have only to consider the blanket of publicity in the spring of 1991 revealing that the president's White House chief aide had used government planes over an extended period for numerous flights for personal and family reasons and that countless congressmen have benefitted from such and other "perks" as a routine matter. Did the president's man report, or will he on his next return, that "compensation" as income to the satisfaction of the IRS and the public? If there is a difference in impropriety, and even legality, between these activities and Moon's I fail to see it.

Pak, obviously much to his disenchantment, hit the headlines in another way in September 1984. In New York he was kidnapped by a group of his own countrymen when leaving the Grand Hyatt hotel, and he was whisked away some fifty miles to State Hill. There he was held hostage for one million dollars ransom, and threats were made against his family in McLean, Virginia. Pak was released after agreeing under torture to pay the ransom, and several weeks later the FBI arrested six Koreans for their complicity in the affair.

Reverend Moon has served his time in prison for his tax "offenses" and was released in the late 1980s. Both he and Pak are still around and active in their pursuits, one of which is owning or operating the *Washington Times*, one of the two major daily newspapers in the capital. The largest daily newspaper in Washington is the *Post*, and it is well known for its liberal positions. The *Times* presents another viewpoint in its editorials and elsewhere and thereby provides the reading public with some degrees of balance in news coverage. Who, therefore, could disagree that these two Korean gentlemen are providing a necessary and worthwhile service to the public?

One can argue as to whether the operations and activities of Reverend Moon and Colonel Pak, and certain other Koreans in the United States, are helpful and in the public interests here. There can be no denying, however, that they do keep Korea and Koreans, for good or not, in the public eye and in so doing help to keep alive the knowledge that there was once a Korean War in which America was deeply involved both during the fighting and long after it ended, in fact if not officially.

With respect to the political activities of Korean demonstrators, radical or otherwise, over the several decades since the war ended, I make no judgments on the merits, if any, of their positions as we slide into the last decade of this century. I leave that to the Koreans or to those far wiser and more knowledgeable than myself.

Suffice it for me to say that in my judgment it is particularly and especially tragic for a new and aspiring country, in which my own country has been so heavily involved in so many complex ways, and where our nation's youth has shed its blood, to be denied the peace and living enjoyment of which it is so richly deserving and fully entitled. I wish my country's involvement had been more productive.

Koreans, regrettably, have every justification for continued pessimism over their country's political future both domestically and internationally. Nevertheless, their cause is not entirely hopeless. On April 9 and 10, 1991, the news services reported that South Korea had announced its intention to join the UN and that the country's political dissidents were united to challenge the government in the coming 1992 elections.

The articles also reported that the South Korean prime minister, Ro Jai-bong, had sent a message to his North Korean counterpart, Yon Hyong Muk, suggesting an early meeting for another round of talks on Korean unification. The request for UN membership could be seen as a significant step toward achieving unification, since the North Koreans do not want two Koreas in the world today.

These developments might well be particularly beneficial to Korea. Organized and peaceful elections, unification of the two Koreas at long last, and inclusion in the world family of nations through membership in the international United Nations organization could be the much needed catalyst to move the country well past the devastation of the Korean War of the 1950s and its brutal aftermath. Friends of Korea and its people will be watching and waiting and cautiously hoping for the best.

I have not been very successful in pinpointing the current whereabouts of comrades mentioned here in my narrative. Most of the higher ranking, and thus usually older, officers or senior NCOs have at this writing passed on. Taps for them has sounded. Colonel Freeman, later a full four-star general at the time of his retirement, and a major player herein, died on April 17, 1988, incidentally, on my daughter's birthday. His obit in the *Washington Post* was especially informative on his post-Korean assignments and activities.

Majs. George Russell, Sammy Radow, and Albert Metts, with whom I was very close and friendly and rotated with, have retired. My efforts to locate and communicate with them through the locator service at the Army Records Center in St. Louis have been unsuccessful.

Although I am a member of the relatively new Korean War Veterans Association and have attended annual reunions in Arlington, Virginia, I have not encountered any of the comrades herein mentioned. No doubt Taps has also sounded for some.

America has been slow and almost reluctant or reticent to show much, if any, appreciation for the sacrifices made by her men who fought in the Korean War, although experiences may vary from veteran to veteran.

Some vets, to include Blaine Friedlander, the Congressional Liaison member of the Korean War Veterans Associations's Board of Directors, report that they were individually well received when returning home during or after the war. Friedlander narrates that when he was spotted as a Korean War vet he was wined and dined and warmly and emotionally greeted with drinks or other expressions of gratitude.

Sadly, however, Friedlander's experiences seem to have been the exception rather than the rule. For the most part there were few, if any, parades and little media or other attention. The war to most of the country had and has become the "forgotten war," as labeled by Clay Blair and some other writers.

In many ways it appears the country is still embarrassed by the Korean struggle, which many considered a lost cause and a war not won, since it ended in a stalemate and since it did not chase the Communists out of all of Korea or even China also.

It seems that many Americans would be content, as until recently with the Vietnam War, to simply sweep the Korean War under the rug and let it all go away, if such were possible. The loss of over fifty thousand killed or missing there, and many times that number disabled, does not make such convenient disposition practicable.

Nevertheless, some recognition worth mentioning, albeit quite belated, for Korean vets has occurred. In April 1990 there was a one-thousand-dollar-a-plate black tie gala tribute for Korean War vets at the plush Omni Hotel in Washington. It was attended by Bob Hope, the President, about fifty congressional Korean War vets, and many other big-name people. The proceeds were to be used to help establish a Korean War Memorial.

Additional attention for the Korean War, and its vets, resulted from the acclaimed PBS miniseries "Korea—the Unknown War," which was aired late in 1990 and already is being rerun. Although that documentary became somewhat controversial because of a claimed pro-Communist slant, it nevertheless did serve to inform and direct attention of many, especially young, viewers to the tribulations of the Korean War.

The Korean veterans, unlike the Vietnam vets, do not at this writing, almost half a century after the war, have a memorial in their honor. In contrast, the hallowed and inspiring Vietnam Memorial on the Mall in the nation's capital, now visited by millions each year, was built barely ten years after the fighting in southeast Asia ended.

In the mid-1980s a drive was launched to design and raise funds for a privately financed Korean War Memorial in Washington, and it appeared for a while that this symbolic pat on the back for Korean vets might at long last be within grasp. But the road has been long and rocky and filled with potholes. At this writing it is by no means certain that the monument will ever be erected.

The April 1990 issue of the Korean War Veterans Association newsletter reported on the then accepted design and planned location of the Korean War Memorial. It would be placed on the Mall opposite the existing Vietnam Memorial between the Lincoln Memorial and the Washington Monument.

Obtaining permission to erect a memorial to the Korean War and its vets, and approval of an acceptable design, has been an uphill struggle, at times very frustrating, by General Richard Stilwell, his Memorial advisory board, the Veterans Association, and other supporters. The enabling legislation was introduced by Virginia Congressman Stan Parris, and for months the proposal wound its way slowly through numerous governmental, historical, cultural, battlefield monuments, and other involved agencies of the federal and Washington municipal bureaucracies.

The last significant roadblock in the establishment of the memorial was thought to have been overcome on April 4, 1991 when the National Capital Planning Commission gave final approval to the memorial and its overall design. Memorial supporters were elated. That action was critical, since further deliberation, or alteration of design, and delay would most likely have prevented timely ground breaking by October 1991, the deadline set by the congressional authorization. Proponents pointed out that any additional delay would probably mean construction costs would constantly increase and exceed available contributions and might well kill the whole project.

Then, on June 28, 1991, came the devastating news that the Washington Commission of Fine Arts had reconsidered the matter and flatly and unanimously rejected the proposed design for the Korean War Veterans Memorial. The Commission Chairman, J. Carter Brown, was quoted in the media as saying that the planned "38 bronze ground troopers set against a mural wall . . . was all too much," that they were "too representational" and should be made more "sculptural." I have not yet, personally, been able to determine just what all that means artistically, aesthetically, practically, or otherwise. At its next meeting on July 25, the Fine Arts Commission considered the matter again and stood by its earlier rejection.

The following day, July 26, members of the Korean War Veterans Association at their annual meeting in Arlington, Virginia, loudly and unanimously voiced their disappointment and outrage at the delays in establishing a monument to the Korean War. By resolution the assembled members authorized and directed their leadership to go directly to the President of the United States in an effort to speed the completion of the memorial.

At this writing, the impact of these developments on the realization of a memorial to the Korean War vets has yet to be determined. In the five years of the campaign to establish the memorial the estimated cost has dramatically risen from a little under $5 million to about $15 million because of inflation, disagreements, litigation over design, and other factors.

Although only a little more than half the $15 million memorial construction costs have been raised, supporters expected that the remainder will be realized from the sale of a special Philadelphia Mint commemorative coin if there was no more delay or costly redesigning.

Some of the vets involved in the memorial effort have told me that although they were not completely satisfied with the design as proposed by the Pennsylvania State University architectural team that won the design competition or later alterations in the original designs, they were not opposing the designs. They felt that further redesigning and delay would accelerate costs to the point where they would exceed available funds and the project would never get off the launching pad. In short, they said, better a less than perfect memorial, after fifty years, than no memorial at all during the lifetimes of the ever-decreasing number of veterans of the war that are still around.

A national monument, if ever established, to the memory and honor of the Korean War vets will not, of course, go very far in compensating those, living or not, who gave so much for their country in that struggle.

A memorial, however, in the nation's capital, which is visited by so many millions each year, may help to some extent to prevent future generations from asking, "Korean War? When and where was that?" as many of our youngsters in school are already doing.

Addendum

As this book was being finalized for publication the Commission of Fine Arts in Washington, D.C., on January 16, 1992, gave its final approval for the modified design of the Korean War Memorial.

The final design, subject to minor changes during construction, consists of 19 "free-standing" statues of servicemen in a field (half the originally proposed 38 in allusion to the 38th parallel), bordered by a 172-foot-long granite wall etched with the faces of support troops as a background. The wall ends in a triangular peninsula piercing a round pond set in a commemorative grove.

Retired Marine general Raymond Davis, chairman of the Memorial Advisory Board (who replaced recently deceased board chairman Gen. Richard Stillwell), called the Art Commission's action "welcome news after a long and concerted effort."

Although approval must yet be obtained from the National Capital Planning and Memorial Commissions, supporters foresaw no opposition in those agencies. Ground breaking is scheduled for Memorial Day, 1992, and dedication in July 1993, on the fortieth anniversary of ending of the fighting in Korea with the signing of the cease-fire at Panmunjom.

Bibliography

I am not including an extensive bibiliography with this narrative. For those interested in further research and information, the computers of any first-class library, public or otherwise, will contain far more authorities and publications on the Korean War than I could assemble.

I list only the following authors and works that I have found to be especially scholarly and thorough and that I have relied on extensively to refresh my memory on dates, names, places and other details.

Blair Clay. *The Forgotten War*. New York: Time Books, 1987.

―――. *Ridgway's Paratroopers*. Garden City, New York: Dial Press, Doubleday and Co., 1985.

Butcher, Lloyd M., USN. *Butcher: My Story*. New York: Dell Publishing Company, 1970.

Clark, Mark W. *From the Danube to the Yalu*. Blue Ridge Summit, Pa.: Tab Books, 1988.

Hastings, Max. *The Korean War*. New York: Simon and Schuster, 1987.

Hinshaw, Arned L. *Heartbreak Ridge, Korea 1951*. New York: Praeger Publishers, a division of Greenwood Press, 1989.

Kim, Illpyong J., and Young Whan Kihl. *Political Change in South Korea*. New York: The Korean PWPA, 1988.

Marshall, S.L.A. *The River and the Gauntlet*. Nashville: Battery Press, 1987.

Middleton, Harry J. *A Compact History of the Korean War*. New York: Hawthorne Books, 1965.

Munroe, Clark C., Lieutenant. *The Second United States Infantry Division in Korea 1950–1951*. Tokyo: Toppan Printing Company, Ltd., 1951.

Office of the Chief of Military History, United States Army. *United States Army in the Korean War*. Washington, D.C.: United States Printing Office, 1972.

Pettigrew, T.H., Jr. *The Kunu-ri Incident*. New York: Vantage Press, 1967.

Poats, Rutherford M. *Decision in Korea*. New York: McBride Company, 1973.

Sandusky, Michael C. *America's Parallel.* Alexandria, Va.: Old
    Dominion Press, 1983.
Steinberg, David I. *The Republic of Korea, Economic Transformation
    and Social Change.* Boulder, Col., and London: Westview Press,
    1987.
Wilkinson, Allen Byron. *Up Front Korea.* New York: Vantage Press,
    1968.

Index